EDWARD THOMAS

Selected Letters

EDWARD THOMAS

Selected Letters

Edited by

R. GEORGE THOMAS

Oxford New York

OXFORD UNIVERSITY PRESS

1995

Oxford University Press, Walton Street, Oxford OX2 6DP
Oxford New York
Athens Auckland Bangkok Bombay
Calcutta Cape Town Dar es Salaam Delhi
Florence Hong Kong Istanbul Karachi
Kuala Lumpur Madras Madrid Melbourne
Mexico City Nairobi Paris Singapore
Taipei Tokyo Toronto
and associated companies in
Berlin Ibadan

Oxford is a trade mark of Oxford University Press

Published in the United States
by Oxford University Press Inc., New York

British Library Cataloguing in Publication Data
Data available

Library of Congress Cataloging in Publication Data
Thomas, Edward, 1878–1917.
[Correspondence. Selections]
Selected letters / Edward Thomas; edited by R. George Thomas.
Includes index.
1. Thomas, Edward, 1878–1917—Correspondence. 2. Authors, English—20th century—Correspondence. 3. Poets, Welsh—20th century—Correspondence. 4. Soldiers—Great Britain—Correspondence. 5. Critics—Great Britain—Correspondence.
I. Thomas, R. George. II. Title.
PR6039.H55Z48 1995
821'.912—dc20 [B] 95-38211
ISBN 0-19-818562-6

1 3 5 7 9 10 8 6 4 2

Typeset by Joshua Associates Ltd., Oxford
Printed in Great Britain
on acid-free paper by
Bookcraft Ltd.
Midsomer Norton, Bath

To Jess
for enduring affection

PREFACE

In 1928 the Welsh bard-theologian Gwili first introduced me to the poetry of his friend Edward Thomas. Since then, my knowledge of the poet has been extended by meetings with Gordon Bottomley, J. M. Thorburn, Rowland L. Watson, and three generations of the poet's family. Invaluable were discussions with his widow, Helen, during her last five years and, since 1967, the generosity of her daughter Myfanwy. She was responsible for the magnificent Edward Thomas Collection at the University of Wales, Cardiff, on which this selection is based. When publication was first discussed with John Bell and Kim Scott Walwyn, the late Professor A. J. Smith offered to share in the work. His death in 1991 was a severe loss to the entire project. His sound judgement would have helped in the complex integration of recently acquired Thomas material with the letters previously used in my portrait of the poet.

In March 1915, in a letter to Walter de la Mare, Thomas said of his own poetry: 'I wrote (if anything) with a feeling that I did use the Morse code. This is a fact. I only hope someone besides myself will catch the accent.' I hope this selection will further that process.

R.G.T.

ACKNOWLEDGEMENTS

THIS selection is indebted to the generous help of the people and institutions who own and control the original sources on which it is based. I owe a special debt of gratitude to the poet's widow Helen, his daughters Bronwen and Myfanwy, his grandson Edward, his nephews Edward and David, and to the family of Rowland L. Watson. Thanks for permission to publish this material—often for the first time—are due to them and to the following: the C. C. Abbott Collection, University of Durham Library; Battersea Public Library and Gervase Farjeon; the Berg Collection, New York Public Library; Anthony and Christian Berridge; the Bodleian Library and Lincoln College, Oxford; Norman Colbeck and the Colbeck Collection, University of British Columbia, Vancouver; Dartmouth College Library, Hanover, New Hampshire, and Alfred C. Edwards, the Jones Library, Amherst, Mass.; the Edward Thomas Collection, Humanities Library, University of Wales, Cardiff; Penny Ely; the Humanities Research Centre, University of Texas at Austin; the Lockwood Memorial Library, State University of New York at Buffalo; the National Library of Wales, Aberystwyth, and Daniel Huws and Nia Henson. Irene Fawcett, Jason Freeman, Brian Ll. James, and Frances Whistler gave unstinted help in the final preparation of the book. Despite much sustained support, the errors and misjudgements are entirely my own.

R.G.T.

CONTENTS

INTRODUCTION

PHILIP EDWARD THOMAS (3 March 1878–9 April 1917), born in London of Welsh parents, was the eldest of six sons. His ambitious Civil Servant father was an exponent of Comte's Positivism and a well-known lecturer in Humanist circles. As his family grew he had moved successively outwards to houses in Lambeth and Wandsworth until he settled finally at Rusham Gate in Balham. Edward's formal education was in small private schools, Battersea Grammar School, and then, for one year, at St Paul's School. In his leisure he explored the grounds of the diminishing large estates and the neighbouring Commons with a quasi-religious devotion to the study of birds, trees, flowers, and all forms of nature study. Before he was 17 his essays on rural topics had been accepted by many of the newly emerging weeklies. Across Wandsworth Common he visited the eminent critic and editor James Ashcroft Noble who helped place his essays, supervised his reading, and encouraged a friendship between Edward and his second daughter Helen. Before Noble's early death (April 1896) Edward had gained his father's reluctant permission to abandon a prospective Civil Service career in order to prepare for an Oxford scholarship. He then spent a year in Oxford as a non-residential matriculant and gained the senior History scholarship to Lincoln College in March 1898.

During his three years at Oxford, he earned about £80 annually from his writings and was overwhelmed by his passion for Helen Noble. Unknown to their parents they married in June 1899 at Fulham Registry office. Soon after, Helen agreed to live with his parents until a son, Merfyn, was born in January 1900 and Edward had graduated with a disappointing Second Class in History that June. Supported by Helen, he had decided to live by writing and to rear their family in the country. There followed a few years of meagre earnings (less than £100 p.a.), the pressure of bad Oxford debts, and a tendency to occasionally severe bouts of depression. In 1902 their daughter Bronwen was born and, in the autumn, Edward succeeded Lionel Johnson as literary reviewer for the *Daily Chronicle*. He was commissioned to write books on

Oxford and Wales and seemed to be in demand as a writer on descriptive travel and country life. Restlessly he lived in three different houses near Maidstone and in the Weald before he finally settled near to Bedales School and Petersfield in 1906.[1]

Strained by overwork, he accepted medical advice to leave home for Minsmere in early 1908 in order to write a study of his idealized naturalist writer Richard Jefferies. At Minsmere he was suddenly tormented by an 'unthinking passion' for the 17-year-old school-girl, Hope Webb,[2] to whom Helen had been a governess in 1897. It seemed to be an entirely one-sided affair and came to nothing, although he returned to the episode at least three times later in his writings. It was probably, I think, the severest test of his marriage and one which, on the evidence of their frequent letters, Helen generously helped him to sustain. In subsequent working absences from home his letters to Helen are consistently concerned to keep her in close touch with their own shared interest in natural sights and sounds.

Merfyn and Bronwen were educated at Bedales and a second daughter, Myfanwy, was born in August 1910 in their new custom-built house above Steep village, close to the sarsen Edward Thomas Memorial Stone. Thereafter, his regular sources of income diminished while his bouts of depression and introspective self-absorption increased. His favourite expedient was to undertake commissioned books of travel which occasioned long walking periods away from home, studiously devoted to intense note-taking. These were followed by five to six weeks at home of concentrated writing and revision of his texts. This pattern, accompanied by piecemeal reviewing and a decline in the intensity of his belief in the healing properties of his response to nature, resulted in an almost complete breakdown in the autumn of 1911. Eventually he accepted a gift of £100 from his Oxford friend E. S. P. Haynes and, as so often before, fought his way out of despair by accepting more stringent deadlines and recording the severe process of introspection in his diaries and notebooks. As he turned away from books of travel to books about writers, he concerned himself more and more with the nature (for him) of the precise connection between the written and the spoken language.

Between 1911 and 1914, in support of his family, he wrote many books at speed and for ridiculously low sums.[3] To write them—and to maintain contact with publishers and editors—he spent longish spells away from home as a paying guest with friends or recent literary acquaintances. He gave up his new house above Steep (Wick Green) and settled his family in a cheap, inconveniently small cottage in Steep village closer to Bedales. Helen assisted at the school and involved herself in various discussion groups. She relied on his letters and his brief visits home, as he forged his growing reputation as a valued critic of the new 'Georgian' poetry. His visits to Harold Monro's Poetry Bookshop led to an instant friendship with Robert Frost whose robust, apparently extrovert manner—and shared explorations of the interaction between poetry and the spoken language—acted as a catalyst upon Thomas's rather hesitant search for a personal style.

In February 1914, early in their fruitful friendship, Thomas was awarded a grant from the Royal Literary Fund to help balance his loss of earnings during 1913. In consequence he returned to Steep. Apart from a few visits to Wales and to Dymock (chiefly to continue his critical discussions with Frost), the Thomas family remained together until his enlistment in June 1915 and his final departure for France from High Beech in January 1917.[4] By then his own poems were ready for publication and he had become a surprisingly efficient and enthusiastic soldier. It is no surprise to me, even now, that his poems, which rely so unmistakably on his autobiography, should draw so consistently on the country surrounding Steep and memories of his long walking tours. His mature poetry, half of it composed as a soldier in training in England, is convincing testimony of his ability to come through debilitating weakness. His letters to Helen, especially those at the beginning and the end, rest on an undercurrent of belief in the tensile strength of their marriage, despite its numerous ups and downs.

Particularly during the last thirty years, his quiet-voiced reflective poetry, which draws so firmly on his entire life experience, has found a wider audience in a society that seems lacking in cohesive purpose. In time, surely, critical attention will extend to a thorough consideration of the underlying philosophy scattered throughout his essays and prose books.

While completing this selection of his letters, I reread once more all his letters in the Edward Thomas Collection at Cardiff. It made clear—as do isolated sections of his prose—his constant search for ways to share with others that idealized devotion to the natural world which coalesced with his belief in the vital role such an understanding could play in the enrichment of the life of a rapidly developing urban industrial society. Apart from the long period of indecision (between August 1914 and July 1915) that ended in his sudden enlistment in the Artists' Rifles (at the age of 37), he espoused no causes, political or otherwise. Yet he had pursued his elusive ideal for a manner of writing directly to others, like a pilgrim, hesitatingly, and without didactic purpose. Gradually, as the market for open-air books declined, he was ready to combine minimal adequate support for his family with a determination to share his half-hidden views with a wider audience. Once, late in 1913, he wrote revealingly to his agent Cazenove:

> Can you conceive me going to Australia or New Zealand or Canada and writing a book about what I see of men and places and also getting people to read it? . . . I am quite prepared to go but chiefly because I want work. I would much rather go about England or Wales, which however nobody wants me to do. What about a compromise—sending me to a Welsh coalfield or an English pottery district and letting me suffer to the tune of 80,000 words? That I should very much like to do. You once spoke of Tonypandy. . . . P. S. Dent wouldn't, I suppose, care for me to do what I might have done in *The Heart of England* and give a really conscientious picture (not for agriculturalists) of England as it is, and called 'This England', showing what England means as one might show what 'The South' or 'The East' means, but chiefly the visible things.

He came close to this idea in his wartime anthology, *This England*, and in two articles in *The Last Sheaf*.[5]

To prepare this necessarily restricted selection, nearly 2,700 autograph letters have been examined and at least another 500 have been read cursorily in libraries overseas or in some earlier accounts of Thomas. Recently the National Library of Wales, Aberystwyth (NLW), has acquired numerous letters between Edward and his wife Helen and many letters between him and her father, J. Ashcroft Noble. These letters to Helen are mainly from the periods of Edward's working absences from home, as well as the lovingly supportive ones to her which he sent from France. Equally significant are his diaries from 1902–14 which supplement others in the Berg Collection (in New York) and in the Edward Thomas Collection (ETC) at Cardiff. A few of these NLW diary entries are included in this selection. They throw light on his often repeated remarks in letters to Harry Hooton and Gordon Bottomley that he should desist from the unfruitful habit of introspective self-analysis.

The final selection was complicated by the long runs of parallel letters to a few correspondents extending over most of his active writing life. There were 400 to Helen, 328 apiece to Edward Garnett and Walter de la Mare, 240 to Gordon Bottomley, 178 to Ian MacAlister, 177 at least to Harry Hooton, 270 to his agent C. F. Cazenove, 78 to Jesse Berridge, and, during his last four years, 203 to Eleanor Farjeon. In addition there are between 40–60 each to John Freeman, Harold Monro, W. H. Hudson, and John Haines, plus the remarkable run of 59 letters to Robert Frost.

Some months before his sudden death in December 1991, Professor A. J. Smith outlined his proposed selection of the letters to Frost, to John Freeman, and to his parents. At that time he hoped to check the ETC transcripts against holographs held in Oxford, Durham, and Battersea, believing that such a selection would concentrate on Thomas's life as a poet and soldier. However, the subsequent availability of the NLW letters and diaries emphasized the value of a selection that would reflect Thomas's entire writing life. The earliest letters to J. Ashcroft Noble required some inclusion, while the wide-ranging Cardiff collection (ETC)[6] was a reminder of the sustained, if often frustrated, progress of Thomas's writing from his early essays to the final letters from the front line at Arras.

A majority of the present selection have not hitherto been published. They supplement those available in the works of John Moore, Robert P. Eckert, and William Cooke, in the various separate editions of Thomas letters to Jesse Berridge, Gordon Bottomley, and Eleanor Farjeon, and of those printed in *Poetry Wales*, 12/4. There is a wealth of Edward Thomas material for further study: in Great Britain—in London, Oxford, Durham, Aberystwyth, and Cardiff; in the USA—in New York, Hanover, Buffalo, and Austin; in Canada, at UBC, Vancouver. Some letters already published in memoirs have not been used, especially those to E. S. P. Haynes and Ernest Rhys. Various others exist only in draft form, and those to W. H. Davies and J. Hartman Morgan have not been seen.

A small circle of friends recorded their memories of Thomas for

Rowland L. Watson in 1946–8, as they had done earlier for John Moore and Robert Eckert. Most of them had met Thomas frequently on his London visits. Letters were unnecessary—postal collections were frequent and punctual, and postcards and letter-cards were sufficient. Regrettably, the two-way business correspondence between Thomas and Cazenove fell largely outside the scope of this present selection: it remains an invaluable guide to the role of publishers—and the treatment of authors—in the decade before 1914. Obliquely, too, it testifies to the doggedness with which Thomas stuck to the chosen writing path that led directly to the sudden emergence of his poetry in late 1914. (I found it impossible to illustrate this from a selection of isolated letters and notes, but the evidence is there in abundance in the C. C. Abbott Collection at Durham University.)[7] Another quite different approach to Thomas awaits more attention in the substantial Eckert Collection at the Bodleian Library in Oxford and the Colbert Collection in UBC Vancouver.

For ease of reading the Biographical Register provides information about the people often cited; this is followed by a list of works in progress as mentioned in the letters, a list of Thomas's numerous prose works, and a list of journals that published his essays. There is also a list of the earliest publications of his poems under the pseudonym 'Edward Eastaway'. Notes to the letters seek to provide necessary information in support of particular letters; at times they draw on letters to or from Thomas with occasional quotations from his own diaries or the recorded memories of close friends. A list of abbreviations is included as a guide to the abbreviations used in the notes and Biographical Register.

Apart from his distressed incomprehension of the frequent uncontrollable irritation set up between the demands of writing and his domestic conditions, two subjects occur repeatedly in his frank diary confessions. The first was his inability to converse honestly and sincerely with more than one person in a group: a reflection perhaps of his persistent search for a close friend with whom to share his innermost thoughts. The other was a deep revulsion at the role he assumed in general London conversation—especially his repugnance against the ideas he put forward without conviction or belief. The diaries, the letters, his discontent with his many books, hint repeatedly at a profound unease with his chosen occupation. When first presented as synopses to his agent, his books seemed fruitful of ideas closely linked to his absorbing concerns. This initial enthusiasm adds momentum to the early chapters of most of his books, to be diminished later by a veiled contempt for sheer 'bookmaking' as he tried to meet the fancied demands of potential readers, publishers, and reviewers. Perhaps this is one source of his frequent statement that he had no power for the sustained formulation of intellectual ideas. His books, it would seem, were an unsatisfactory concomitant of his search for a one-to-one conversation with an ideal listener. And eventually, they, too, displeased him, as so much of his London-based conversations had done.

The transition from profitless introspective records to thinly disguised autobiographical fiction—which became the essence of all his poetry—took shape as he worked away from home at East Grinstead in December 1913. In response to Eleanor Farjeon's offer to type for him, he sent her the manuscript which was published in 1937 as *The Childhood of Edward Thomas*. He seemed pleased with the work: 'It's very lean but I feel the shape of the sentences and alter continuously with some unseen end in view.' His letters, which read as one-to-one conversations untroubled by any need to publish, seem to carry a similar seal of approval.

Thomas was a faithful and assiduous correspondent. Each friend was a chosen listener for particular needs and purposes: Harry Hooton (and his wife Janet—a lifelong friend of Helen) for domestic difficulties between himself and Helen; Ian MacAlister and Jesse Berridge for personal and modest financial help in his earliest post-Oxford days as an impecunious journalist; Gordon Bottomley, and then Edward Garnett and Walter de la Mare, as fellow writers with whom he could discuss critically (and unflinchingly) his numerous books, essays, sketches, and other projects. Later still, he attracted a group of younger writers—John Freeman, Harold Monro, and, more closely, Eleanor Farjeon—whose practical aid he enlisted to bolster his growing reputation as an independent critic of 'Georgian' poetry. Finally, late in 1913, Robert Frost came to embody all his needs for a close friend and literary mentor, who could sympathise and understand, as an equal, his sudden emergence as a poet.[8] After his friend's death Frost often stated that Thomas was the only 'brother' he had ever had.

Some letters seem initially to be merely concerned with arrangements to meet or to visit long-standing friends or family members. They include those to 'Dad' Uzzell, his early guide to country lore in the Jefferies country; to the theologian-bard Gwili and the schoolmaster John Williams of Waun Wen, essential ports of call in South Wales; to John Haines, the Gloucester solicitor-botanist friend of Robert Frost through whom Thomas kept a secondary link with the American after his return to the USA. The handful of letters to Helen's elder sister, Irene, and her husband are specially valuable. They throw a little light on the constant use Edward made of the homes of his parents, brothers, relations, and very old friends when he spent many working days at the British Library. These reveal the same familial tone as the letters to his aunt Margaret Townsend in the USA and to his own parents in his constant letters from France. They reflect, but do not echo precisely, the frank tone of direct, open friendship which characterized all his letters to Helen, and ended with the factual, consolatory ones from France.[9] In them, perhaps, he fulfilled adequately his hopes for complete communication outlined in his 'How I Began' article in *T.P.'s Weekly* (January 1913):

Presently, also, myself and English, as she is taught in schools came to a conflict, and gradually to a more and more friendly arrangement through the necessity of writing long letters daily to one who was neither a schoolboy nor an elder, the subject of the letters being matters concerning nobody else in the world. Now it was that I had a chance of discarding or of adapting to my own purpose the fine words and infinite variety of constructions which I had formerly admired from afar and imitated in fairly cold blood. There is no doubt that my masters often lent me dignity and subtlety altogether beyond my needs.[10]

His hundreds of letters to Helen—all faithfully preserved from 1896 to 1917—make abundantly clear what those needs were. They anticipated the demands he later placed upon his poetry:

I should use, as the trees and birds did,
A language not to be betrayed;
And what was hid should still be hid
Excepting from those like me made
Who answer when such whispers bid.

('I never saw that land before', May 1916)

But the moment unveiled something unwilling to die
And I had what I most desired, without search or desert or cost.

('The Ash Grove', February 1916)

Whatever wind blows, while they and I have leaves
We cannot other than an aspen be
That ceaselessly, unreasonably grieves,
Or so men think who like a different tree.

('Aspens', July 1915)

The voice of the poet and the voice of the letter writer are in close harmony, inviting us to listen to their subdued message. This was the informed perception of Edward Garnett in his 1927 preface to the Gregynog Press *Selected Poems of Edward Thomas*: 'No poems reinforce one another more insidiously than Thomas's, each being a fresh refraction of his elusive thought and personality. . . . Each of his poems in turn leads us deeper and deeper into the charmed atmosphere of their creator's inner life . . . mirrors some fresh aspect of nature's character and prodigal loveliness.' Similar glimpses of his character and central preoccupations underlie his personal letters and diaries. Here is man rarely at ease with himself, yet relentless in pursuit of self-understanding, even in the twists and turns of his love for, and continued friendship with, Helen. Their relationship—incomprehensible to others but shored up by her tolerant acceptance of his absolute devotion to the claims of his daimon—was noted by Helen's sister Irene in 'her clearest and vividest recollection of him. For I took the opportunity of speaking of his treatment of Helen. My spirit burned within me, and I felt I *must* say what was in my heart. I shall never forget how he took it,—admitting everything, extenuating nothing. His humility melted me, and I felt drawn to him in a way I had never felt before.'[11] Irene was an early advocate of women's independence and had known Edward from his first letters to her father in 1895 until his last evening in England in January 1917. Her reluctant testimony and her gratitude 'that he had that year or two of happiness and freedom at the end' provide a quiet corollary to the portrait of Thomas given by these letters, especially so in the contrast between the tone of hesitancy that marks the first seventy-five and the firm contours of the remainder.

Early in 1911 Edward had asked Helen to keep his long letters home as a necessary supplement to his notebooks. He repeated the request to her (and to his parents) from France. Clearly, along with his War Diary, they were to form the basis of new works he had hoped to write about his front-line experiences. Nor should there be any surprise that so many of his non-combatant friends kept his letters. When reading his diaries in NLW and the field notebooks in the Berg Collection (in New York) and in the ETC, one feels close to the wrestle between a creative writer's initial ideas and their final published form. The letters here give a similar impression. Many of them appear to answer directly a comment he made when discussing Maeterlinck's *Serres Chaudes*: 'Any writer whose words have this power may make a poem of anything—a story, a dream, a thought, a picture, an ejaculation, a conversation . . . Anything, however small, may make a poem; nothing, however great, is certain to. Concentration, intensity of mood, is the one necessary condition in the poet and in the poem.'[12]

Eventually, when he appeared pseudonymously as a poet, he chose a family name, 'Eastaway', which epitomized for him the semi-itinerant craftsmen of his parents' families in and around South Wales and the Bristol Channel in the post-Napoleonic period and later. His firm belief that the pseudonymous poems would find an audience is typical of the confident soldier who also seems to have reached the quiet conclusion in France that he would explore the possibilities of a writing career in the USA when the war was over. His is a challenging story. These letters allow us to overhear, if not fully to understand, his abundant reflections upon his life's experience. In those from Arras we hear a mature voice—so sadly missing from post-war English poetry—which is based not on cultivated eccentricity or slavish conformity, but on a humble yet alert acceptance of things as they are:

But now that there is something I could use
My youth and strength for, I deny the age,
The care and weakness that I know—refuse
To admit I am unworthy of the wage
Paid to a man who gives up eyes and breath
For what can neither ask nor heed his death.

('There was a time', June 1916)

NOTES

1. 'Thomas's successive places of residence were: 61 Shelgate Road, Battersea Rise (1896–); 113 Cowley Road, Oxford (Oct. 1897–June 1898); Lincoln College, Oxford (Oct. 1898–June 1900); 117 Atheldene Road, Earlsfield, SW (Nov. 1900–Feb. 1901); 7 Nightingale Parade, Nightingale Lane, Balham, SW (Feb. 1901–Oct. 1901); Rose Acre, Bearsted, nr. Maidstone (Oct. 1901–Mar. 1903); The Green, Bearsted, nr. Maidstone (Mar. 1903–Feb. 1904); Elses Farm, The Weald, Sevenoaks (May 1904–Oct. 1906); Berryfield Cottage, nr. Ashford, Petersfield (Dec. 1906–Nov. 1909); Wick Green, Petersfield (Dec. 1909–July 1913); Yew Tree Cottage, Steep, Petersfield (July 1913–Aug. 1916); High Beech, Loughton (8 Oct. 1916–Dec. 1916). From time to time Thomas, and his family, stayed at his parents' last home—13 Rusham Road, Nightingale Lane, Balham (Rusham Gate). From Apr. 1909 until mid-Aug. 1916 E.T. used a 'hut' in the grounds of Wick Green as his study. There he made huge bonfires of his letters and papers during weekend leaves in Aug. 1916.
2. Hope's parents were cousins of Janet Hooton (née Aldis), Helen's close friend. The Webb and the Aldis families occupied seven former coastguard cottages at Minsmere, near Dunwich. An eighth cottage, a weekend home for Harry and Janet Hooton, was offered to Thomas while writing his *Richard Jefferies*.
3. For E.T.'s books (and his numerous publishers) see the long list of his published prose works, pp. xlv–xlvii.
4. Thomas chose the cottage at High Beech because Merfyn was apprenticed to an engineering firm in Walthamstow and he could then live at home.
5. Less directly, I believe, Thomas developed this concept of the 'meaning of England' in his personal long essay *The Country*.
6. Formed by the generosity of the poet's daughter Myfanwy and now professionally arranged and catalogued by Brian Ll. James at the Library of University of Wales College of Cardiff.
7. These letters are chiefly about proposals from Thomas of books he would like to write and Cazenove's replies about the reactions of various publishers to them and to Thomas. Many scattered notes and pencilled comments form a useful insight into the difficulties of both agent and Thomas in convincing numerous publishers that there was a ready audience for E.T.'s dominant interests. Thomas emerges as a clear-headed business man, determined to give his children a good education and to put by a 'small nest egg' against a rainy day.
8. Most of the selected letters to Frost are taken from an initial selection made by Professor A. J. Smith who checked the ETC transcriptions of the Frost letters at Dartmouth College, of the John Freeman letters in the Berg Collection, and the typescript version of E.T.'s letters to his parents from France, which I believe (on hearsay evidence) came from originals once held by Julian Thomas. They are still untraced.

9. Edward preserved all Helen's letters to him during his lifetime and, as she told me in her last year, she relied entirely on his letters to her and kept them 'as a lifeline'. The two-way correspondence was found by her daughters after her death. When they are read in their entirety, I think it becomes clear how firmly they had guided Helen when she subsequently wrote her two remarkable, thinly disguised, memoirs of their life together: *As It Was* (1926) and *World Without End* (1931).
10. For a thorough discussion of the fruitful, necessary commerce between the written and the spoken word—before he had ever met or heard of Robert Frost—see E.T.'s study of *Walter Pater*, especially 'The Essay on Style', 196–211.
11. Between 1946 and 1948, Rowland Watson invited all Thomas's friends and relations to send him their memories of E.T. He hoped to round off his devoted work as secretary of the Edward Thomas Memorial committee 1935–7 by publishing them as a tribute to 'Thomas the man'. He failed to find a publisher and two typescript copies of the memoirs are in the ETC. Irene McArthur sent him her short succinct memoir but stated that it was not for publication then. The extract I have quoted is the only piece critical of E.T. in the short memoir.
12. This quotation is part of E.T.'s extended argument about the name and nature of poetry in his *Maurice Maeterlinck*, 27–9.

LIST OF LETTERS

CHRONOLOGY

1878	3 March	Philip Edward Thomas born at Lambeth in London, the eldest of six sons of Philip Henry and Mary Elizabeth Thomas.
1883–93		Attends various board-schools, private schools, and Battersea Grammar School.
1894	January	Enters St Paul's School. A frequent visitor to home of James Ashcroft Noble.
1895	Easter	Leaves St Paul's. Essays published in various journals. Friendship with Helen Noble.
1896	April–September	Works first for Civil Service Examination and then for entry to Oxford University.
1897		His first book, *The Woodland Life*, published.
	October	Matriculates as a non-collegiate student at Oxford; lodgings at 113 Cowley Road.
1898	March	Wins a History scholarship to Lincoln College. Continues his journalism during Oxford career.
1899	June	Edward and Helen married in London at Fulham Registry Office.
1900	January	His son, Merfyn, born. Gordon Bottomley begins his correspondence with Helen and Edward.
	Summer	Gains a 2nd Class in Final Honours History Schools. Decides to become a writer and not enter the Civil Service.
	August–	Penurious existence as a writer, first at Atheldene Road, Earlsfield, and then at 7
1901	August	Nightingale Parade, Balham, London, SW.
	September	Moves to Rose Acre Cottage (one mile outside Bearsted), near Maidstone, Kent.
1902	October	Elder daughter, Bronwen, born.
	November	Becomes a regular reviewer for *Daily Chronicle* on the death of Lionel Johnson.

1903	February	First commissioned book, *Oxford*.
	July	Moves to cottage on Bearsted Green.
	September	Consults a specialist about ill health and exhaustion.
1904	May	Moves to Elses Farm, The Weald, near Sevenoaks, Kent. Continues reviewing and works on *Beautiful Wales* (second commission).
1905	Summer	Physically and mentally exhausted. Experiments with 'ejaculations in prose'.
	October	Invites W. H. Davies to share his small study cottage.
1906		Meets W. H. Hudson, Walter de la Mare.
	April–July	Walking tours; more reviewing; more commissioned books.
	October	Notice to quit Elses Farm. Stays in London.
	November	Regular reviewer for Hilaire Belloc with *Morning Post*.
	December	Moves to Berryfield Cottage, Ashford, Petersfield, near to Bedales School.
1907	April	Visits a specialist about his 'melancholia'.
	August	Walking tour with Helen in 'Jefferies Country'.
1908	January–February	First draft of *Richard Jefferies* completed at Minsmere, near Dunwich, Suffolk.
	August–December	Assistant Secretary to a Royal Commission on Welsh Monuments. Lives in London; continues to review and write books; resigns for health reasons.
1909	January	Returns to Ashford where a new house is planned.
	April	Enters new study at top of Ashford Hanger; work begins on new house.
	Autumn	Merfyn and Bronwen attend Bedales; Helen teaches there in the Kindergarten.
	Before Christmas	Moves into new house, Wick Green, Petersfield, Hampshire.
1910		Continues to write books and to review for *Daily Chronicle*, *Morning Post*, *Saturday Review*, and *The Bookman*.
	August	Second daughter, Myfanwy, born.

	September	Cycling tour with Merfyn. Visits Conrad, Belloc, Ralph Hodgson, Rupert Brooke.
1911	January	Follows a strict vegetarian diet.
	March	Low in health and spirit.
	April–August	At work on six books of various kinds.
	September	Severe breakdown caused by overwork and financial worry. Accepts money from E. S. P. Haynes.
	October–December	In West Wales and Laugharne; writes *George Borrow*.
1912	January	Begins fortnightly visits to London in search of literary work. Writes for H. Monro's *Poetry Review*.
	April	Stays with Clifford Bax in Somerset and is treated by Godwin Baynes (a nerve specialist).
	May–June	Near Bath. Treatment and writing continue.
	July	Begins reviewing for the *English Review* and the *Nation*.
	August	Cycles with Merfyn in Somerset and Kent. Long walks with Baynes.
	November	Leaves Wick Green; stays with Vivian Locke Ellis as a paying guest at Selsfield House, East Grinstead. Writes *Walter Pater*. Begins fiction, *The Happy-Go-Lucky Morgans*. Meets Eleanor Farjeon.
1913	January–February	His health much worse. Travels a great deal in Wiltshire and Somerset, preparing *In Pursuit of Spring*.
	March–May	At work on various books, reviewing for monthlies, quarterlies, and *Daily Chronicle*.
	July	Sells books before moving to a small cottage (Yew Tree Cottage) in Steep village, near Petersfield.
	August	Moves to Steep village; retains hilltop study.
	October	Introduced to Robert Frost by Ralph Hodgson.
	December	Begins his autobiography at Selsfield

		House, East Grinstead, Sussex. Meets Frost again.
1914	January–February	Chiefly in London; working on his autobiography. £100 grant from Royal Literary Fund.
	March	In Steep, reviewing, proof-reading, writing articles.
	April	Travels to Wales and then to see Frost in Herefordshire. *In Pursuit of Spring* published.
	June	At Cartmel with Bottomley, then Herefordshire with Frost.
	July	Reviews Frost's *North of Boston*. Helen and Edward visit Frost at Ledington.
	August	Thomases on holiday with Frosts at Ledington.
	September	Cycling tour in Midlands and the north of England, preparing articles for the *English Review*. Visits Frost and plans to leave with him for USA.
	October	Monthly and quarterly reviewing. Cycling in Wales and then back to Ledington.
	November–December	At Steep, begins prose versions of earliest poems. Earliest poems written and sent to Frost.
1915	January	Confined to Steep with severely sprained ankle. Writing poetry. Eleanor Farjeon begins to type them.
	February	Unable to walk. Merfyn leaves with Frosts for USA. Thomas sends poems to friends and, unsuccessfully, to some editors. Adopts pseudonym of 'Edward Eastaway' for his verse.
	March–June	Writing poetry and *The Life of the Duke of Marlborough*. Preparing anthology *This England* for the press.
	July	Enlists in the Artists' Rifles. Poems sent to Bottomley for inclusion in *An Annual of New Poetry*.
	August–September	Billeted with his parents at Balham.

	October	In camp at High Beech, near Loughton, Essex.
	November	Moved to Hare Hall Camp, Gidea Park, Romford. Promoted to Lance-Corporal. Acting as map-reading instructor.
	December	Merfyn returns from USA.
1916	January	Still at Hare Hall Camp.
	February	A convalescent leave spent at Steep.
	March	Promoted to Corporal. Frequent leaves; continues to write verse. *Keats* published.
	June	Awarded a £300 grant instead of a Civil List Pension. Applies for a commission in the Royal Artillery. Asked to leave his study at Steep.
	July	Granted £1 a week by the Civil Liability Commission (to cease if he becomes an officer). Declines to stay on the permanent staff at Hare Hall Camp.
	August	Roger Ingpen considers publication of a selection of his verse.
	September	An officer cadet with the RA in London. Stays often with his parents at Balham, begins to arrange the typescripts of his poems. Moves his family to High Beech, near Loughton, Essex.
	October	Moved to firing camp in Wiltshire, near Trowbridge.
	November	Commissioned 2nd Lieutenant; posted to 244 Siege Battery, RGA Lydd, Kent. Visits Cartmel and Gloucester before returning to High Beech.
	December	Volunteers for service overseas. Sees proofs of *An Annual of New Poetry*. Sends duplicate set of poems to Frost.
1917	January	Embarkation leave, then final firing practice at Codford, near Warminster, Wiltshire.
	13 January	'Last poem' written in his diary.
	29 January	Embarkation from Southampton.
	4 February	Leaves Le Havre area for front line.
	11 February	Settles into positions near Arras.

9 March	After a spell at Group HQ returns to his Battery. Begins duty at the Observation Post (Ronville).
26 March–	Positions moved up beyond Achicourt in preparation for forthcoming Battle of Arras.
8 April	Under constant artillery fire.
9 April	On duty at the Observation Post. Killed by the blast of a shell at 7.36 a.m. during the first hour of the Arras offensive.

BIOGRAPHICAL REGISTER OF CORRESPONDENTS AND PERSONS FREQUENTLY CITED

ABERCROMBIE, LASCELLES. Poet, critic, later Professor of English. Close neighbour (near Dymock) of Wilfrid W. Gibson where they collaborated on the journal *New Numbers* devoted to the poetry of Brooke, Drinkwater, and themselves. Invited Robert Frost to live near them in 1914.

Army colleagues of Edward Thomas. (1) With the Artists' Rifles at Hare Hall Camp, Romford: NCOs, chiefly map-reading instructors—Benson, Mason, Nash, Pearce, Robins, Vernon, and the artist John Wheatley. E.T. also taught there G. Blanco-White, R. A. Scott-James, and Paul Nash who were his fellow Artillery officer cadets at RA Barracks, Trowbridge. (2) In France, at 244 Siege Battery, E.T.'s fellow officers were: Major Franklin Lushington (as 'Mark Severn', wrote *The Gambardier* in 1930); Captain Horton (ex-regular NCO); three young subalterns, named Berrington, Rubin, and Smith; and the older J. M. Thorburn, subsequently a teacher of Philosophy at University College, Cardiff.

ARTHUR. See Hardy.

BAX, CLIFFORD. From a wealthy artistic Hampstead family: poet, dramatist, editor of *Orpheus*, a Theosophical journal, organizer of cricket festivals at his country house. With his second wife, Olga, gave hospitality to E.T. in early 1914. His brother, the composer Sir Arnold Bax, published stories as 'Dermot O'Byrne'. Their mother had 'adopted' Godwin Baynes and seen him through Cambridge. Through her brother, Bertie, Eleanor Farjeon met Bax who invited her to write for *Orpheus* and published her first volume of poems. (EF, DG)

BAYNES, GODWIN. Fashionable, but restless, doctor; an early student of Jung. Through Bax became deeply concerned with E.T.'s 'depressive state' during 1912 but with little lasting effect. (EF; see *Morning has Broken* by Annabel Farjeon (1986))

BELLOC, HILAIRE. E.T.'s senior at Oxford and his lifelong friend, practical supporter, and walking companion. A clear portrait of him as anonymous undergraduate in Thomas's *Oxford*.

BERRIDGE, JESSE. Poet, initially a bank clerk, then clergyman. Annual walking companion and lifelong friend of E.T. and Helen along with his wife, Edna, and his sons Dell, Denys, Christian, Wilfrid. (*JB*)

Berrington, Lieutenant. See Army colleagues.

Blunt, Wilfrid S. Poet and active publicist for nationalist causes.

Bottomley, Gordon. Poet, dramatist, close friend of E.T. and active proof-reader for him. Dogged by ill health, kept up (along with his wife Emily) a voluminous correspondence with E.T. (*GB*)

Brooke, Rupert. During 1907 a frequent visitor to Steep and the Thomases while he courted Noel Olivier (at Bedales); later a friend and collaborator with Abercrombie.

Cazenove, C. F. E.T.'s literary agent 1905–14 except for nine months amicable separation September 1912 to July 1913. Their continuous two-way correspondence is in Durham University Library.

Chandler. Reserve soldier and small farmer near Ledington where E.T. and family spent August 1914 as paying guests close to the family of Robert Frost.

Clayton. Tom, a friend of E.T. from schooldays; his brother, Rolf, a publisher's reader. Friends of Berridge and other lifelong London friends E.T. tried to visit before his final embarkation for France. (*JB*)

Conrad, Joseph. Often visited by E.T. for short stays; his *Walter Pater* was dedicated to Conrad.

Cornish. An outstanding athlete, at St Paul's and Oxford with E.T.

'Dad'/'the old man'. See Uzzell.

Dalmon, Charles. Poet, much admired London-based friend of E.T. Known as 'Dal', was the inspiration of Thomas's *A Friend of the Blackbird*.

Davies, H. B. At Lincoln College, shared in many of E.T.'s drinking excesses, and was a frequent visitor to E.T.'s early homes. Later took Holy Orders and, during the 1937 E.T. Memorial activities and later, studiously refused to comment on their student days.

Davies, W. H. The Newport-born 'tramp poet', highly praised in E.T.'s reviews; then shared E.T.'s small Egg-Pie Lane 'working' cottage—paid for by A. Martin Freeman—while Edward and Helen Thomas encouraged him to write his autobiography and gathered money for him from their friends. Introduced to the London literary luncheons by E.T.

de la Mare, Walter. With Gordon Bottomley, Edward Garnett, and later Robert Frost, one of E.T.'s closest literary friends whose opinions on his work he valued. (*AP*)

Drinkwater, John. Poet, editor, dramatist. Associate of Abercrombie.

DYALL, FRANKLIN. Actor, friend of Dalmon and other of E.T.'s London friends with whom he occasionally stayed briefly before his move to Berryfield Cottage.

'EASTAWAY, EDWARD'. The pseudonym—based on a family name—which E.T. adopted for his poems. He wished to retain it until his poems had established themselves in their own right without the support of friendly reviewers. (*AP*)

'EDWY'. Family name for E.T.—also used by the Hootons.

ELLIS, VIVIAN LOCKE. Wealthy poet and dilettante editor. E.T. spent two longish periods with him and his wife, Dorothy, at East Grinstead, as a paying guest 1913–14. (*AP*)

ELSEY, W. EDWARD. Known as 'Lucy'. An undergraduate at Lincoln and cox of the boat for the 1900 Torpids. A short, intense friendship with E.T. following Thomas's 'strange longing, but unsexual passion for this year's History scholar (Brook)'. Both friendships fizzled out; neither could share E.T.'s intellectual interests.

EVANS, FREDERICK H. Bookseller and fashionable photographer. His work extravagantly praised but his portrait of E.T. was not liked by his family or close friends.

FARJEON, ELEANOR. See Bax, Baynes, John Freeman. She first met E.T. in 1913 at C. Bax's Broughton Gifford Cricket Week. Soon after she visited Helen at Yew Tree Cottage, Steep, to assure her that her own overwhelming love for Edward would not be allowed to threaten their marriage. She remained Helen's friend and became a favourite 'aunt' to the Thomas children. As she did for other writers, she typed many of E.T.'s MSS—including his poems—during 1913–16. In retrospect she recognized the citadel of reserve E.T. preserved around himself. Although he came to rely on her repeated offers of friendship and practical aid, it seems unlikely that she ever entered his narrowly confined private life. Her *The Last Four Years* contains all his letters to her. (EF, HT, *AP*, *GB*)

FLINT, FRANK S. Poet, associated with Pound, Frost, and the Poetry Bookshop group. (*HM*)

FREEMAN, A. MARTIN. E.T.'s Lincoln College and lifelong unobtrusively supportive friend and walking companion. Amateur naturalist and authority on Irish literature.

FREEEMAN, JOHN. Poet, critic, novelist and businessman. A friend of Roger Ingpen and de la Mare, and a member of the Poetry Bookshop group. With Eleanor Farjeon saw *Poems* of 'Edward Eastaway' through the press. (*GB* and *AP*)

FROST, ROBERT. American poet, discussed E.T.'s prose works and critical ideas exhaustively during 1914, before and after their long discursive walks in August 1914. According to E.T., 'the onlie begetter' of his poetry. His wife Elinor and their surviving children (Lesley, Carol, Irma, Marjorie) sustained contact with Helen Thomas and her three children after E.T.'s death. (*AP*)

GARNETT, EDWARD. Influential critic, editor, dramatist, and publisher's reader. David, his son, a frequent visitor to E.T. (See his *The Golden Echo* (1953))

GIBSON, ASHLEY. Journalist, critic, reviewer; member of luncheon groups with E.T.

GIBSON, WILFRID W. Poet, friend of Abercrombie, E.T., Frost, R. Hodgson.

GUTHRIE, JAMES. Artist, writer, editor. Friend of Bottomley and E.T. First publisher of some of 'Eastaway' poems, see 'Edward Eastaway', *Six Poems*, The Pear Tree Press, Flansham (1916). (*GB*)

GWILI. Bardic name of Revd John Jenkins, a distinguished Welsh poet and Oxford theologian. An early and lifelong friend of E.T.

HAINES, JOHN W. Gloucester solicitor, amateur botanist, poet; friend and correspondent of Frost and E.T.

HARDY, ARTHUR YORK. Close friend of E.T. and Helen from schooldays. Later paid many visits to them when on leave from the South African Police.

HAYNES, E. S. P. Fashionable society solicitor and writer of vivid memories of E.T. Oxford and lifelong supportive friend of E.T. at times of crisis. (*GB*, RPE, *AP*)

HELEN [THOMAS]. See under Thomas and Noble.

HODGSON, RALPH. Poet, praised by E.T.; editor (C. B. Fry's *Magazine*), member of literary and artistic luncheon groups.

HODSON, C. F. Master at Bedales; later Headmaster of Bablake School, Coventry. (*AP*)

HOOTON, HARRY. One-time colleague of de la Mare in banking, he suffered business disappointment in mid-life. A firm friend of E.T. from 1898. His wife Janet (née Aldis) was Helen's chief school friend (and adult confidante) and witnessed her secret wedding. The invaluable Hooton letters, and his annotated copies of all E.T.'s prose works, are in the Colbeck Collection, UBC, Vancouver. (*AP*)

HOPE [WEBB]. See under Webb.

HORTON, Captain. See Army colleagues.

HUDSON, W. H. Most distinguished writer and naturalist, maintained weekly meetings with Edward Garnett and E.T. whenever he was in London.

HUEFFER, FORD MADOX. Later F. M. Ford: writer, editor, novelist.

INGPEN, ROGER. Boyhood friend of E.T. and brother-in-law of de la Mare. Editor, reviewer, war correspondent, and the publisher of E.T.'s first volume of poetry.

JANET [HOOTON]. See under Hooton and Webb.

JONES, S. Friend and one-time banking colleague of Hooton with whom E.T. got to know him. Later, when he was British representative at a Parisian bank, he persuaded E.T. to visit him in Paris.

LOGAN, Mrs BEATRICE. Later Potbury. Close friend of Helen Noble and Janet Aldis, keen advocate of women's rights. Helen spent the early months of her pregnancy with her and E.T. joined her there from Oxford. Mr Potbury witnessed the Thomas marriage. Later, Frank Dalmon married Phyllis, one of Mrs Logan's daughters. (HT)

LUSHINGTON, Major. See Army colleagues.

LUPTON, GEOFFREY. Builder and master at Bedales. He built Wick Green, Froxfield, which was rented by E.T. The house, with adjacent 'study' and large garden, is near to the 1937 E.T. Memorial Stone above Steep.

MACALISTER, (Sir) IAN. At St Paul's and Oxford with E.T.; along with Hooton and Haynes a most supportive friend at times of crisis. A frequent port of call for E.T. when in London. Eventually Secretary of RIBA. (*AP*, *JB*)

MCARTHUR, IRENE. See under Noble. With her husband, Hugh, offered E.T. frequent hospitality and discreet practical aid.

MASON. See Army colleagues.

MARSH, (Sir) EDWARD. Influential friend of the Georgian poets and editor of volumes of *Georgian Poetry* (see WC). He supported E.T.'s applications for Civil List grants but did not publish E.T.'s poetry. (See Christopher Hassall, *Edward Marsh, Patron of the Arts* (1959).)

MONRO, HAROLD. Poet, editor, founder of Poetry Bookshop. (*HM*)

MOORE, T. STURGE. Influential poet, brother of philosopher G. E. Moore.

MORGAN, J. HARTMAN (Brigadier/Professor). Welsh friend of E.T. at Oxford and later, especially during his early struggling years as a reviewer, when Morgan too was partially employed by the *Daily Chronicle* and *Manchester Guardian*. Politically influential proposer of Civil List awards for E.T. (and after his death for Helen). Their correspondence still unlocated. (JM)

Mrosowsky, Peter. Bedales pupil and holiday boarder with Helen; he was Merfyn Thomas's companion with the Frost children at Dymock in August 1914. (HT)

Nevinson, H. W. Influential literary journalist/editor. Member of key luncheon groups and literary editor for *Daily Chronicle* until 1903. E.T.'s 'greatest patron'. (*GB*, JM)

Noble, James Ashcroft. Helen Thomas's father. Journalist, critic, and editor in Liverpool and London (*Pelican Papers* (1873); *Sonnet in England* (1893)). Criticized and influenced E.T.'s reading and writing until his early death in April 1896. Helped place E.T.'s numerous adolescent essays and encouraged his friendship with Helen, though, later, Mrs Noble attempted to hinder the subsequent rapid relationship, revealed in their correspondence now in ETC (Cardiff) and NLW (Aberystwyth). There were four Noble children: Irene (McArthur), Helen, Mary (Valon), and a son Lance. Mr Noble frequently stated that E.T. 'replaced' a son Philip who had died in early childhood. (JM, HT, *AP*)

Oldershaw, Lucian. St Paul's and Oxford friend, related by marriage to G. K. Chesterton. Editor of undergraduate journal *JCR*.

Pearce, Maresco. See Army colleagues. A book illustrator known to Bottomley. (*GB*)

Perris, G. H. Boyhood friend of E.T., connected with various journals and publishers. *Bookman* reviewer and war correspondent.

Pound, Ezra. Much involved during 1913–14 with other poets (F. S. Flint, Frost) and the Poetry Bookshop. At first E.T. strongly praised his early poems. With Frost, Pound recommended E.T.'s poetry to Harriett Monroe for her *Poetry* (Chicago).

Ransome, Arthur. Journalist and novelist friend of Bottomley. Met E.T. January 1904; they shared London digs September 1904. Married his first wife, Ivy, in 1909 (one daughter, Tabitha) and lived near E.T. Although the men's friendship cooled, Ivy and Helen remained close friends. (See A.R.'s *Autobiography*, ed. R. Hart-Davis (1976).)

Rathbone, George. Musician and folk-song collector. (*GB*)

Reynolds, Stephen. Member of luncheon groups, writer on social problems (Cornish fishermen), valued friend whom E.T. frequently sought out on his long 'travel' walks.

Rhys, Ernest. Author, editor, publisher (*Everyman* series). A supporter of E.T. for Civil List awards and with editorial commissions. (See his *Wales England Wed*.)

ROBERTS, HARRY. Well-known socialist East End doctor. With his sister, Winifred, neighbours of E.T. at Froxfield, sharing his interest in Welsh and English folk-songs.

RUBIN, Lieutenant. See Army colleagues.

SCOTT-JAMES, R. A. Influential critic and literary editor. With E.T. at Oxford, he frequently commissioned reviews and articles from him. Vivid memorialist of E.T. in the Artists' Rifles and as an Artillery cadet. (*AP*)

SCOTT, RUSSELL. Nephew of C. P. Scott (*Manchester Guardian*), junior master at Bedales. Later emigrated to USA where he taught Merfyn Thomas practical subjects in 1915. (*AP*)

SECCOMBE, THOMAS. Military and cultural historian at Sandhurst and frequent walking companion of E.T. In *The Athenaeum* (16 April 1920), E. Garnett recalls a small circle of *habitués* lunching nearly every Tuesday: 'W. H. Hudson, Thomas Seccombe, R. A. Scott-James, Stephen Reynolds, E.T., W. H. Davies, Hilaire Belloc, Muirhead Bone, Ford Hueffer, Perceval Gibbon, occasionally John Galsworthy, and rarely Joseph Conrad.' (*GB*, *AP*)

TAYLOR, C. M. E.T.'s batman in 244 Siege Battery in France.

THOMAS family. Philip Henry Thomas: Edward's father. Civil Servant, Positivist writer, Humanist preacher, local Liberal politician, and, after retirement, unsuccessful parliamentary candidate. His wife, Mary Elizabeth (née Townsend); six sons—Edward, Ernest, Theodore, Reginald, Oscar, Julian (HT). Many first cousins of P.H.T. lived at Pontardulais, regularly visited by E.T. and often by Helen, and still later by Merfyn and Bronwen. E.T. and his brothers spent school vacations with their paternal Welsh-speaking grandmother at New Swindon, where E.T. made friends with 'Dad' Uzzell and developed his knowledge of Richard Jefferies country. (*AP*)

THOMAS, HELEN (née Noble). The second daughter of J. Ashcroft Noble, was very conscious of being 'less bright'—in academic attainment—than her sisters Irene and Mary. Encouraged by her father, she joined Edward Thomas ('the young genius', the Nobles called him) on his wide-ranging nature walks, absorbed the country lore he taught her, and, after her father's early death, followed Edward's suggestions to widen her reading. Her passionate attachment to Edward—clearly reciprocated—is best expressed in *Under Storm's Wing* which charts the rapid progress towards their 'secret' marriage while he was at Oxford and her subsequent repeatedly tested support for his difficult, tortuous career as a journalist-critic and multiple book maker who, without admitting it to himself, wished to be a poet and at the same time provide adequately for his family. The switchback movements of their marriage are fully chronicled in R. George Thomas, *Edward Thomas: A Portrait* (1985; 1987), 148–59, 189–96, 211–14, 230–2, 302–3.

Edward was meticulous, inward looking, intensely self-critical: Helen was a happy extrovert, devoted to children and home-making, and quite careless of formal domestic expectations and minute financial matters. The bedrock of her love for him—reinforced by her belief in his genius—was proof against his self-absorption in his work and his devotion to nature—and the irritability with her and the children that accompanied it. It also survived his infatuation with Hope Webb and, much later, the intense interest that Eleanor Farjeon showed in him.

During Edward's profitless 'wanderyears' (between late 1910 and early 1914), Helen found some congenial employment at Bedales School and became involved in various discussion groups and local causes in Steep and Petersfield. But the supreme joy for her during his absences from home was his frequent letters. With his regular visits home they kept alive their friendship and love—although 'love' was a word he used charily. After his final return to Steep early in 1914, with the sudden birth of his poetry and, then, his numerous weekend leaves from the Artists' Rifles, she was once again reassured of the strength of his affection for her. This, she once told me, was amply confirmed by his constant letters to her from France. His chief concern was to reassure and inform her without unnecessary alarm.

His death was a shattering blow and she seemed to suffer a severe long-delayed breakdown until she wrote, in 1926 and 1931, her two moving accounts of their life together. Until her death, aged 90, in 1967, she was sustained by the firm, cheerful conviction that despite the many stresses of their marriage everything had come right for them in those last testing years.

Helen and Edward had three children: Merfyn (often Mervyn), Bronwen, and Myfanwy ('Baba').

THORBURN, J. H. See Army colleagues.

TOWNSEND, MARGARET. E.T.'s aunt. A secretary-companion in London and Oxford and later when settled in the USA. See her letters in Bodleian Library. (RPE)

TREVELYAN, R. C. Poet, friend of Bottomley, editor of *An Anthology of New Poetry*, 1918, with poems by 'Edward Eastaway'. (*GB*)

UZZELL, DAVID ('Dad'). Countryman, gamekeeper, poacher, Salvation Army convert. Friend and early mentor of E.T. during adolescent stays in Swindon. Three sons—Charley, Bill, Tom. (HT, *AP*)

VALON, ARTHUR and MARY (née Noble). Bronwen Thomas spent two terms in 1914 at their daughter Margaret's school in Chelsea. (HT)

WATCYN WYN. Bardic name of Watkin H. Williams. (*GB*)

WAUGH, ARTHUR. Literary review editor of the *Daily Chronicle*, later a publisher's reader. (*GB*)

WATTS-DUTTON, T. W. Solicitor then literary critic (*Athenaeum*); friend and adviser of Swinburne in his later days.

WEBB family. Janet Hooton's father (James Aldis) was uncle to Josephine Webb whose husband (William Trego Webb) had worked in Darjeeling and Tasmania (?as an academic/missionary). The Webbs returned to Margate in 1896 where Helen Noble was nursemaid-governess to their four children, Phillis, Paul, Hope, and Alice. In 1907 Dunwich Town leased eight Minsmere coastguard cottages to the Webbs, the retired Aldises, and Harry Hooton who offered his cottage to E.T.—then under a strict medical regime for 'neurasthenia'—while he wrote his *Richard Jefferies*.

WEBB, HOPE. The 17-year-old schoolgirl daughter of the large Trego Webb family to whom E.T. was strongly attracted during the Christmas vacation of 1907. E.T. was much involved with the Webbs and the Aldises because Helen Thomas had once (in 1896) acted as governess to four of the Webb children at Margate, soon after the Webbs had returned from abroad. Hope was then her favourite pupil. There is no suggestion of any improper relationship between E.T. and Hope. As he repeated in letters to Harry Hooton, Bottomley, and de la Mare, he was simply bowled over by a powerful, 'unthinking feeling of attraction' that had rarely happened to him before.

For a full discussion of this episode, and its positive effect on the Thomas marriage, see R. George Thomas, *Edward Thomas: A Portrait* (1985; 1987), 144–54, especially Edward's comment to Helen about some of his verses in January 1916: 'There would have to be two to make a love affair and I am only one. Nobody but you would ever be able to respond as I wished. I don't like to think anybody but I could respond to you. If you turned to anybody else I should come to an end immediately.'

When Hope returned to school, E.T. sent her his *Pocket Book of Poems and Songs for the Open Air* (through her mother) and they then exchanged a few letters. When Helen visited Edward at Minsmere in late January 1908, Mr Webb insisted that the correspondence must cease. E.T. recalled the affair to Harry Hooton in March 1908: 'I know I was foolish, but the punishment as it always is is excessive. It is a small consolation that perhaps Hope is serene enough and even that may not be true.' She went on to read English at Westfield College, London, and gained a First Class Honours degree. Later, she taught in a state and then in a private school (together with her sister, a correspondent once informed me some years ago). She never married and there is no mention of her in the surviving correspondence between Helen and Janet Hooton. Hope is described, I think, in 'The Fountain', *Rest and Unrest*, 138–43, and a more muted description of E.T.'s initial response is woven into his *The South Country*, chapter 6, 81–3. (See Martin Haggerty's account in Newsletter 26, E.T. Fellowship; and HT, *AP*.)

WILLIAMS, A. DUNCAN. Undergraduate fan of E.T., who offered help with translations for his *Maurice Maeterlinck*. (*GB*)

WILLIAMS, J. WILLIAM (often called 'the Deacon'). Headmaster of Waun Wen School, Swansea. Related to J. Hartman Morgan. Once Gwili had left the Pontardulais area, E.T. usually made Waun Wen the base for his many repeated visits to Wales between 1909 and 1914.

WILLIAMS, T. C. (called 'Duncan'). Originally from North Wales, a socialist friend of William Morris. A LCC Civil Servant, and folk-song collector. E.T. first met him through Berridge, Dyall, and Dalmon. His home remained one of E.T.'s favourite ports of call when in London. (*JB*)

CHRONOLOGICAL LIST OF WORKS IN PROGRESS WHEN FIRST MENTIONED IN LETTERS

1896/9	Essays appearing in *New Age*, *Globe*, *Speaker*, *Literature*, *Junior Common Review* (Oxford).
1900	*Olivia Patterson*, with E. P. S. Haynes, an unfinished novel.
1901	Two essays in *Crampton's Magazine*; some essays rejected by *Outlook*.
1902	Reviews in the *Daily Chronicle*; articles in *Week's Survey*, *Atlantic Monthly*, *Illustrated London News*, *Academy*, and *Literature*. E.T. succeeds Lionel Johnson on *Daily Chronicle*.
1903	Constant reviews for *Daily Chronicle* (until 1911/12); *Oxford* (1903).
1904/5	Reviews in *Week's Survey*, *Academy*, *Speaker*, *World*. *Beautiful Wales* (1905).
1906	Constant reviews in *Morning Post* (until 1911) and *Bookman* (until 1910); some reviews in *Saturday Review*. *The Heart of England* (1906).
1907	Edited *The Pocket Book of Poems and Songs for the Open Air* (1907) (called 'Anthology').
1907/8	Edited *The Book of the Open Air* (1908).
1908/9	*Richard Jefferies: His Life and Work* (1909); *The South Country* (1909); *Rest and Unrest* (1910); *Light and Twilight* (1911)—'Welsh tales'.
1910	*Feminine Influence on the Poets* (1910); reviews begin for *English Review*.
1911	*Maurice Maeterlinck* (1911); *Celtic Stories* (1911); *Isle of Wight* (1911). Reviews reduced in *Daily Chronicle* and *Morning Post*.
1912	*Lafcadio Hearn* (1912); *The Icknield Way* (1913); *Algernon C. Swinburne: A Critical Study* (1912); *George Borrow: The Man and his Books* (1912). Frequent reviews in *Daily Chronicle*, *Bookman*, and *Saturday Review* (until 1913).
1913	*Walter Pater* (1913); *The Happy-Go-Lucky Morgans* (1913)—called 'a fiction'. 'Proverbs' which eventually became *Four-and-Twenty Blackbirds* (1915).
1913/14	Series of review articles on contemporary verse for *Bookman*.

	Autobiographical attempts—see especially *The Childhood of Edward Thomas* (1938) and 'a fiction' half now in ETC, University of Wales, Cardiff. Tales and sketches included in *Cloud Castle and Other Papers* (1922). *In Pursuit of Spring* (1914); *The Last Sheaf* (1928); *A Literary Pilgrim in England* (1917)—called 'Homes and Haunts'.
1914	Articles on the war (in *The Last Sheaf*); *This England: An Anthology from her Writers* (1915). Prose version of his first poem ('Up in the Wind') begun 16 November; Poems 1–15 (as numbered in *Collected Poems*) written by 31 December.
1915	*The Life of the Duke of Marlborough* (1915). Poems 16–93 (as in *Collected Poems*). Adopts pseudonym 'Edward Eastaway' for 'Manor Farm' and 'Haymaking' in *This England*, for poems in *An Anthology of New Poetry* (1916), and all poems published during his lifetime.
1916/17	Poems 94('Rain')–144('Last poem', 13 January 1917). Embarks for France 29 January 1917. Receives reviews of *An Anthology of New Poetry*, 5 April; killed outside Arras Easter Monday, 9 April 1917.

LIST OF PROSE WORKS

The Woodland Life, two editions (1897).

Horae Solitariae (1902).

The Poems of John Dyer (Number 4 of *The Welsh Library*, edited by Owen M. Edwards), edited by Thomas (1903).

Oxford (*Black's Colour Book Series*), painted by John Fulleylove, RI, described by Thomas, with 60 illustrations (1903). Reprinted (1911); revised, with 32 illustrations (1922).

Rose Acre Papers (Number 2 of *The Lanthorn Series*) (1904).

Beautiful Wales (*Black's Colour Book Series*), painted by Robert Fowler, RI, described by Thomas, with a Note on Mr Fowler's Landscapes by Alex J. Finberg, and with 74 illustrations (1905). Second edition, entitled *Wales* and with 32 illustrations (1924).

The Heart of England, with 48 coloured illustrations by H. L. Richardson (1906). Second edition (in *The Heart of England Series*) (1909), third edition (in *The Open Air Library*), with a Foreword and 10 wood-engravings by Eric Fitch Daglish (1932 and 1934).

George Borrow (Number 151 of *Everyman's Library*), *The Bible in Spain*, with an Introduction by Thomas (1906).

George Herbert, *The Temple* and *A Priest to The Temple* (Number 309 of *Everyman's Library*), with an Introduction by Thomas (1908).

Richard Jefferies: His Life and Work (1909). Second edition (1911). Reissue (1978) edited by Roland Gant.

The Plays and Poems of Christopher Marlowe (Number 383 of *Everyman's Library*), with an Introduction by Thomas (1909).

Richard Jefferies, *The Hills and the Vales*, with an Introduction by Thomas (1909).

The South Country (in *The Heart of England Series*) (1909). Second edition (Number 12 of *The Aldine Library*), with an Introduction by Helen Thomas (1932); edited R. George Thomas (Everyman, 1993).

Windsor Castle (*Beautiful England Series*), described by Thomas, pictured by E. W. Haslehurst (1910); as volume i of *Our Beautiful Homeland Series* (1919).

Rest and Unrest (*The Roadmender Series*) (1910).

Feminine Influence on the Poets (1910).

Rose Acre Papers, Including Essays from Horae Solitariae (*The Roadmender Series*) (1910).

Light and Twilight (1911).

Isaac Taylor, *Words and Places in Illustration of History, Ethnology and Geography* (Number 517 of *Everyman's Library*), with an Introduction by Thomas (1911).

Maurice Maeterlinck (1911). Second and third editions (1912 and 1915).

The Tenth Muse (Number 2 of *The Coronal Series*) (1911). Reissued (1916) and, with a memoir of Thomas by John Freeman (1917).

Celtic Stories (1911). Second and third editions (1913 and 1918).

The Isle of Wight (*Beautiful England Series*), pictures by Ernest Haslehurst, described by Thomas (1911); as volume ii in *Our Beautiful Homeland Series* (1919).

Lafcadio Hearn (*Modern Biographies Series*) (1912).

Norse Tales (1912). Second edition (1921).

William Cobbett, *Rural Rides*, 2 vols. (Numbers 638 and 639 of *Everyman's Library*), with an Introduction by Thomas (1912).

The Pocket George Borrow (*Authors for the Pocket Series*), passages chosen from the works of Borrow by Thomas (1912).

Algernon Charles Swinburne: A Critical Study (1912).

George Borrow: The Man and his Books (1912).

The Country (*Fellowship Books Series*) (1913).

The Icknield Way, with illustrations by A. L. Collins (1913). Second and third editions (1916 and 1929).

The Happy-Go-Lucky Morgans (1913).

Walter Pater: A Critical Study (1913).

In Pursuit of Spring, with illustrations from drawings by Ernest Haslehurst (1914).

George Borrow, *The Zincali: An Account of the Gipsies of Spain* (Number 697 of *Everyman's Library*), with an Introduction by Thomas (1914).

Four-and-Twenty Blackbirds (1915).

The Life of the Duke of Marlborough (1915).

Keats (Number 126 of *The People's Books*) (1916). Second edition (1926).

A Literary Pilgrim in England (1917). Second edition (Number 95 of *The Travellers' Library*) (1928).

Cloud Castle and Other Papers, with a Foreword by W. H. Hudson (1922).

The Last Sheaf: Essays by Edward Thomas, with a Foreword by Thomas Seccombe (1928).

The Childhood of Edward Thomas, a fragment of autobiography with a Preface by Julian Thomas (1938).

The Friend of the Blackbird (written by Thomas in October 1911) (The Pear Tree Press, Flansham, Sussex, 1938).

The Prose of Edward Thomas, selected by Roland Gant with an Introduction by Helen Thomas (1948).

Edward Thomas on the Countryside, a selection of his prose and verse, edited by Roland Gant (1977).

The Chessplayer and other essays, with an Introduction by R. George Thomas (Andoversford, 1981).

A Sportsman's Tale, with an Introduction by R. George Thomas (Edinburgh, 1983).

A Pilgrim and Other Tales, selected and introduced by R. George Thomas (Everyman, 1991).

Numerous essays, sketches, tales, reviews and prose extracts by E. T. appeared between 1896 and 1915 in the following journals:

Academy
Athenaeum
Atlantic
Bookman
Country Life
Courier
Daily Chronicle
English Review
Globe
Illustrated London News
Junior Commonroom Review
Morning Post
Nation
New Age
New Numbers
New Statesman
New Weekly
Outlook
Pall Mall
Poetry and Drama
Poetry Review
Poetry (Chicago)
Saturday Review
Speaker
T.P.'s Weekly
Thrush
Tramp
Times Literary Supplement
Venture
World

Thomas's own selections are in 5 volumes in the ETC at Cardiff. (*GB*)

SOURCES OF EARLIEST PUBLISHED POEMS

(Unless otherwise stated these poems are attributed to 'Edward Eastaway'.)

Root and Branch, ed. J. Guthrie (1915).
This England (1915).
Form. A Quarterly of the Arts, ed. Austin O. Spare and Francis Marsden (Apr. 1916).
Six Poems, printed by J. Guthrie (1916).
An Annual of New Poetry (1917).
Poetry, A Magazine of Verse, ed. Harriett Monroe, 9/5 (Chicago, 1917).
Root and Branch, ed. J. Guthrie, 2/2 (1917).
Edward Thomas [Edward Eastaway], *Poems* (1917).
Four Poems (28 Apr. 1917).
Root and Branch, ed. J. Guthrie, 2/4 (1918).
Edward Thomas, *Last Poems* (1918).
Twelve Poets: A Miscellany of New Verse (1918).
In Memoriam: Edward Thomas, The Green Pasture Series, 2 (1919).
Edward Thomas, *Collected Poems*, foreword by Walter de la Mare (1920).

For more detail see *The Collected Poems of Edward Thomas*, ed. R. George Thomas (1978), pp. xx–xxix, 423–6, 435–59.

LIST OF ABBREVIATIONS

AP	R. George Thomas, *Edward Thomas: A Portrait* (1985; 1987)
CP	Edward Thomas, *Collected Poems* (1920)
DC	*Daily Chronicle*
DG	David Garnett, *The Golden Echo* (1953)
EF	Eleanor Farjeon, *Edward Thomas: The Last Four Years* (1958)
ETC	Edward Thomas Collection
GB	R. George Thomas, *Letters from Edward Thomas to Gordon Bottomley* (1968)
HM	Joy Grant, *Harold Monro and the Poetry Bookshop* (1967)
HT	Helen Thomas with Myfanwy Thomas, *Under Storm's Wing* (1988) (includes *As It Was* (1926) and *World Without End* (1931))
JB	Anthony Berridge, *The Letters of Edward Thomas to Jesse Berridge* (1983)
JM	John C. Moore, *The Life and Letters of Edward Thomas* (1939)
NLW	National Library of Wales
RPE	Robert P. Eckert, *Edward Thomas: A Biography and Bibliography* (1937)
WC	William Cooke, *Edward Thomas: A Critical Biography* (1970)
UBC	University of British Columbia

To James Ashcroft Noble

61 Shelgate Rd Battersea Rise | London SW | 11 January 1896

My dear Mr Noble,

I am just back from Wimbledon and have been reading your letter. It gave me intense joy for a moment in a day of misery—comparative misery. In truth though I am not ill, I am worse today. Want energy, and weakness, stiffness and languor, and have no plans, hardly any ideas, for tomorrow. I trust it will find me away somewhere. The idea of being permanently glued to a stool at a London office is horrible just now. For though I fear I cannot say.

My love for Nature is as old as I, with increasing health—and I am getting better—my intense love for the open air, my—feeble though it be,—sympathy with everything about me increases too. Badly thought and expressed again, but I may learn something from Emerson and my favourite(?)—Thoreau.

I would wish that I might not be classed with 'Provincials', 'Dissenters', 'Very Middle Class' people, 'Phlegmatic' cusses or other—I was going to say 'dramatic'—aversions.

Now I think I had the symptoms.

My brothers could not—would not—come with me today, and I did not feel strong enough to go far, so I went off to the Common after dinner. Of course, my pleasure on the walk was great, but a sadder, a serener pleasure perhaps than usual. Many things I saw, and among them such a band of blue tits—and quite close to me. They were chattering in their usual merry fashion, and hanging in the strangest attitudes on the birches. I do hope Helen and I will see another such band on Monday. No weakness could deter me from that walk!—and I may be well again. I did not walk more than nine or ten miles, nor was I tired, but my shoulders are very stiff.

Should I see Arthur* tonight or tomorrow I will give him your kind message.

I am glad I am not 'Very Middle Class'.

When you mentioned Mary's* watch I was astonished for a moment, but I have it safe and will bring it with me on Monday.

I shall be sorry if it has inconvenienced her. The glass is cracked, but I forget how it was when I had it.

I have finished Leland, saving only the 'Spells' and a 'Short History'. It has pleased me immensely and it only adds to my indebtedness to you for introducing to me such a charming and interesting book.

I should like you to have this note by tonight, so must bring it to a sudden end.

Love and kindest regards to you all from

Yours ever affectionately | Edward Thomas

To James Ashcroft Noble

19 Cambria Place | New Swindon | Wilts. | 21 February 1896

My dear Mr Noble,

I was very sorry indeed to hear of your continued illness, so bad as to keep you in bed. I do hope you have been feeling better and are improving now, that I may have a better account of your health.

I am loth to trouble you with my affairs, but you will be able to judge in a moment whether the paper has a chance. I am bewildered in attempting to give a title to it. I think—though I may be wrong—that the Gypsies should be mentioned in the title. 'Gypsies and (or in) Wiltshire Meadows'; 'Round a Gypsy Camp'; 'Meadows and Gypsies'; each of these has something to be said for it though they are very clumsy. It was extremely kind of you to suggest a magazine and I would have tried without troubling you at such a time, but I thought you might see better where to try by looking over the article. After all, it is not very long, but there seems to me *more* information than I can generally give.

My note book would show you that I am not wasting my time—out of doors at least. I have written another paper and hope to be able to write two a week regularly. Father in his letter suggests that I should try the *provincial daily press*, but I know nothing of it, though it seems worth some trouble.

We are having some lovely clear weather now and every day I have been out for long walks. I wish I could hear that yourself had been tempted out by the sun, as you would have been today if better. Though I like the old man's company* I really enjoy walks alone best and seem to feel the companionable stillness of the woods, and get more intense calm and pleasure thus.

My reading, beyond Civil Service work, is limited to: 'Hypatia' and 'Selborne' and a snatch at Jefferies rarely as yet.

Besides studying the wild creatures of the fields I have gone so far as to make the acquaintance of a 'hedger and ditcher' and a shepherd on the downs. All of them cry out on the farmers who 'put no money in the land' and send everything to London; they say that the farmers even forget how to make cheese!

Arthur is in no hurry to write but I suppose he is waiting to let me know the result of his exam.; I hope that by this time you will have heard of his *success*.

Again hoping you are already better or well and with kindest regards to all I remain, my dear Mr Noble,

Ever your affectionate | Edwy Thomas

To Helen

113 Cowley Road* [Oxford] | Sunday 14 November '97

Thank you very much for the stamps, dear.

My dearest Friend,

I am very happy with you, very content, and very hopeful, but little inclined to write. In fact I sat several minutes before I could 'think what to say'. The happiness and content and hope is in a magic and higher place of our own: to write a letter means to leave that place, sweet heart; and leaving it I have doubts, frettings, hopelessnesses. That is why I hesitated at the beginning: and I write that you may have no least misgivings. Perhaps you are not likely to have them? Then I find it is because I should be a little discontented if I wrote nothing to you for long. So I write.

Your last letter was kind, it was gracious and sweet and gave me joy. I thought of it, and even read it again, as I walked in the quiet fields today. It is fine and mild; the last few days have been a little wet; today is the tenderest of all. Not a bright sun, but a cloudy sky pleasant to look upon, and most of all where it meets the thick woods of the horizon. Little flights of larks were singing and darting about in the last gardens of the town and the first fields of the country. Short snatches of blithe song—for indeed the birds were too lively and eager to fly, to sing much. In the wet grass, there were daisies, one here, one there, but half closed—for the day is too dull to open them. A mistiness in the air—hardly a wind—a healthy languor everywhere—a day when it is good to be alone, to walk slowly in the loneliness, not to think but merely to live, if our souls are calm enough. I was not calm and therefore did not enjoy it to the full; but I became calmer, and was the sweeter for the walk. My head is so full of littleness; now I think of history and coin an 'idea', now I think of what is about me and stupidly write in my notebook, and nothing ever long; in fact, a sort of madness. I want an object which shall concentrate my life, gather up the flying edges and trailing ends, and purge away a good deal, too. For I find myself with a lot of minor interests, encouraging now one, now another, and not really developing any. My writing vexes me, too. I don't know what my papers are coming to, except prose fancy. If I ever had any power of description, it is entirely gone now, not a particle left. I am become a mere word spinner—almost always. Yesterday for example I put my hand to the perfecting of a halfdone paper, thinking it would absorb my brain for a while. Instantly I began to spin and spin things that were never in my brain before the moment: I was led away now by a thought of somebody's verse like a word spinner; and so went on producing not a whole at all, but patchwork, where, besides, not one patch is silk, nor even honest cloth, but rotten finery. However, I grant you I may not be an entire fool, and so leave the matter.

I wrote Mr. Hooton a long letter yesterday and Friday: in fact so long that I feel you might be justly angry. But you know why it was long, and yours short:—all is uncertain, and unknown between me and him:—we have no uncertainties. Therefore you are content, sweet Helen?

The most beautiful thing I could do, would be to draw your picture in my fancy, you as you are at this moment among the shaking birches. I see you indeed. If I were to choose one thing and then die; it would be to really see you now as you are, happy and well, you say, and enjoying the wild air, feeding on your own sweet mood. I only wish my head were cooler and clearer, to see you the better, to see you perfectly. You alone are beautiful. I can often doubt whether what I see on the earth is beautiful; but I know

[*unfinished state*]

To Harry Hooton

113, Cowley Road, Oxford | 10 January 1898

My dear Harry,

You must have known how sorry I was on Saturday not to be able to call as I had hoped; but there is surely no need for me to talk of a disappointment so slight in comparison with the delight of yesterday; indeed you have probably forgotten. I hope Janet was as well on her arrival as she was happy, and I hope she came in good time. Surely I shall see her when I get back?

It is a weakness of mine that in any but the most fitful conversation I lose my head and my power of memory and even of reasonable speech; but immediately I am once more alone I recollect the subject and torment myself with a regret that I did not see this and that. One or two things occurred to my mind after leaving you on Friday. For example, it seemed to me that, desiring as you do an unbroken progress of character which death cannot affect, modern Science, with its doctrines of development, and Christianity, with its trust in a constantly beneficent God, should help you, at least by their inspiration of hope. But will you object to this, that it degrades the egoistic idea? Surely not; for what I suggest would be an action not more obtrusively outside action than what in life affects us from the outside,—surely a great force, even for the most self-centred egoist. This is vainly longwinded, and quite enough. Nevertheless, I will mention another thought that occurred at the same time. You considered the total cutting short of a character in the process of arduous development one of the most pitiful results of death to be contemplated. But is it not a question, a matter of opinion, whether we live to mould the abstract beauty of a character for itself alone, or whether only for its service to surrounding human nature? The results of well doing and the enjoyments of sweetness are positive enough to be the reward of any exertion, I am inclined to think; and added to them, if one still dreads the shattering of this lovely thing character, there is at least the trust, if not the certainty, that, as I before suggested, a beneficent God or a natural process will carry on the development to its perfection, which is of course infinite. There remains, however, the sad consciousness which a person of strenuous and lovely character must possess, that a very miserable portion only of his strength has by outward forces been allowed to strike itself into the soil; then as to the remainder, which has been wasted or unused; surely it has not been futile, whether seemingly resultless, or even never exercised? There comes in the Egoist's assurance and delight in himself, even if he stand perfectly alone.

I am almost enjoying myself here, though I certainly shall see no friendly creature before I return. In fact, I find quite a keen pleasure in the competition. I will try to go in full of hope.

Did you read any of Richard Jefferies on Saturday night, I wonder? I should be very glad to find you could enjoy him.

Helen goes to Bedford Park today, and it is about time; for I was beginning with ground to fear for her health. She should have a month's ease there, and need be in no hurry to find another place, though never forgetting that end. What happy times are still promising for us. You make it so pleasant that we have quite a debate to decide whether to go to you or to Wimbledon. Goodbye! I will tell you when I definitely come back.

Edwy

To Helen

113 Cowley Road | 14 June '98

My dearest Friend,

Your letter this evening gave me such a warm sense of quiet bliss. I half expected you would have been miserable after my one note. You mistook me favourably once, however. As if I meant Irene! How could I have had enough experience of her to find my 'friendship' with her 'accursed'? No. I am not her friend, nor is she mine.

I hope to return by a train leaving here at 4.20 on Thursday. I don't know when it gets to Paddington; rather before 6 I should guess: but you could look it up, and if able, meet it. We might have a quiet, if not a private hour. Never mind if you can't. Still, I will watch for your brown face, sweet heart. If I don't see you, I will write to arrange for Friday. Don't wear a white dress if you meet me at Paddington.

This is really Wednesday and I have copied so far from a letter written last night. Half the exam has passed successfully, but then it was the easier half.

You are probably right as to the verses: and I will attempt to mend the part you dislike. For heaven's sake tell me if—dispassionately and unbiassed—you find my verses boshy—those at the head of my articles, for instance. Did you think them ludicrous? Say! for I want to know, though it is true I wrote them for you. Mind to tell me.

I spent a short unpleasant evening with MacAlister yesterday, Fyfe having once more disappointed me: I enclose the note he left in his room as an apology.

My dear Helen, I hope you haven't got hard visible muscles. Girls ought not to have them, and can be quite strong enough without them, you know.

How unreasonable you are to say Cornish doesn't interest you! You would stare and talk a long time about a stone Apollo—and here is one much lovelier in red and white, and you say he doesn't 'interest' you. Never mind.

That is delightful news about your holiday. I shall possibly go to Wales when you go to Holmwood; I will manage it so: but I shan't go anywhere if I fail at Responsions.* Still I could sometimes ride or walk to Holmwood, if you go there, and perhaps stay a night.

Your health and spirits make me so glad. It means spirits and something by which to live, for me also.

Such a union as you speak of for Janet and Mr. Hooton is scandalous. Did they intend sometimes sleeping together? Have they already? It would be taking a mean advantage of a law (which they affect to despise).—You are mistaken in one point, nevertheless. People don't avoid having children in order to show they can restrain themselves, but because they can not afford to keep the children. Therefore they are entitled to use any preventive. If their object were self restraint, then of course it would be immoral to use artificial preventives; but it is not; their object, as I said, is to avoid natural consequences; and they are taking the surest means. Whether they take advantage of the ineffectiveness* of their embraces, and indulge themselves like beasts, is another matter. But indeed, Helen, it is impossible to reason on this. I don't believe any reasoning will bring us to a right conclusion. We must let nature take its course: and *be sure that if we are noble and sweet by nature we shall do nothing together which shall bring shame or evil result*. Think of beautiful souls like Milton, Plato, and the best Puritans; think how they would behave: and consider if you could be like them: and if you, too, would behave modestly as they would, then yours is true morality; for I believe beautiful natures have desires which never forget themselves and run wild; so that if we are not beautiful souls, it is vain to reason ourselves into restraint. But know this, that when once people indulge themselves for mere pleasure, *they can never have enough*. And there is much in the understanding between man and bride. But here I feel unsure and dim, and will go no farther.—One truth is becoming clearer to my mind every day, which is, *This century thinks too much, certainly talks too much, of love. Human beings need many things as well as love, if not more. They need action, change, experience etc.* But perhaps I am vague, though I doubt not I am right: someday I shall say more of this; and it needs saying, because people go about talking as if love were the only aim of life,—which leads to prostitutes, I think, since love let *entirely free* becomes lust, and *excludes all else*; while love *not entirely free* remains love, and *has need of something else*. There's philosophy for you, Helen! but I have written the very first part too carelessly, and yet have not time to copy it out.

I must post now, sweet heart. Goodbye. I kiss you quite happily, and with a smile. You, too, I see are entirely happy. How you fly as you walk. Goodbye—Goodnight it is as you read this. Then Good-night! I am in life your truest and fondest friend Edwy and you ever my own sweet little one, Helen, my anemone maiden, Good-night!*

To Harry Hooton

17, Woodville Street | Pontardulais* | South Wales | 17 August 1898

My dear Harry,

The good Welsh people here have changed me into the animal I always potentially was. I eat and sleep, and my most serious work was yesterday—binding the sheaves of wheat in a strong sun; I really did work hard, and at the end had tea sitting round a cock of wheat with the reapers and binders. That is what they do with me. Sometimes they pretend I can work, but put me into a room so absurdly encumbered with cheap decoration that I can't do any good work there. So you will excuse my negligence, if you cannot pardon it. The fact is I would rather not write to anyone that can endure without a letter,—that is write to Helen alone; yet I should like to know how you are, and how Janet is; if you are busy, or if I might drop in any evening; if you have done much writing lately—and made money by it. And I shall be away until September the seventh, very likely. Then, do let me come at least once a week until I go up again.

I wish ignorance was not so flattering as it is. I mean—the ignorant people here flatter me in every conceivable way, so that if I respected them only a little I should blush all over, as is my way. The worst of it is, too, that I have in me the seeds of the meanest of all kinds of conceit; so that if only my reason would be quiet, I should settle down in content with a sort of microscopic lionism. The only man of any reading and intellect is a Welsh bard* of whom I have probably told you before this. But he has the same damnable lenience, tolerance, concessive gentleness, that spoils one, and is as painful as the opposite treatment I get at home. He is reckoned the best bard in Wales, though only 24; but his heterodoxy—perhaps paganism—makes him barred a lot in this second Palestine. But his English verses lack originality altogether,—like Burns's.

So I am not encouraged to write. The only things I have completed, in nearly three weeks, are a few odd sentences about this and that; the copying of a story from Greek history in dialogue form (which Helen found at least interesting, though it is still uncorrected:—in fact I will enclose it even as it is, if only to ensure a letter back with it very soon); and the beginning of another of my birthdoomed Arthurian transcrips from Mallory [*sic*]—enlargements—or what you will, about Elaine; the incident always delighted me and fed my imagination; it is where Elaine goes collecting flowers 'to make a bain' for Lancelot,—that is all Mallory says, then leaves it.—I had a paper in last week's *Speaker*, but could not get a copy here, and so miss it, in uncertainty: I was forced by the Editor to hack it down to suit his columns.

Helen seems to be entirely happy even at Holmwood with the Andrewses, where she must feel more separated than ever. For some reason or another we are happier now than ever before, and cannot stop wondering aloud at it to one another. It is a happiness so mild and cool that it is like a kind of saintliness after passion; yet it is not satiety.—Janet must be gone away now. Do you see her often? And Helen can not come to look at you. Yet I hope you are not miserable, but enjoying this brilliant summer, at least at evenings and on Sundays, when you escape the heat, which I hear has been terrible.

The flowers here! And in another way I notice them, for I am adding to my knowledge of at least the names,—which is useful as far as it goes, I am sure. And by the way, you did not mean it when you talked of the unhealthy love of flowers, the healthy love of locomotives? Though it often is true. Nevertheless Helen is surely a proof the other way; for if she has any unhealth, it is from me; and that more on her lips than in her heart.

I write in a noisy kitchen which will give me no sweet thoughts. I am at least well; that you can be sure of: and I wish you were the same.

Goodbye now! | Edwy

To Helen

Lincoln College | Oxford | 3 February '99

My dearest Friend,

I can understand that you found nothing very charming in my last letter; but can't understand how you expect anything else.

Consider the life I lead here. The greater part of it in bed and at meals, the rest spent in getting ready for sleep, in digesting, in violent exercise, foul conversation and dull work. I don't even have time or inclination to write. How then could I write to you? whom I can only satisfy by my best self. Remember that last line in the last verses I wrote: 'We cannot always love!' As a rule it is impossible I should write to you except as a friend willing and even anxious to hear just the bare facts of my life. Oxford is not a place for friends (so far). I almost forget what it is to have a friend at my side. Naturally therefore I cannot write in a truly friendly way; and especially as my life is such as to dispense with the needs of friends—it is so humdrum and unadventurous.

Anyhow!

Of course I only want you to talk about yourself in your letters. Of whom else? I am not concerned with the Pooles* or anybody there. What else could you write of? Nothing. I want to hear nothing but your innocent talk, expressing the laughter which is natural to health purity and happiness.

I want that *J. C. R.** returned at once; if possible by Sunday. The Editor has asked for more, but I don't know what to send until I examine my note books.

All this week I have been unable to row. My wrist is not painful, but swollen and weak. A doctor has painted and bound it, says I ought to be able to row soon. Certainly I shan't row till Monday; if not then—not at all, I fear, for the races begin on Thursday week, and I should be out of training after such a rest. I should be sorry to lose a chance of getting my colours this year. Except for my wrist I am very well indeed. Did I tell you I ran to Nuneham and back (10 miles) on Tuesday, without exhaustion. It was a strange experience: the cold day; hazy, but still with a wide landscape; very still; the full swift river; and the solitude—for I left the others behind, and the boat was some way ahead. My running with Arthur served me well.

Since my mishap, I have taken to walks, one with Haynes and one with MacAlister. They were both new walks and very pleasant—especially one through Bagley Wood with Haynes (trespassing). I like Haynes, and yet detest the brilliant, vicious society at Balliol. Haynes himself is utterly immoral; but still with many fine feelings and purposes, I think . . . We found no daisies, though. You were lucky; and kind to send me the daisy you first found. Sweet Helen! If I did not know you, I should by this time be the most abandoned of creatures up here. As it is—did you see me as I am, I fear you would think me sadly fallen from my sentimental well-intentioned babyhood, two years ago.

I am going to try to write a page or two, or remake an old thought, perhaps for the *J. C. R.**

Goodbye, sweetheart. In life I am your truest fondest friend Edwy and you ever my own sweet little one, my anemone maiden. Goodbye, Helen—Adieu.

P.S. My aunt* is not here yet.

To Helen

Lincoln College | Oxford | 11 May '99

My dearest Friend,

I can do little more than say I am well and more cheerful than before, and then answer what requires to be answered in your letter.

You remember you said that on no account must my people know:* well, they would know, if yours knew; so that before attempting to get the £150, it must be certain that you can do it without the knowledge of Mrs. Noble. I hope that is clear. Have you ever thought of asking for a part—if only £5 or £10—just before leaving home? It would help, and I should think an excuse would be simple.

As to leaving home, things have turned out luckily, but I suppose it is still uncertain what you can do when you leave the Logans in July? You say you will be among kind friends at the Logans—have you any reason for expecting they will help you? Is Mr. Potbury rich?

Now as to my coming to town. Of course the chief object would be what you say, and I suppose the money can be got somehow. You must let me know when you go to the Logans; then ask Mrs. Logan*—if you think she has room etc.—whether she can put me up for a night, and on what day; the day must be a Tuesday, or Thursday a week after you write, so as to give me time to ask leave at College. I think I shall cycle, for we really can't afford fares. Would there be any reason against our sleeping together at the Logans'? The ceremony—or whatever you call it will take place on the morning after I arrive. Why is the fee so much as £2? Will it be by special licence, and can Mrs. Logan be witness? I don't know from whom we can borrow £2.

You ask me if I know anyone who might help us in the point of money. Well, I have not told Haynes anything yet; in fact I haven't seen him since the Wednesday night before you came. But when I had told [J. H.] Morgan, and we were talking about finances, he said Haynes might be ready to help, as he had already offered Morgan one or two hundred pound to help him at Oxford. I shall tell Haynes everything sooner or later; but money help from him is very uncertain.

You ask if I too feel any joy at the thought of a child. I confess I have felt it considerably, but I do not know if it is a decent joy.

I am managing to work fairly well, and am writing just a little at 'The Caryatids'. The *Speaker* hasn't paid me yet, nor said anything about my article which they are considering. It is hard; Davies* is earning far more than I at work, not his best and which even he despises, and his powers are inferior to mine. I wish I could get a kind of secretaryship or else a tutorship in the Long Vac . . . I suppose I could not teach Mrs. Logan's children? Perhaps she has friends who have need of such a person in the Summer.

I suppose Mrs. Hooton visits Mrs. Logan and will then learn the news.

Give my love to Mrs. Noble, please. I am too busy to write. I await the future.

Goodbye, sweetheart. Ever and wholly yours, my own sweet little one

Edwy | Adieu.

To Helen

Lincoln College | 20 November '99

My dearest Friend,

I want you to send me Morley's sketch of English Literature,* a fat gloomy book which is most likely on the top shelf of my cupboard. Pray do not look too closely at my cupboard, if you go to it, dearest.

Such a good account of you as I had this morning was most welcome. Yesterday began with fog as it seems to have done in town, but it cleared up here and became a dry bright day, in which I enjoyed a long riverside walk to Sandford. There I lunched with Davies and two others. The lunch was expensive but excellent, and ended by mulled port which warms your very soul. Then in the evening after actually doing a few lines of composition, I enjoyed two or three hours of young Brook's company. Not, however, before being reduced to such depression as to force me to take *a little* opium for the first time this term. But I was none the worse; in fact I was able to talk rather better than usual and to relate quite a number of respectable stories.

Today is dull and damp. Your letter is the only sunshine, and alas! how short; just long enough to make me crave unbearably for you, body and soul. That poor body! I can easily understand how the sight of it pains you. I hope it is not very prodigious, also that it will not interfere with us when I return. Will it do you think? for a weight upon it might do great harm.

Give my love to Mary. To Irene I have not yet found time to write. Remember me to the people at Said House—I have just been looking for Ambrose's brother, but he was out.

ABROAD: not ABROARD.

I fear I cannot influence Haynes. He probably could not live without having women. He must not marry when he is just entering business: besides it would be unwise, especially for Haynes to marry in a hurry. And then the women he does have may always chance to have the terrible disease, however careful he is about their appearance. But as for marrying and 'increasing his intellectual powers', it is almost universally agreed that the truth is as a rule the reverse of this.

'Atheism' is not taken for granted in a place like Lincoln where there are very many mediocre people of inordinate piety; and even the worst of them are as a rule strict churchgoers and in a way religious, blaspheming only occasionally and always ready to prove the existence of God and the divinity of Christ etc. etc. It is quite likely that I am an atheist, but I certainly never call myself one.

Now I am going to try and write a few lines. You will have this tomorrow and then I hope you will write back a long letter to me.

So goodbye my own sweet little one, Helen.

Ever and wholly yours Edwy | Goodbye

Give my love to Janet and Harry.

To Helen

Lincoln College | Oxford | 21 May 1900

My dearest Friend,

I promised you a letter, but I don't see what in my present condition I can write. If I could only give you a description of Oxford on Saturday night you would not be so disappointed with this letter as now you will be. The whole of the City and University were in the streets.* Some of the Oxford streets are the broadest in England and there huge bonfires were lit which we supplied with rafters etc. while the city crowd stood peacefully and uselessly by. On such occasions the City acknowledges its inferiority. All the women, married and otherwise, allow themselves to be promiscuously kissed etc. by the University: in fact most men employed themselves in recording as many kisses as possible. Nearly everyone was drunk, except the citizens, who looked on with the utmost complacence; and two of whom brought me home when, after an exciting evening, I at last succumbed to the wine I had taken. For universal good temper you never saw such a night. Although all were taken very ill and 'cheap' the next morning, few regretted it and I certainly did not tho' it was an absurd occasion for so unpatriotic a man.

Maine* stayed at home and 'read strange volumes' as he says. He was ready to greet me when I arrived home.

Yesterday (Sunday) I had a short walk in the morning with Elsey.* It was the finest day we have had this May and the country was exquisite and new, but he had even less to say than usual, while I was somewhat handicapped by effects of Saturday. He then returned to finish his paper on Miracle Plays which I have been helping him to write for the Davenant.* In the afternoon I took a long walk with O'Brien and Curran to Godstow where there is a charming inn called *The Trout*, covered with blue periwinkle flowers: near by is the nunnery of fair Rosamonde and the river flows between. This time I did nearly all the talking; for Curran had been fearfully bad the night before.

I am going to write a volume of 'Mafeking Nights entertainments' and really such of my adventures as I remember were much like the Arabian Nights.

With kisses for Merfyn.

Ever and wholly yours my own sweet little one   Edwy

To Ian MacAlister

c/o Mrs Howells Pleasant View | Tirydail
Amanford S Wales | 30 August 1900

My dear Mac,

After many changes I came hither 10 days ago, and your letter following me about has just arrived. I am delighted to hear from you, and can easily 'forgive' your use of my 'Christian' name, notwithstanding that the somewhat solemn music was long ago reduced to the feeble but endearing term of Edwy. In turn, I will if I may adopt your synonym for George Ian MacAlister, though its rhymes with smack, etc., suggest a rude bonhomie which I never associate with you. I am glad too that you 'have had nothing to say.' Happy is the man that has no history. My own vainglorious epitaph is to convey, That I had nothing to say, and said it in the aptest terms—with which you will by no means agree!

As to our villain's handwriting, I have a curious specimen of it, in the shape of a pseudo-subtly dishonest letter to my wife, showing very well his way of going to work. If I had not been in Oxford at the time, he should have been answered in terms of the horsewhip.

My Spanish trip was abandoned partly because I was kept waiting too long, and partly because I wrote an unanswerable hostile letter to Morgan. It was my first angry letter. The cause was a lady to whom our friend had made love under the pretence of giving her a higher education, viz., literary. Morgan made rather a bad figure in a final difference with her, which I witnessed in Berkshire during my viva visit. The girl had interested me, and as she had seemed to be really passionate, while M. was preoccupied, I wrote to her and sent her a copy of 'Wuthering Heights' to read. After encouraging my correspondence in an amused way, M. suddenly ordered me to bring it to an end, in a tone that convinced me that his attitude was one of patronage, maintained with some real friendliness because I had a certain ready sympathy with his vitals, e.g. liver. But let us agree that we were incompatible persons.

After all, Wales is good for me. In spite of my accidentally Cockney nativity, the air here seems to hold in it some virtue essential to my well-being, and I always feel, in the profoundest sense, at home. Anyhow I am vastly better, though still unable to walk the three or four miles necessary to reach the nearest waterfall among trees, or the nearest Castle—Careg Cenen, which has a site as imposing as Edinburgh Castle, as I hear from those who know both. But the Castle is a fearful place, and glimpses through its shooting-gaps on to a plain about 400 feet sheer below, leave my body like a telegraph wire in a high wind. I still wait for a visit from my prosaic Muse; and have to fill up my hours of solitude with writing distasteful scraps of a novel, at which Haynes and I are collaborating.* Perhaps when I write to you next, the Muse, or, if you think that too professional, some genial spirit of the place will breathe upon my letter.

My wife and the child (who bears with some grace the names Philip Mervyn) are with me here and afford a constant undercurrent of deep joy, despite my weakness, irritability, anxiety, disappointment. But you will write soon, won't you?

Ever yours | Edward Thomas.

P.S.—I don't know yet, how long I shall stay here.

To Ian MacAlister

7 Nightingale Parade | Nightingale Lane | Balham | London SW |
12 March 1901

My dear Mac,

There is nothing to say except that your letter was very welcome. Postman's Knock is out of fashion just now especially on Monday mornings, so I was cheered by the event. But you don't seem quite yourself. You make me anxious about your father. Perhaps you will tell me more next week. Better still, perhaps all will have turned out happily.

Meantime my own affairs don't change. I feel more and more helpless. I tried to get work from George Newnes on Thursday; but he didn't think I should make either a merchant or a baronet, and dismissed me. He wondered I didn't try his magazines! I allowed myself to have another venture with the C.O.S.* and again unsuccessfully I think. Haynes (who is continually making suggestions) is sounding the librarian of the House of Lords on my behalf: I can't be hopeful, however. You see, I have not yet gone to sleep, tho' I might as well. A librarianship would suit me, and I am sure my interest and experience would make me not incompetent!

So would a sub-editorship—on a weekly, for preference. The one I applied for came to nothing.

There is no news yet from the Americans. Success there would be a boon indeed. The Malory scheme drags on slowly. I am hampered by the fearful ignorance of the publishers. They know nothing at all about Malory and are consequently very suspicious of everything I say. They suggest 'Explanatory notes' for the edition. Poor Malory was not clever enough to write anything that needed explanation: but what am I to do? However, my correspondent says there is no hurry and merely says now that the edition will be put in hand 'within eighteen months.' I may prepare it from the workhouse, therefore.

I am very happy now and then with some old books of travel I have discovered. I am also still busy with your Elizabethan dramatists and have got almost a volume of notes, etc. There are a hundred things I could do—a dozen things I could do well—but I haven't the pluck, when I know they won't be read, far less be printed. So I just polish essays I wrote months ago, and day by day write a sentence or two as near perfection as is possible for me, to keep my hand in. I read Virgil daily: he is the best training for the ear that I know. (N.B. *Have you got a Claudian?*)*

Today (I mean yesterday: I write at 2 in the small hours) I have been carpentering. I began at 10.30 a.m. and at 8 p.m. I had nearly finished the frame of a big lounge for my wife's sitting room. It is to be a sofa, an alternative for 3 chairs, and in case of need an extra bed. I have now only to fit it with a mattress, and drape it. It is a great saving of cash and the making gave me a rest; it also amused Philip Mervyn.*

P.M. is now wonderfully well and develops apace. *Nulla dies sine linea*. You should see him saying 'Hark!'

What was C. P. Scott's son like? I owe his father a grudge. He encouraged me to hope for work on his paper* and then let me slide without any reason.

I am glad to hear of your brekker with Cornish, whose performance I have been following. Did he talk much? I presume he has forgotten me: I hope at least he has forgotten my faults. Nobody from Lincoln writes to me now. Several wrote one effusive letter at the beginning of the term, promising more, and I wrote back, very happy to be remembered. My only refuge is to read 'Thyrsis' and 'The Scholar Gipsy' and enjoy my tears.

A clock has just chimed two with a deep voice almost like 'Tom'* and you must forgive me if I dedicate the night now to reading and Oxford dreams; nor shall I forget you. Write before you go down and fix a day to come and dine with me.

Ever yours | Edwy.

P.S. If you do see Morgan or Maine remind them that I love them.

To Ian MacAlister

Rose Acre | Bearsted nr Maidstone | 29 October 1901

My dear Mac,

Perhaps I am in the promised Land, as you say; but there are still the Canaanites, not to speak of Philistines. That is why I have not written before, in spite of your most welcome letter; I celebrated it, I assure you, like a prodigal's return. I have had troubled times—no work and much expense. I have nevertheless stuck at it in a way that would show bravery in anyone else. Have sent out over 20 articles to journals and magazines. 12 have come back: the other 8 will stay longer because they are with magazines whose decisions take the length of an elephant's pregnancy. I haven't scored one success; yet, showing you how stubborn I have been, the 'Globe' and 'Pall Mall' between them have rejected 8 articles in a fortnight! And I go on smoking clay pipes and playing with Mervyn who is now going to sleep to the sound of the Bearsted bells. The country is exquisite: yet in a way it soothes me too much and encourages a mild despair which is my favourite vice. Helen and the heir and I have just spent the afternoon out of doors with deep enjoyment, he eating blackberries; I stealing young trees to plant in the garden. As to the garden, now is almost the busiest time. I have turned all the soil up; planted roots, shoots and bulbs; dug a ditch 540 feet long and thrown up a bank the same length; and weeding, etc., illimitable. I suppose you haven't much garden; if you had, I should ask you to send me roots or cuttings.

And you—I hope you will soon have something that will relieve you from 'reading for the bar'. If only you could get a tutorship near here! But I fear the Oxford Appointments' Committee will not help you much; they send me announcements about every 3 months; they seem to enjoy a very long vacation.

'Affec.ly.'—why do people abbreviate the most important part of a letter? I envy you yours from the Malvern boys. The only boys who write to me are grown-up boys at Oxford, and I find the nicest of them all the more foolish because they are old. Still, all Oxford letters are precious to me; and I glance at the post-mark like a philatelist who has got a treasure. You are partly mistaken when you say I valued Oxford more than the people there. It was only because the place acknowledged my love; the people so rarely did. Those that did are far more than the place to me; but a child could count them—1, 2, I can't go on! Now that I am far away, even acquaintances who were unkind or (worse) flippant seem like friends, and now and then I write them letters from my heart; they never reply. Why only lovers understand passion (of any kind) I shall never quite know. And older people—they are never tired of rebuking me. They put melancholy down to crumpets and the like and laugh; they fail to realise the simple fact that 'there it is'. I know now, of course, that melancholy is largely due to physical causes; only it doesn't seem to me any the less psychical for that.

I shall be very glad if Blackie gives me work, and am most grateful to you for writing to him. I suppose you never meet Crossland of the 'Outlook'? If you do, tell him he owes the price of a review done last March, and that he promised me more work. He won't pay and he won't give me work.

It's bad news of Fyfe, but I suppose Garrod was a better man, at any rate by his achievements.

Write again soon especially if you have good news of yourself,

With love from us all, | Yours ever, Edwy.

To Ian MacAlister

[Rose Acre] | 5 April 1902

My dear Mac,

I wish I could send you news, facts instead of thoughts, as you ask. But I haven't any, and I have always had an (unconscious) dislike of facts; or rather, I can't handle them. You should see, for instance, my attempts at narrative on paper. I can't progress at all. I simply jump from one picture to another. And so in my existence, what happens is soon lost in a mist of what I think about and around it. In fact I think so much about things that I forget very soon what set me thinking.

The only events in my life now are the arrivals of envelopes from the 'Chronicle,'* to announce that books are being sent for review. They come more often just now, but not often enough. For I have to live on the 'Chronicle' almost alone. I told you that I sent my things all round Fleet Street and elsewhere. I can do so no longer, because there remains no paper or magazine to which my much-travelled M.S. has not gone in vain. And I have nearly ceased to copy out fresh works for sending out. I have to depend on the two or three editors who know me, and they take my work very seldom indeed. I have had two papers in the Illustrated London News and one in The Academy this year. That is all. And yet it is more painful to write this down than the actual experience is, because I have learned to drift. Nevinson of the 'Chronicle' tells me that my position (or rather, he spoke of a position similar to mine) is 'unendurable'. I believe it and ignore it.

Haynes wants me to plan some critical or autobiographical work.

7 April

I have already made plans, but today I feel as if I could never work them out. One is—to trace the element of 'Nature' from Chaucer to the present day in English poetry. I should like it; it would be fairly new; and perhaps in after years I could do it pretty well. But today, as I say, I feel quite hopeless. It is one of my mad days. I am unaccountably nervous and anxious, as if something were going to happen. (N.B. I know from endless experience, that nothing will happen). All the morning I worked hard at a review and at dinner I planned a walk to a quiet and distant pub. But I walked half a mile; turned back; emptied a brandy bottle left by last week's guests; worked furiously in the garden most of the afternoon; and now inflict my transparent pessimism on you. The brandy, remember, was an afterthought; I am trying hard to think why I didn't keep out of doors. I suppose the fact is that I must have a bad day now and then while my position is so precarious; for no calm, affected or real, under really anxious conditions, can be quite unbroken.

9 April

It is obviously time for me to put a stop to this letter. It is quite inexplicably damned. I have done a lot of work in the intervals, and now I am expecting the last visit of my oldest friend* who is going out to South Africa after enlisting in the S.A. Constabulary. We shall just plant a tree and drink some whisky and leave unsaid the things that will occur to us when he is over the Equator.

Just a word more. If you do go to Oxford next term—it will be my last possible term, too,—would you let me join you. I shouldn't worry you because our ways would be different.

I know I have left your letter quite unanswered, but as I have nevertheless left out everything else I wanted to say, you will forgive me, because my ineptness is so symmetrical.

With love from all of us,

Ever yours | Edwy

To Ian MacAlister

Rose Acre | Bearsted nr Maidstone | 25 December 1902

My dear Mac,

It was very great joy to have even a gloomy letter from you. And on Christmas Day, too. The feast never meant much to me as a child, except from the books and stomach-aches I received. But every year it becomes more and more a remembrancer, and I make up the books of friendship and thought with a sombre pleasure whatever the balance. So you have been with me all day, whether I was playing with Mervyn or drinking hot ale and ginger along with nuts. We had no frost, yet a great fire—and the logs were as idols.

Since I wrote I have had a pretty continuous supply of books, enough to keep me almost continuously employed and to put a stop to original composition; and yet not enough to prevent the quarterly alarm about my rent. I had—but tell it not—Milton's latest book, '*Nova Solyma*,' to do for the 'Chronicle.' And that reminds me that I heard unofficially that I am now to get the review-books which used to go to Lionel Johnson who died last month. I don't know whether to be elated or desperate; for he was a fine scholar and (tho I have only just found it out) a writer of the most beautiful prose.

We are pretty well. Helen is at work now as usual. Rachel Mary Bronwen (for that is her name) grows more agreeable in appearance. Her eyes are changing in the direction of brown, and her hair is to be dark brown, a constrast with Mervyn, who has conspicuous blue eyes and fair yellow hair in long waves. He is a nice boy at times, and by the way he sends you two kisses. He has already quite a store of knowledge—about animals, natural effects and colours, etc., and is a good talker, and most hearty lover of life, with just a tinge of reverie along with a short sharp temper. He runs and climbs and walks often 5 miles a day. He will be 3 next month. I know you would like to see how joyous we can be while he hears me 'singing' Welsh airs or 'The Old Gray Fox' or 'Widdicombe Fair' or 'The Lincolnshire Poacher.'

Still my progress towards the state of family man is not smooth or invariably pleasant. I often want to go away and walk and walk for a week anywhere so long as it is by an uncertain road. For tho I like to stay in one piece of country I don't like (as I have to, in England) to meet continually some respectable acquaintance with whom I must stop to bore and be bored. I am not a bit of a wanderer, but I like to be thought-free and fancy-free as I can't be in this sweet domestic country. Also my melancholy 'grows old along with me.'

You don't give me any notion of your work, and so I can only be sick at heart to think of your difficulties. Write to me oftener and talk before your heart gets too full.

Everything you say to encourage me in my work encourages me, partly because I know you used to be unsympathetic. I don't despair because my work is unrecognised. What makes me desperate is the little leisure (from reviewing and much thinking about money) left me to write my best in. In the last three months I have written about 1000 words exclusive of reviews. Yet my head has been so full that I might have done 10,000 much better than I did 1000, and tho' some of that was at the rate of 40 words an hour. Moreover, when for a time I am free from all business, tho my tendency then is to write, I am not always willing to. For I must have some time in which to be non literary, free to think or better still not to think at all, but to let the wind and the sun do my thinking for me, filling my brain. However, that is a trifle and will not be even that when I am part of a great calm under nettles and yews and grass.

Well, I seem to have spent much ink in getting myself on paper. I had better have sent my photograph.

I hope you like 'Coldstreamer'* a little. He is now in a 2nd edition, so you can at least make half a crown per head.

We all send our love and good wishes.

Ever yours, dear old Mac, | Edwy

To Jesse Berridge

13 Rusham Road | Nightingale Lane | S.W.* | 12 February 1903

My dear Jesse,

I have come alone to live in town for an indefinite length of time, because I am in debt, and am not earning much nor likely to, for some months. Could you meet me *outside* the Pharos Club at 5.45 tomorrow (Friday)? Anyhow, I will be there. I shall probably not have anything to do in the evening, but don't want to go to Southfields because of the railway fare. I have only a few shillings until I get work. So if you know any journalists, or any likely persons, please introduce me.

Ever yours | Edward Thomas

To Helen

8 p.m. | New Swindon | 16 September 1903

My dearest friend,

I am now back from a walk of nine hours with the old man. As I left the house with that nasty letter* to you in my hand I fell violently and was punished all day by pain in the head. Still I thought it was better to let you know what I felt than to wait for a day and send a honeyed note. And yet I am not sure, because you will probably misunderstand me, and also because I really cannot myself explain why I was so much annoyed and with such fury, unless perhaps I vaguely resented your liking for a person whom I think little or poorly of, and unless also I thought it an insult that he should wish you (and you consent) to go with him as ballast on a journey to his paltry acquaintance. When I am at home it is different. But I can't endure the idea of my being here and you at Ramsgate and the children with Emma alone.

All this is very solemn, I perceive. What it means is that I had one of my innumerable fits of indignant annoyance and that had I thought you would laugh at it or ignore it I could have murdered you. Such I am, unhappily for you and me. And let me admit that you have just as much right to go to Ramsgate or anywhere else as I have and much more right than I have to drink or talk indecently or take opium. What a muddle headed ass am I! and how I wish I were dead and stinking, though that will not be until I have far greater cause to wish it than now.

All this is written after a long day in the open air spent with greater pleasure than you can imagine in spite of everything. We walked past Coate with its 'Sun' and 'Spotted Cow' and on to another 'Sun' at Lyddington where I had cider and bread and cheese and raised the suspicions of the landlady somehow. Then we spent half an hour in Lyddington church and churchyard and entered the fields and so up on to the downs to Lyddington beeches whence we could see fifty miles of beautiful, waste, rounded downs and now and then a part of the manoeuvring army. We sat and talked about 'the old-fashioned times' in the Roman camp on the hill, where Jefferies began 'The Story of My Heart'. The old man poured out 'old-fashioned bits', about herbs and poaching and women and this style of story:—

Parson: 'Where does this lane go to, my lad?'
Lad: 'I don't know where it goes to, but 'tis always here when I comes along.'

Three or four miles farther on from there, at Chiseldon 'Patriot's Arms' we had tea and then walked steadily on past Burdcrop and down Ladder Hill and in sight of Coate again to beastly Swindon after 18 or 20 rough miles. Now I am hardly at all tired.

The review of the policeman's poetry was mine: also that of Besant's 'Essays and Historicities'. I have two others to appear, and 3 more books to review for the 'Chronicle'.

I am interrupted by my Grandmother. She is reading the 'Oxford' proofs and alleges that I have written several things two or three times over! Of course she is mistaken—I now find she has been doubling the sheets over and reading the same set twice. But I can't convince her of folly any more than you can convince me!

Perhaps the cider is the cause of the portentous solemnity and the rambling twaddle of the end of this letter. At least, I partly think so, and you would be wise to agree with me and think no more about it. Yet I fear I have hurt you; and I only persist in sending this, lest I should deceive you without your knowing it. Bear with me, sweet heart, even though you know I shall show little gratitude if you do.—Was ever a fool so conscious of his folly as I? and yet so helpless in it that perhaps I am not also a knave?

Tomorrow I must work a little and have another walk with the old man. Then on Thursday I shall think about returning and shall be home not later than the 8.10 on Friday. Say, 8.10 on Friday, though it may be Thursday. I hope Davies has not returned to my bedroom because I want to be able to use it: and perhaps Merfyn had better sleep in his cot, as before. Here are kisses* for him and Bronwen to share with you as distributor.

Try to believe me, my own sweet little one, ever and wholly yours

Edwy

To Ian MacAlister

Bearsted Green | 1 November 1903

My dear Mac,

I wanted to write some weeks ago but wisely held my hand. For I was and am in a bad way, but then I was hopeless, except that I hoped for death: now I am not quite hopeless. The improvement comes of seeing a good and sympathetic London doctor.* I so rarely see doctors that I retain my childish belief in them; and when this one told me I must do this and not do that, and said 'I want you to get well,' I was more moved to a strong effort than I had ever been by the advice of friends or my own conviction. So I am to take cod liver oil, and arsenic and strychnine, and much meat (which I hate), and special foods; and I am to be as regular as possible in my habits, never to get exhausted (!), to try to divert myself (e.g. by cards), and to see many people (which is impossible). I begin badly by being left to complete silence and solitude for 5 days while Helen and the children are in London. So this letter is written because it is better to think and write than merely to think, about myself.

I really can't say what is wrong with me. The doctor of course wants to make me fat and thinks I shall then smile. But I am not physically weak. I sleep very well and long. I can walk 25 miles in a day or fish for 12 hours and then walk 10 miles without much discomfort. On the other hand, I am sometimes terribly fatigued by half a mile or by 2 hours writing, and I sit down and wish I could sleep for ever: sometimes I sit for hours and can do nothing but submit to the play of the imps that bring into my mind the most mad and trifling and undesired thoughts—a whole medley of them as disconnected as Tit-Bits and as revolting. When I am free from these thoughts, I consider what can be the cause of my misery and incapacity. Let me be methodical. And be patient—I am sure you will, since it pleases me sadly.

First, I wonder if my indiscretions and intemperance in alcohol, opium and tobacco, have at last taken effect. They have been serious, but 2 years ago they became far less so, and in the past 9 months I have lived moderately in every way, unless (which is unlikely) I have worked or walked too much.

Second, has continued journalism at last destroyed my always slender capacity for writing what I like? At first I always tried to leaven my reviews with some thought or fancy which was often irrelevant but often gave me the satisfaction of thinking that I have at least written one or two decent sentences and uttered a part of myself. But those thoughts and fancies had to be very brief: I could not follow them up. So I got, perhaps, into a habit of jerky and unconcluded thinking and imagination. The result *seems* to be that when now I try to write an essay I cannot do more than 2 or 3 sentences: they do not, as they used to do, flow one from the other in a rosary. I hope I am mistaken. Anyhow, the symptom which makes me most wretched is my inability to write an essay. I sit down with my abundant notebooks and find a subject or an apparently suggestive sentence: but nothing moves me.

Third—am I losing my religious attitude towards 'Nature'? That is too painful to admit. Yet it may be so. Perhaps my love was not as deep as it seemed. But I seem to notice a change when I sit down to write. One little note used to recall to me much of the glory or joy of former days out of doors. Now it is barren, and that means a great deal, because I cannot bring myself to write about anything else, or at any rate about anything which 'Nature' does not unavoidably enter. I argue thus to myself: 'I have cared more for Nature than for anything else, therefore if I can write at all, Nature will move me. If, on the other hand, I am unworthy or insincere, if the years of days and nights which I spent in rapture or awe out of doors now mean nothing to me, then I distrust myself wholly and will at least refrain from serving another mistress.'

Fourth, shall I ever get used to what I consider the dirtiness and confusion of my house? Practically not an hour of my day passes without some violent irritation caused by this: and either I sit down and curse or I vainly attempt to put things right. In other people's houses I can be contented; never in my own. Some tell me this irritation is an effect of my state of health and mind. Perhaps so: I believe it is the cause and apparently it is ineradicable.

Well there I am writ large. Other things trouble me, lack of company, lack of money (due to small extravagance and great mismanagement). But I have said nearly all—and now I don't feel any better for having told you so much, because I know you will want to help and you can't.

The book* is delayed but I hope not for more than a fortnight.

Work is bad, for Nevinson (my greatest patron) has left the 'Chronicle' for good and is in Macedonia, and W. J. Fisher, the editor, is not fond of me. So I am advised to look out for something else. But what? Librarianship at a private library would perhaps suit me, but I am unqualified. Who would have me as schoolmaster or secretary? I shall stick to Bearsted as long as possible. Anyway, you will write, I hope: and will you tell, by the way, whom to ask for on the 'Outlook'? You remember saying that your father might help me there.

Goodbye. | I am ever yours | Edwy

To Helen

c/o. Mrs. Labrum | Warminster | 8 December 1903

My dearest Friend,

The Shelley have just arrived. I expected them earlier: that is why I sent the postcard. And by the way, you will be interested by that. I heard from Nevinson this morning—he had mysteriously mentioned the subject before—that he was giving a dinner at 'The Florence' to his friends on the *Chronicle*. It will be pleasant and perhaps useful, and in any case such an invitation from Nevinson is law. So I shall be in London on Saturday the 19th. Well, Morgan has now decided to stay here until January 4 in order to complete a portion of the *Annual Register*: the rest he has given up. After that, his plans are vague. He may go to Tintagel, however, and if possible I should like to join him there. So I now think that I shall not return to Warminster but come on to Bearsted on the 20th and stay with you for a week or two until I can decide to join Morgan at Tintagel or visit Mr. Bowman* at Walmer. What do you think? Remember that I shall be very lonely at Christmas, especially as Morgan will be working—he must work now. Remember too, that until either Black* plays up or MacAlister sends some money, I shall be very hard up for the rent will soon be due. I should also like to be able to run up to town just after the New Year to see Donald. There is a new literary editor* at the *Chronicle* and I am trying to find out who he is. Morgan forgot to ask—much will depend on him.—Of course, I think it is possible that I shall find myself well able to go on with my usual work after a few days after I get back to Bearsted. I shall be more careful of myself in the future, particularly in the matter of exercise. Hitherto I have overwalked or in some way tired myself nearly every day at home. My limit for some time must be 6 or 7 miles a day. Even 4 miles here is tiring in spite of my increased weight. And I must sleep more and also more regularly. So if I do return to you on the 20th I shall be rather wiser, at any rate, and I hope I shall be less nervous too, and altogether more hopeful or less desperate. But tell me what you think, tho I think I quite understand what you have already urged in favour of my staying here, and tho I know—you need not have said it—that you would rather I kept away until I am quite restored. I shall have been away for 4 weeks all but a day. If you wish it, however, I will return to Warminster after Nevinson's Dinner. Or I will come to you just for a day or two.

Please send me *The Man of Genius* by Lombroso. It is with other books of Irene's. Morgan wants to see it. You might send it with my handkerchiefs.*

Kiss Merfyn and Bronwen for me and goodbye my own sweet little one.

I am ever and wholly yours Edwy

QUOTATIONS FROM EDWARD THOMAS'S DIARY OF 1903

27 August Helen to Cartmel. I home again tired and nearly insane. To bed 11.30,

28 August Up at 7.30. Packing, writing, and fussing all day. I hope to go to Swindon tomorrow and get back my capacity for quiet. I am never concentrated on anything—except Merfyn and Bronwen—now—and in the midst of reading and writing (which I can rarely ever attempt) my forehead burns or throbs with a thought or a vague disquiet totally irrelevant.

26 September I am now more than ever tired, restless, irritable, uninterested, bored. I am never interested by review books now. I hate it. Only once in 6 weeks have I been able to look at the Aeneid and once or twice at Don Quixote (mechanically). I don't want to walk either or to talk. I hate seeing anyone except occasionally Merfyn and Bronwen. And I am so irritable and weak and stupid on rising in the morning that I invariably begin the day by being rude (on account of nothing) to Helen. I smoke less, eat less, drink less, copulate less. When I am not reading or gardening (and often when I am) I am occupied with the most ridiculous brood of trivial disconnected thoughts and imaginations and never one of them is with me more than 5 minutes: e.g. in this order, I imagine myself fighting so and so and get excited over it (planning etc.)—or playing a large fish,—or I think about my personal appearance or about the real merit or demerit (if either) of *Oxford*—about what people really think of me and what I really am and so on: my head reels to think of them seriously. And as for my usual self-distrust and hopelessness and lack of ambition it is extreme. How can I ever write an essay again or get passionate (except with anger) about a thing.

Harry [Hooton] came. Like a fool I told him many symptoms; like a coward I did not tell him nearly all possible causes. He had the insolence to recommend self control. A walk through the hop gardens in evening. To bed 11.

24 October Up at 7.45. Writing in morning, afternoon gardening and reading. I am now, in my fruitless despair, taking courses of Persian opium. It does little good, except that it teaches me how dull I am, since my dreams are as dull as my existence. How unreal must be my reading when it touches my dreams not at all. I can't recall the substance of one just now, but I awoke several times last night with such a feeling of contempt for myself that I wanted a pencil to record the dreams, yet was too slack to fetch one.

27 October 1903 Morning writing. Afternoon a 6 mile walk with Merfyn in rain and wind. Merfyn happy and I, too, perhaps: but once I got home I could have fallen into bed and have slept forever. Day by day I wish for that. Trifling debts—no money—little but countless dirtinesses and untidinesses in the house—lack of forcible company—lack of ambition—inability to write except pitiful reviews, e.g. one of Lord Cromer's Translation for anthology etc, all make me powerless, isolated and yet indifferent, discontented and yet inert. I cannot kill myself and fate will not. No one knows how difficult I find it to live with Helen, though I admire her, like her, perhaps love her. Or does Mother know and we conspire not to mention it? How will it end? What shall I do 3 years hence?

Is it that I cannot reconcile myself to the possible fact that I am ceasing to care for Nature so religiously as I used to do? For when I try to write I fail most in attempting to write as I did in 'Isoud' and 'November' and that embitters me. My notes no longer inspire me and make my pen overflow with memories. I get nothing but ink out of the inkpot. My first sentence no longer begets a family of generations of others.

Or is it that 3 years of reviewing has unfitted me for writing essays? I try or used to try to console myself for the cheapness of my Criticism by getting in—however unjustifiably—a sentence or two on some point that really moved me: seldom more than a sentence or two, for I never have space to track a thought to the death. Have I thus lost any power for continuous, if allusive, reflection?

Or have opium, wine, and *other indulgences* some of them so lengthy, at last rased a brain that was never very firm, I think.

If I walk 25 miles and have fishing or forcible stimulating company at the end of it, I am almost happy. If I walk ½ a mile or less, come home and find Helen sympathetic I am fatigued and almost dying, calling for death. Only 2 or 3 things now engross me happily even for a short time—a letter from Mac—a play with Bronwen, or (in a less degree) with Merfyn—fishing—or some rare intercourses with Helen. To bed. 11

29 October Saw Dr Segundo. . . . But when he asked 'were you happy in married life?' I said merely 'No'. Whereas I fear my discontent with sluttishness at home is really a cause not an effect of my misery.

13 November Segundo tells me to cultivate self control, cheek; to go to Boston for 5 years and then send for my family; or to move to London and work in the Silence room of a club, which is impossible. Fisher is to leave Chronicle; but Lawlor Wilson says I am safe enough. Talked to Jesse [Berridge] about my 'religion' and to his wife about education of children (conventional beliefs etc.).

2 December [Staying with J. H. Morgan]

After supper a talk about greater frequency of spirituality in sexuality among women than among men. Yet the common physical side in friendships of pure women for other women—and also the extent to which one actually changes or enlarges one's real nature by such mimetic adaptations to the character of one's usual society, as e.g. in the case of my Oxford life. I am yet, I think, essentially sentimental, craving for a few passionate friendships, and not as cynical as my conversation (on sex e.g.) often suggests: thus I can with Mother and even with others talk as if my follies of the past 6 years had never been, and that without hypocrisy. I regard much that I do say as distinctly out of accordance with what I believe to be my real nature. Why am I shy or silent and (when speaking) stupid in the company of two or more, even when they are not strangers, and yet not altogether so with one? I suppose: I know that I know nothing properly and unconsciously realize that detection is more likely among a number; or is it that the unaccustomed sound of my own voice frightens me and reminds me of my real loneliness and reminds me how poorly my conversation represents my thoughts in consequence of my long silences.

11 December A long talk with Morgan—he tries to get out of me the cause of my sorrow as apart from physical weakness—non compos mentis. I want an aim in life. Not to have all my days arranged for me by the necessity of getting a living. I want to make the means of getting a living an end in itself, which is impossible: therefore I wish for a librarianship which would give me fair leisure; and that is almost impossible, since I have to keep reviewing, and that takes all my energy and so prevents me from preparing for a library and specializing. Therefore I am without hope and still wish for death as a solution. Still, 3 months on a sailing vessel, if I could cease to be worried by lack of letters and distance of Helen, might give me leisure to think out a more moderate solution. But I don't see that is possible. Morgan says 'don't worry' and urges me to multiply such means of oblivion as conversation (books no longer give it) but that is impossible. So I went sighing to bed after a digression to show that Nevinson has not got 'temperament'. To bed 11.30.

29 December Up at 8. Writing and copying in the morning. Afternoon a walk with Helen and we decided I am not likely to be able to work in the same house with children (small house). Therefore I may take room in town for work, perhaps at Irene's.

To Helen

[With Hugh and Irene McArthur] Monday | 8 February 1904

My dearest Friend,

Just after I posted my letter to you on Saturday, I went off to see Jesse,* but when I got there I was so tired that I was not comfortable even lying doubled in a chair. So I did not stay long. Jesse also was tired after a week of Bank and theological lectures and he worried me, as I probably worried him; and I found myself talking for an hour after I had risen to go, about the fruitlessness and stupidity of my life, not forgetting the things which make it impossible to leave it. I got back before 10 and was in bed at 11. This morning was at first very cold but by the time Haynes and I got out into the fields beyond Upper Watlingham the South side of all the hedges was full of Spring and we enjoyed it. We wasted most of our time in foolish talk, foolish whether serious or not, and when nearest seriousness I was only endeavouring (half unintentionally) to entertain Haynes by humouring some silly notion in a smart way. For me, society is only the dullest form of solitude. Nevertheless, the evening with Dal and Frank* had its pleasures. It was the Annual Dinner of the Yorick at the Monico Restaurant, there was much good singing by good people and one good fiddler and pianist—the latter a Balliol man named [Donald] Tovey whom I remember hearing at Oxford, and an acquaintance of Haynes. He was asked whether he or his brother who sat near to him was the elder: and replied, 'Well, Duncan has lost more opportunities': I drank moderately and could not talk at all. So that the pleasure was much like lying in front of a very hot fire and too near it. It lasted until 2 and now I go to bed.

Monday.

This morning I have little to say except that your letter makes my misery clearer. You evidently don't understand my life in town* and as I am no longer an essayist I can't explain it except in speech. I now think of living at Rusham Road if I may, and working too, coming to town 3 or 4 evenings a week to see Milne* etc. I am struggling to write a review of *The House of Quiet* and have not very much time, since Ambrose has asked me to dinner.

What a bad review this is of Henry Murray's.

I almost forget why I like my evening at Harry's. But I suppose it was because we were really intimate, with much silence and no unnecessary talk. Harry is really far more a friend than Haynes. In a way, I wish Haynes were dead, because I want to be away from him and dare not while he is alive.

In great haste and just back from Ambrose's and am sleeping tonight at Dal's because the bedroom here is impossible. Damn—Damme (!)

Goodbye. Kiss Merfyn and Bronwen.

I am ever and wholly yours | Edwy

To Helen

[London] 9 February 1904

My dearest friend,

I have been at Rusham Road this evening and the result of talking with Mother and Father and of other things is that I think of retreating from my attempt to live in London. In fact I may return to you tomorrow. I will try to work at Bearsted and if I can I shall content myself with going to town every Wednesday to see Milne, and perhaps a week-end every now and then. It would take hours to explain why I am doing this. I don't like being away from you and I don't like being in London. Also, I live a foolish life that is unsuited to my mind, and I think the blank condition which the London streets produce is if anything worse than the brooding I may have to endure in the country. Dal and Frank want me to live with them and kind and delicate as they are I don't think I can.

For perhaps months of this life might make me unfit to enjoy quiet retirement while it would not by any means change me so completely that I could thoroughly enjoy London. I must try harder than I have done, to be calm if not contented, and to imitate the ideal character which I have sometimes written about—like Fitzgerald or Philip Amberley. That is my only possible achievement, and if I don't go mad (as my extreme egotism sometimes make me expect) it is possible, I think.

I have much work in hand and must begin it as soon as I reach home or rather on Thursday, working morning and evening, and walking with you or alone or with Merfyn in the afternoon. As I write, of course, I am aware of the possibility of failure or rather of the difficulty of attempting.

Goodbye my own sweet little one. Kiss Merfyn and Bronwen and a special kiss for Merfyn's letter.

I am ever and wholly yours | Edwy

To Helen

16 April 1904 | Well Knowe [with Bottomley]

Dearest one,

I have just been asleep for an hour (it is 4) because I did the same yesterday and then had the clearest and happiest hour I have had since I came, as I was walking back from the post across 'the Park'. Yet your letters were enough (one letter and a parcel containing another letter arrived together at 9.30), and I was more sweetly dissatisfied than usual; only I was still tired and thought I would call sleep to the aid of your letters—sweet one, dearer letters they seem than you ever have sent and I have no language but my body to thank you with and that is glowing with thanks even yet. If I could only love *you* and show my love as much as you deserve how happy would you (and I) be! But with all my silly head and trembling body and rotten soul* I do love you, and Merfyn and Bronwen will love you as you should be loved. How gay your letter is with your happiness and theirs. As I write this, I feel keenly how stupid it is not to be off to you at once. Yet I am getting more out of my visit than I thought I should. I can't and don't walk at all except to the post, but my talks (though far too littry and all that) are getting easier and deeper and more satisfying, and a few expressions of violent dislike of men and books have cleared my mind a good deal. I now find I can say to Gordon what I cannot say to most people with the exception of some bad language. Mr Bottomley came back last night and we have had some three-sided talks.—I admire and could like him, but he emphasises too much his 'literary tastes' and dislike of 'commercialism' and though they are part of a real refinement, in themselves they are a little laughable. He and everyone speaks so lovingly (and more than that) of you.

I have spent 1d. since I came here, and got three clay pipes for it.

Goodbye dear old sweet and beautiful one. Keep yourself as neat as you have made the house and I won't grumble ever again; and don't wear your glasses. Kiss Merfyn and Bronwen for me many times and get them to kiss you back for me.

I am ever and wholly yours, my own sweet little one | Edwy

To Jesse Berridge

The Weald | 8 August 1905

My dear Jesse,

I did call at the Bank last Wednesday at 10 minutes to 5 and was sorry to find you gone. I half expected to see you at the Vegetarian Restaurant between 5 and 6. I am almost always there on every other Wednesday. But I fear you were still unwell—I hope you are right now. Perhaps I shall feel more equal to meeting [G. K.] Chesterton later: if I do, I shall want you to take me.

I am glad to have your letter tho I do not know what is the 'one cure' for me. I can only think about 'cures' when I am fairly well and then I can't think very seriously. The one thought which may in the end be comforting is that there is certainly no hope from myself in the tenderest friend.

Of course I know books and reviews are not important, but vanity prevents me from treating them quite lightly as well as badly.

What I really ought to do is to live alone. But I can't find courage to do the many things necessary for taking that step. It is really the kind Helen and the children who make life almost impossible.

Freeman* and I started for Canterbury on Saturday but we only did 25 miles because my foot became blistered. We had one good night sleeping under corn sheaves in a field not far from where you and I slept one day—on the Pilgrims' Road. I meant to have asked you to come and strangely forgot.

Yours Ever | Edward Thomas

To Gordon Bottomley

c/o John Williams | Waun Wen School | Swansea | 23 November 1905

My dear Gordon,

I got a promise at *The Academy* and *Chronicle* of your book and probably I shall get it from one of them. That was on Monday. On Tuesday I came here and I have been fiercely bored ever since. Swansea is a big rather notably ugly town and what with my not very intimate acquaintance with my host I am being reduced to inanition. Everything is against me. A mile off lives an old Aunt whom I remember seeing when I was 4: two miles off is an old Lincoln friend whom I had not seen since 1900. I have seen them both and they have plunged me into languid and unpleasant reminiscence, and although the Welsh mutton is good my food is thus not altogether bracing. Also the merriest man I ever knew—Watcyn Wyn—the bard who wrote 'The Maid of Llandebie' and 'The Maids of Caermarthenshire'—is to be buried today: and on Sunday I am to be taken in my bowler hat and collar to a Welsh chapel in the town. And I have still a lame foot and cannot confidently start a long walk. Of all those blessings my temperament makes the best as you know it would. So how can I write?

I saw Balmer on Monday and enjoyed an hour or two with him and his brother. His brother is charming—his clean and reddish hands, his shining collar, cheeks and eyes, the perfect white parting of his hair, as he sat at the piano, were fascinating in a way. On Tuesday I saw Ransome for a little while. He read me a story about a tramp, a clay pipe and a wife in which a small pretty notion was insisted upon to distraction. He also talked about the Lady whom he has promised to marry. He complained that he could not 'get anything of himself into' his stories: a natural complaint.

My host is a schoolmaster. The school is adjacent and now I hear a master's whistle assembling a crowd of ragged children and see him with miniature ferocity giving silly little cuts with the cane to boys who are healthy enough to ignore his commands. So I end.

Remember me.

I am ever yours | Edward Thomas

To Walter de la Mare

The Weald | nr. Sevenoaks | 27 August 1906

Dear Sir,

I am very glad to hear you are publishing some more poetry.* If you care to let me know a few days before the reviewer's copies are sent out, I shall ask for it and have no doubt I can do you whatever service praise may be.—But I have never dreamed of collecting my reviews. I live by them and that seems to be wonderful enough without sending the poor things out in fine raiment to beg once more. (For as I dislike writing about books and do it in haste and in such abundance, I assume it is valueless.) It is good of you to ask about my books. I began at an early age in 1897—since then those published:

'Horae Solitariae'	Duckworth	2/6
'Oxford'	Black	20/–
'Rose Acre Papers'	Brown Langham	1/6
'Beautiful Wales'	Black	20/–
'The Heart of England'	Dent	20/– just coming.

But the expensive books were written to order and the little books of essays are very early.

Believe me | Yours very truly | Edward Thomas

To Walter de la Mare

Berryfield Cottage | Ashford | Petersfield | 14 November 1906

Dear Mr de la Mare,

I was very glad to have your letter this morning, you are the only man I do not know who has ever written to me about my reviews and knowing your work I cannot but be happy. And yet I feel that even I could do so much better—about your book, for example—if only I had time. My article was only a hasty review: I have not time to order or make clear the thoughts and emotions your 'Poems' suggested. But to have pleased you is everything and to talk like this is only vanity. So thank you again and may I look forward to seeing you in London. May I call? When I am in London I often happen to be in Anerley (which I shall like a little better now).

I am using 'Keep Innocency' and (probably) 'Bunches of Grapes' and 'The Child in the story awakens'* also in my Anthology and I will mention the publishers.

About 'Ev'n' I think you can count on your readers making it a grave monosyllable without printing it so.

My other review of you—a very scrappy little one—will appear in the Bookman.

Yours sincerely | Edward Thomas

To Gordon Bottomley

Berryfield Cottage | 26 December 1906

My dear Gordon,

The photograph is very good and a good picture too and Helen and I were glad to have it this morning and send our thanks to Emily for it with our love. But I may still regret that you didn't meet F H Evans and get him to inspect you. Perhaps you will this next year. At any rate I wish you the health for a journey. It is nearly a year now since I saw you at Cartmel and I reflect that I have had one sight of you per annum since we began to write. Then with luck I may see you 30 or 40 times again—which makes the future seem quite a desirable reversion. But the present is of the old sort: even a little worse, since I have had but one visit from a friend since I came here, have had so much work that only twice have I been able to walk all day, and for some reason have attained a degree of self-consciousness beyond the dreams of avarice (which makes me spend hours, when I ought to be reading or enjoying the interlacing flight of 3 kestrels, in thinking out my motives for this or that act or word in the past until I long for sleep). Certainly I have a devil as much as any man I ever read of. But if there are devils there are no exorcisers, though a kind friend wrote to me lately to point out the security and sweetness of his refuge in the fat bosom of the Church. I feel sure that my salvation depends on a person and that person cannot be Helen because she has come to resemble me too much or at least to play unconsciously the part of being like me with a skill that could make me weep. It is unlikely to be a woman because a woman is but a human being with the additional barriers of (1) sex and (2) antipathy to me—as a rule. And as to men—here I am surrounded by schoolmasters [at Bedales], while in town I can but pretend to pick up the threads of ancient intercourse, a task as endless as the counting of poppy seeds or plovers in the air.

I think you are right about Davies.* But there are fine things in the new book, 'The Likeness', 'The Ox', 'Music', 'Parted', and others, and I do like 'Catharine'. He will always observe and always feel, I think and whether he grows much or not, it seems likely that he will often attain simplicity unawares. I must think out a just and yet genial comment for his private eye. In print I shall praise him mainly because a reviewer has to shout like an actor if he is to be heard by the audience.

How is your Anthology? I have half expected Guthrie to call (at your instigation). Do you think we could do anything with one another?

Oh, thank you for *The Gem* and the Prayer. I wonder is that Miscellany worthy of its great aim. The soft paper anticipates part of a great millenial scheme of my own.

I have written to Dent asking that a copy of my book be sent to the *Courier* but it has very likely gone there and into other hands already. If not Dent will send it and I trust your man [Dixon Scott] will get it. Salute him for me. He belongs to a very small and very secret society. So far my only intelligent review is from *The Athenaeum* and that is not favourable. It objects to my 'sensuousness', 'love of colour', 'lyricism'. So far no one has discovered 'The Ship, the chariot and the plough' except you and me.

It is alright about your Poetry article. As a matter of fact I am being hurried on by the publishers, but I have only the first $\frac{1}{4}$ to get ready at once and there will be no literary articles therein.

With our love and good wishes to you and Emily and your father and mother and Aunt Sarah, | Yours and Emily's ever |

Edward Thomas

To Jesse Berridge

Berryfield Cottage | Ashford | Petersfield | 1 January 1907

My dear Jesse,

Smoking some of your York River tobacco, but otherwise rather denuded by too long a walk into Sussex in the slush. I thank you for your letter and the tobacco. I am glad you liked the books. If I could possibly help to set Dell* off in a direction of profit and delight I should be happy. I wish I had got to know him. But now he is getting older and aloof I expect. How hard it is to get over the natural boundaries between those even of an age I know, I know; for here I am surrounded by good men, masters at Bedales school, and so far I simply look at them with a 'How I wonder what you are'. How I wish you were a curate—or better still a rector—within an easy walk. Someday you and I ought to walk to Oxford from here. Winchester is a fine day's walk, Selborne is close at hand.

Never mind now about the tunes. I sang them to Freeman and now we have got them all right. You shall have the Anthology* and recommend it to your parishioners as by your brother. The melodies—56 of them—are a fine lot but the poems are perhaps rather obviously chosen by one who didn't want to clash with other anthologies.

Some day I will come to Colchester. Tell me when it is quite convenient and I will do my best.

[W. H.] Davies is cheerful at the cottage and looking out for reviews of his *New Poems* just published by Elkin Mathews. Ransome* is at present in Edinburgh where his mother lives. He is or lately was engaged again and he has plenty of work—did ½ a dozen Xmas books for children, of no great merit. Tom is in Derbyshire, cheerful and serene and puzzling as ever I suppose. Rolf* has a boy baby. Yes I saw Hogg's book and gave it a lift in the *Daily Chronicle*. Some of it was jolly good, clear and original thoughts justly expressed. But I never got the *Virgin Goddess*. I wish I had. Lend it to me some day.

Merfyn had 10 days at school at the end of term, now looks forward to his scarlet cap and school every day with joy. He was a Rat in a musical performance of the Pied Piper of Hamelin at the end of the term!

Helen's love and mine to you and Edna and Dell and Denys and Incogniti Tertius and Quartus.*

Yours ever | Edward Thomas

To Gordon Bottomley

Berryfield Cottage | Ashford | Petersfield | 14 May 1907

My dear Gordon,

It is a beautiful still evening at 7 o'clock and I sit and look at the most luxuriant beechen hill and coombe in the world. I have no need to do any more work today, because I did 1600 words of reviewing* before 3.30, after which I wasted two hours trying to pay calls with Helen but finding my victims out. Then I said 'don't' to the children many times, and finally to myself; then suddenly seeing how beautiful it was, I thought I ought to enjoy it and could not think how. I can't read for pleasure. I tried gardening: it annoyed me, and there was an end to it. It is no use walking, for I do nothing but feed my eyes when I walk, and it has at last occurred to me that that is not enough,—a man in the country must be a naturalist, an historian, an agriculturist, or a philosopher, and I am none of them. I have no 'interests' at all, and I know that beauty can bore and even infuriate one who is seldom passionate. So I am writing to you which is obviously a poor thing to do as it simply clarifies my introspection a little but will not—I know well—lead it anywhere. Oh for a little money, to turn round for a year, to make sure whether there is anything I should want to do if I had not to do reviewing. I tried to get my agent to help me out of reviewing. But he could only suggest fiction, which I can't even begin to think of yet. I suggested a book on the Suburbs, but instead of my little 20,000 words he wants an important work of 60,000 and I know what that means, and he wants a syllabus and I don't know what that means. The *Jefferies* has not been settled yet and I am afraid of it. It is a silly thing to do a bad life of a good man and I shall have no leisure to try to do a good one. I wish I hadn't written this because it is not clear enough to enable you to help, supposing I can be helped. But I leave it, I think, just because I don't like sending you a very short letter and I don't like keeping you waiting very long. Oh, my self-consciousness, it grows and grows and is almost constant now, and I fear perhaps it will reach the point of excess without my knowing it.——

I won't send you my Anthology until the 2nd. impression because it is full of misprints. I simply cannot concentrate my mind on familiar poems so as to detect misprints.

What you say about 'a new movement of Naturalism—naturalism of feeling where Wordsworth's was no more than a naturalism of thought', I believe is well worth thinking about, and I have meant to get conscious of it to some purpose (having long thought vaguely as you do); but positively only reviews and nature ever make me think at all and that in a way beyond my control—things occur to me and I think for about the length of a lyric and then down and blank and something new—if the old idea returns it will not grow, but is only repeated. Perhaps we worry less about conclusions, generalisations nowadays, in our anxiety to get the facts and feelings down—just as science picks up a million pebbles and can't arrange them or even play with them. I am by the way going to plead for a little more playfulness and imagination (if to be got) in archaeology, topography and so on: the way in which scientific people and their followers are satisfied with data in appalling English disgusts me, and is moreover wrong.

About Jefferies—I never read *The Scarlet Shawl* but it is a yellow back and said to be an entirely vain attempt to write an ordinary novel about lords. But I should like to look at it when I come down. By the way, as Helen is a daily schoolmistress from 9 till 10.30 she cannot get away until August and will then most likely go with the children.

I like the idea of blank verse for your Gunnar play,* but then also I should like to see how you would do prose to that extent.

I don't know why de la Mare should not like you, by the way.

Yes; I only smoke about 1½ pipes of tobacco a day. Perhaps I am a little hungrier, but I am neither more joyful nor more wise.

It is past 8 and almost too dark and there is little more time.

I use a stylographic pen now—hence my handwriting.

I introduced Guthrie's landscape to a very clever acquaintance of mine who has money and spends it and most of his time in learning to draw. He likes Guthrie's feeling immensely but says he ought to try working with a fine fountain pen on smooth paper and give up his 'mezzy' methods! But I imagine Guthrie will have to be satisfied with his *results* now, won't he?

Our love to Emily and you | Ever yours | Edward Thomas

NOTES FOUND AMONG HELEN'S LETTERS, DATED 9 OCTOBER 1907

Disappointed because Helen said she would return today but now puts off till tomorrow—which throws me out and gives me no relief for my reading—also I may have smoked and taken too much tea.—So I sat thinking about ways of killing myself. My revolver has only one bullet left. I couldn't hang myself: and though I imagined myself cutting my throat with a razor on Wheatham I had not the energy to go. Then I went out and thought what effects my suicide would have. I don't think I mind them. My acquaintances—I no longer have friends—would talk in a day or two (when they met) and try to explain and of course see suggestions in the past: W H Davies would suffer a little; Helen and the children—less in reality than they do now, from my accursed tempers and moodiness. It is dislike of the effort to kill myself and fear that I could not carry it through if I half did it, that keeps me alive. Only that. For I hate my work, my reviewing: my best I feel is negligible: I have no vitality, no originality, no love. I do harm. Love is dead and lust almost dead.

N.B. These thoughts have come to me at least once a week for 3 or 4 years now and frequently during the last 7—except as to lust.

I wonder how many people are as impatient of impermanence as I am, and who go away from an evening in company with such regrets not so much because it has been pleasant (it seldom is) as that it might have become so. Why when I am on my way to London I always run thro' all the engagements ahead that I have made and as I enter the Mt. Blanc with Hudson and Garnett, see the clock at 1.30 I reflect that at 3 all chances of making myself happy will be over and I shall have to look about for others.

Now and then for about a minute only every day and rarely for perhaps a quarter of an hour on end I enjoy perfect happiness—I am without thought, my body is painless, I am unaware of it,—I move easily and I sing or hum a song or a fragment of one.

How I admire direct expressive natures. This morning I went into ——'s bedroom as he was dressing. He had been rather ill and was not over cheerful but as he was pulling a shirt over his head he talked easily and rapidly in a clear voice, expressing likes and dislikes right out of his heart, without any of the hesitation which I have so often that I really never ought to say or write anything.

I am interested in nothing and would for ever sit still and seek nothing if I had to be continually nailing my mind to something with my nice docility. And yet unawares I am lured into interest as when I found myself today near crying as I read the Iliad to Merfyn.

I believe I can be perfectly humble with a very young child, with no condescension or mere curiosity, simply responding to his emotions as he shows me a picture or a map, and suggesting things to him which are inspired by him and would be impossible to me in a man's company, believing in things I say to this child more than I ever believe in what I write or what I say to Garnett for instance.—This imitativeness goes far. I was with an ordinary 2nd. year undergraduate today and found myself sharing his experiences in talk as if I were in my 2nd year too. Nor does this come from a desire not to displease, though that is (unconsciously) often so strong that when a man opens talks with a remark implying that I know e.g. a certain book I nod assent. Yet again much as I hate argument and am unfit for it I am often lured in talk into an attitude, by some slip of speech or even the other man's misunderstanding, and I keep up the attitude so long that when at last I am beaten I am mortified as I should not have been were I upset in an argument on something I care about. For most people argue to defeat their opponents and not to get at truth.

There are many horsechestnuts by the roadside at Ashford and today (9.x.07) many 'conquers' are falling in rainy wind and they strew the road. I feel a pang as I walk over them and do not like to crush one if I can help it, for thinking of the time when I should not have left the place till I had gathered them all,—15 years ago at Cannon Hill, Merton.

To C. F. Cazenove

Berryfield Cottage | Ashford | Petersfield | 6 December 1907

My dear Cazenove,

Thanks for your letter and receipts. I have not found a Barnes yet—the difficulty is to get one out of copyright, published about 1859 and not later than 1862 or 3.

I can't say I have any very practicable proposals to make. But I should like to do a big book giving a history of the attitudes towards Nature, sport, and country life in English literature from the earliest times, largely by means of extracts.

Then I had thought of a book of extracts from prose and verse from Welsh writers—viz. translations from those who wrote in Latin and Welsh, and the originals of those who wrote in English. This would mean a quite attractive book from a popular point of view as it would include Geoffrey of Monmouth, Gerald of Wales, the Mabinogion, the medieval Welsh poets and romances, some fairy tales, three out of the four greatest religious poets (Herbert, Vaughan, and Traherne), some great preachers and theologians, etc etc. I should only include those who had at least one Welsh parent or whose families had been resident for at least two generations.—I did make a proposal of the kind to Unwin (in answer to one from him) a few days ago, but he was so vague and silly that I would rather not deal with him. The book ought to be about 60,000 words long and at present I don't see how I could do more than an introduction to it. For the next 3 months I shall be quite full up with Jefferies.

Yours ever | Edward Thomas

To Walter de la Mare

Ashford | 16 December 1907

My dear de la Mare,

I liked reading the poems* you sent me. The first poem—the one on top, 'The Puppet Master'—showed at once that he could write and had a special individual feeling for words. Then 'Prayer to my Lord' seemed to me very fine; 'Waterpools' also and in the main 'After Flight'; 'The Men who loved the cause that never died'; and everything of 'Happy Death' except the title. But I find I am going through them all except the last long one—'The Plighted Queen' and that had an untransmuted allegorical feeling that disagreed with me. Often the writing is admirable—I mean that I feel in reading, quite suddenly and with a thrill, that here are words arranged in a foreordained manner which I can't explain. You must be annoyed at my only making these very vague and general remarks, for I am terribly busy trying to get rid of a lot of trivial work before I leave home. That will be on the 27th of this month most likely. If so, can we meet for tea? I will let you know positively as soon as I can. I have just filled a small box with roots and am sending them to you by rail, carriage paid. They aren't as much as I meant but the Michaelmas daisies and other big things are so clotted with moist earth that they would weigh too much. I will send some more in the Spring perhaps. The feathery stuff here and there is a kind of saxifrage, green all the year round with a beautiful ivory flower, and it spreads rapidly. Plant it in loose earth so that it is covered up all but the green tops and it will soon be right. In the bit of newspaper—and I hope not crushed—are some big African poppy roots. At the bottom is one piece of Michaelmas daisy and one piece of a big knapweed. Then there are several pieces of pink, I think some Canterbury bell, some forget-me-not, and at the top several roots of Japanese anemone which I don't feel very certain about, and in any case they will be diffident at first. Also there are 4 roots of hollyhock. In the spring there ought to be many seedlings I could send. Here is a packet of Columbine seeds from our garden at the Weald.

With good wishes to you all | Ever yours | Edward Thomas

PS. I now find the box won't go till Wednesday which is a nuisance, but it might be all right.

To Gordon Bottomley

Berryfield Cottage | 26 December 1907

My dear Gordon,

I don't know when I shall next get a chance to write to you and even now it nears dinner time, I expect Guthrie, and I have still to pack, for tomorrow I leave here for Minsmere, nr Dunwich, Suffolk

where I hope to write about Jefferies. I brim over with little things but have no notion of a good movement and sweep yet. Could you send me the Wilde books there as I understand the new edition is coming early in the year?
—Isn't Nietzsche magnificent?* and so necessary these days? Yet he damns me to deeper perdition than I have yet bestowed myself.

I am glad to hear I was enjoying life. Perhaps my melancholy is a delusion of the surface, a term mistakenly applied by one who is after all only a ½d. critic. I did enjoy yesterday though because Bronwen excelled herself in joy and expressions of joy and even Merfyn was never peevish. We did not over eat, touched no alcohol and I actually laughed as I was getting to bed. The other night I went into the children's bedroom, by the way, and awakened Bronwen by accident—she burst out laughing and fell asleep again. Fancy laughing in bed and at night and on just waking up. I ought to bend all my efforts to live up to her as the Superman.

I was sorry Emily ran off so gaily, but it was all a hurry and it does not rankle.

You are right about Yeats and I felt the same even when I praised *Deirdre* but if he does it again I shall administer an emetic for the laudanum with which he is always drugging big hearty people. But it was so perfect in its kind I couldn't throw stones, though glass houses are really meant for stones. Trench* has a better spirit in his *Deirdre* and the ravishment of Naois is well done; there is a most beautiful comparison in it (I forget where now) of Deirdre's astonishment at sight of Naois—to the astonishment of a man who comes suddenly out of woods upon a vast quiet estuary and his horse's hoofs startle the seafowl that were glassed—with sky and cloud—in the ebb. Oh, glorious. Yet I know I like it because with great good luck I might have done it myself.

Adieu Sylvanus with love to Sylvana from your loving |
Urbanus.

Have you any book that touches well on the mystic trance—its origin—typical visions etc? I ain't a mystic myself and I want to know what is possible before coming to *The Story of my Heart* in which there are some trance-visions or experiences. I know Inge's

Christian Mysticism and Edward Carpenter's chapters in *Adam's Peak to Elephants*.

To Harry Hooton

Minsmere | 30 January 1908

My dear Harry,

I am not cursed at all. I didn't stop work because she* went, but I simply found that as a matter of fact my work went rather to pieces. Of course I am greedy. You might as well blame me for not being grateful that I get my meals daily when some starve, you aged moralist. As to the other children, I see their merits but they do not touch me very closely. So I must console myself with you, aged and masculine as you are. I am very much better for being here and for having a good doctor but I can't lose sight of the plain fact that the world is not made for me.

I wish you luck and Wolff confusion. Let me know that it is all well.

I have now reached *The Story of My Heart* in Jefferies and it is every way the most difficult part. But I look forward to finishing the first draft by the end of February and then Helen wants to spend the last weekend (Feb. 21–5 or Feb. 29–March 2) here—May she if she can? She blesses you for doing me this turn.

I sent Hope (through Mrs. Webb, decorously) my Pocket Book* but have not even had an indirect word in reply.

My love to you and Janet and Joan and Patsy.

Ever yours | Edwy

To Walter de la Mare

Minsmere | 19 February 1908

Dear de la Mare,

[*The first paragraph mentions skulls uncovered at the sinking beech near Dunwich with a promise to send one to de la Mare. Then, after a reference to Thomas's work on Jefferies, the letter continues.*]

I don't think I really have any imagination, certainly not enough to distinguish between it and reality. But I feel sure it is beyond what is called reality, and that is something fit for and even aware of infinite and eternal things. Jefferies and Maeterlinck believe that it is so weak—they call it the soul—simply because we do not as yet admit its existence and have never tried to nourish it and let it have its way. I think it may be found to be life itself to which flesh, mind etc. are only aids, that it is what enables us to feel and know the divine in all things, is itself the divine to which the rest of the universe responds according as we have or have not cut off our communication by pampering flesh and mind: (which is not very clear and may be pure metaphor, I mean bad, metaphor) so that only by imagination can we see things flesh and spirit as they are, only by it understand the life of things, and take images of them above with us for ever. That is the only hypothesis to suit my own experience. You ought to read Jefferies's 'Story of My Heart'. Will you if I lend it to you? I have had nobody to discuss it with so that I have come only to my customary rhetorical and general conclusions about it. When you have read it you will not think of water and wine in the relations you suggest.

I am so glad you have got Energy even if congested. My case is just the opposite, lack of Energy expanded. And so the Jefferies is getting to an end—. I wish you would write more now, and yet when I think of it it is wonderful you write at all after your long days every day in Town.—I would gladly lend you parts of my 'Jefferies' but you have no idea what my MSS are like—something like a lawn intersected with mole runs and dotted with mole heaps and worm casts. I continually add in the margin, on top and between lines: I only indicate the pages of my quotations and I alter the order of paragraphs etc. very often. It will be quite hard work for me to follow all the signposts.

My health began by improving rapidly, but then I began to get very fond of one of the children of my neighbours (they are retired Anglo Indians, friends of friends of mine), and she left a month ago to go to school and the place has become chiefly superficies ever since. She is 17, a particularly lovely age to me because when I was that age I knew only two of my coevals, one I married and the other is in South Africa, and in the presence of this new one I had the sharpest pains and pleasures of retrospection, longing and—I am now making absurd attempts to return to that period by means of letters! You see I have a young head on my decrepit shoulders.

I expect to leave here on March 2 or 3

[*Then arrangements follow to meet in town on 25 February*]

With best wishes to you all | Ever yours | Edward Thomas

To Walter de la Mare

Ashford | February or March 1908

My dear de la Mare,

Thanks for the MS and your letter. I made use of your suggestions as a rule, e.g. putting in a few words about Jefferies' unpopularity at school and suggesting that it was the result of that something repellant in him which you (and Sir Edward Grey to Hudson) see in his writing at times. It can't be defined except by comparing it with a trick of voice or manner that offends. Of course he is emphatic and he is capable of a certain viciousness which one dislikes particularly in a man so pathetically unworldly and alone. A snarl, perhaps you haven't noticed it. Nobody has a really kindly thing to say of him personally. But it may have been the awkwardness of an unsocial animal.

You ask me to define Nature. I used it vulgarly for all that is not man, perhaps because man contemplates it so, as outside himself, and has a sort of belief that Nature is only a house, furniture etc round about him. It is not my belief, and I don't oppose Nature to Man. Quite the contrary. Man seems to me a very little part of Nature and the part I enjoy least. But civilization has estranged us superficially from Nature, and towns make it possible for a man to live as if a millionaire could really produce all the necessities of life—food, drink, clothes, vehicles etc and then a tombstone. I believe some do live so. But I can't write about this being specially busy after walking to Goodwood races* and back yesterday and getting overtired and behind with my work.

Yours ever | Edward Thomas

To Edward Garnett

Berryfield Cottage | Ashford | 11 February 1909

My dear Garnett,

Have you time to look at another sketch of mine? I don't like troubling you again especially with manuscript but I am strongly impelled to because I have now had about six weeks of unusual energy and have written about a score of tales and sketches* real and imaginary such as I have never attempted before, and though I feel a little more confident than I used to I am not at all sure that I am on a wise path—far less a profitable one—and you are the only man I can turn to for an opinion. I have been working so fast that I have only copied out one or two of these things and those only the shortest, or else I should have sent you something of a more elaborate and realistic kind. Perhaps you are very busy—I know you must be about now engaged in arranging for your Icelandic play*—and if so I hope you will return this piece at once and let me show it to you another time perhaps.

Yours | Edward Thomas

To Edward Garnett

Ashford | 13 March 1909

My dear Garnett,

Your letter that came this morning was too flattering but entirely pleasant to me, for I am not exaggerating when I say that I have long hoped to please you and that I now feel glad of whatever praise the book* wins largely because it is some return to you for all your direct and indirect criticism of me and my work. You have been my chief guide to such knowledge as I have of the relationship between life and literature.—But I am too confused with pleasure and shyness to say what I am feeling even on paper. I will only offer affectionate homage. I hope I shall have a chance of talking to you soon—won't you come down here some time before as well as after the new house is built? They are only just digging out the foundations and bringing up the bricks. I am to have a little room right away from the house to work in and that may be finished soon after the beginning of Spring I hope—it looks through trees to a magnificent road winding up and round a coombe among beeches, and to the Downs four miles away south. But I wish and so do we all that you would come before. You can have a bed-sitting room with a fire and work when you want to. But unless you could perhaps come down next week don't trouble to write about this as I shall see you on the 22nd or 23rd I expect.

Thank you for sending my sketch to *Country Life*, but it would look very odd there, I think.

I shall not forget what you say about going forward still more into contact with the world at my gate and over the hills. You mean the world of men, I think. I should like to, equally as a man and as a writer, but the ability grows slowly; I am still very much afraid of men and too easily repulsed from them into myself; and I feel very humble when I think how seldom I can be myself and enter into them at the same time—either I remain sullenly self-centred or I lose myself on the stream of their usually stronger or more active characters.

Yours | Edward Thomas

Merfyn is often asking about David [Garnett] now as he is a 'Scout' and just beginning to enjoy what he vividly remembers seeing David in full possession of years ago.

To Gordon Bottomley

Ashford | 15 March 1909

My dear Gordon,

I was afraid that you were not well as you were silent rather longer than usual and am sorry to know I was right. But I think perhaps you are feeling not uneasy as you are making such big and charming plans for Spring. Don't worry another second about the *South Country*. Dent wants to delay. He says the season is very bad for his trade; but I think the fact is he wants to organise and advertise a series in which my book shall appear. When the proofs do come, be sure I shall very gladly ask you to look at them. I have very little else to tell you about myself. Here is nearly ¼ of the year gone and I seem to have been sitting close up to the fire all the time writing all sorts of things which you shall see some day only I don't like to trouble you with M.S. and the typescript is being thrust upon editors.* I have done a great deal at first under a real impulse but latterly (the long frost having quite undermined me) by force of daily custom as much as anything. I can do almost anything if once I can start doing it every day at a certain hour. And as reviewing has been scarce I have had few interruptions. I feel sure it is better work or in a better direction than all but the best of the old but it is even less profitable and quite impossible to palm off on a publisher as part of a guinea guide book. A difficulty will soon arise unless *Jefferies* brings me offers of work—which it has failed to do except from the Editor of a new magazine who asked me for a short 'semi-poetical' article on 'why I love an out of door life'! I don't live an out of door life and can't be semi-poetical to order so I asked a prohibitive price and so got out of it. Meantime I get articles returned on every hand. *The New Age* printed a thing last week. Did you see it? But it was written a year ago nearly.—Evidently I am developed into a worse kind of bore at any rate. Put it down to the big fires which I have to sit close up to in this weather.

I am very glad 'Gunnar' is soon coming. If I were sending out review copies I should not go beyond *Times*, *Chronicle*, *Daily News*, *Telegraph*, *Manchester Guardian*, *Saturday*, *Outlook*, *Nation*, *Bookman* and, perhaps, *English Review* (tho they review very little). I don't know if I can decently review a book dedicated to me but I will do it indecently, if not.

The English Review may perhaps help me if it lives.*

I wish I could talk to you about Edward Garnett. (I shall doubtless; and by the way it seems likely I shall be walking out of Yorkshire into the Lake country in June or there abouts, and if so I should like to stay a day or two with you, if you are at home and free.) Certainly his talk is far better than his writings. I hardly know a poorer writer of any ability at all. I don't know which Turgenev preface you mean but there again I should like to talk about naturalism—writing would weary me—I've had a day of it and woodchopping and reading to children (who have chicken-pox; Helen being away) and walking etc. I don't know anybody who seems to see literature and life as a whole so well as he, judging from his talk. But nevertheless I think that my respect for his opinion *of my own work* is possibly exaggerated by feeling that he was at one time reluctant to like it and even perhaps antipathetic to me and it; so that I had something to break down before reaching him and to succeed in that would always please my vanity. He is like the one sinner who repenteth. The man who readily sympathises with my work and says he likes it I am with insistent cursedness, inclined to suspect, on the other hand. There's a grand fire now and my legs are burning.

Tell me why you frown on the later Symons?* I suppose you detect in his broadening out also a thinning down. But I should have said that, allowing bulk to count, he hardly had a superior living as a critic combining instinct and scholarship. I don't think he had any originality, but then that is true of his other work too. But I thought a few of the later poems* as good as anything he had done before, tho not better than (of their kind) the earliest. I imagine he could never be what I should call quite sincere, that is why he had not style; but in the later attitude all the flimsy avoidable insincerity had gone. But I don't possess *London Nights** and I am writing on the strength of perhaps very wrong early impressions.

Then we kiss again with tears over Poe. Hawthorne I know little of, I have read some very indifferent creepy stuff of his tho it didn't produce a creep.

Arthur Ransome is married, I hear, and is coming to try to live for the Summer near here.* I met his lady. She belongs to the higher orders and no connection of hers has ever been in trade. She paints herself. She has many rings. But she is pretty and spirited and clever*—but not clever enough to do her own hair. Unfortunately I never venture to limn the higher orders in my sketches . . .

It is 10. I must read about the Zeno of the London Celts. You haven't got to—please, when you are well write again a long letter. I can't. You can: also you have, at least perhaps you have, more time. Please do

Yours ever | Edward Thomas

To Gordon Bottomley

Ashford | 16 July 1909

My dear Gordon,

Thank you for your letter. I ought to have said it before and would have done had I known I was to glide into such a languid desperate condition as I am in now. Yet I ought to have known for by referring to diaries* I have at last found out what I suspected before that I get periods of depression particularly once a month for a week or so. But this is enough of the natural history of ET for the present.

I have seen the Book* and it looks very well and fitting. The printing is not first class and the house at Lithend has come out rather badly, but the pictures are very good—I like the horse's head at the beginning. It is good of you to promise me a Pullman edition and I quite understand how that may be delayed. Mrs Guthrie seems worse than ever and was to undergo an operation this or next week if no better. I haven't seen them for months, perhaps not this year, though Helen has. I don't like going into the house where there is so much disease and pain, especially as the house seems to suffer too.

If only you were here now you would see de la Mare. He is staying fairly near and we see him and his family often. You would like his singularly (sometimes comically) restless and curious and innocent mind. Our other neighbours* we scarce ever see. They frequent Petersfield and other pubs enlivening the countryside with song. We like the 'painted lady' less and less and call her the Unicorn because she has a small ivory horn in the midst of her forehead. We feel very bourgeois beside them but deferentially expect *Bohemia in Froxfield*.

What do you think of Arthur Wor* now after his review in the D.C.? Do you think he is not altogether fool. Still you won't care, after Sturge Moore's opinion which I am glad to hear.

We have seen Garnett's play acted.* The middle was slow and was full of the smell of old skins which the family was beating while awaiting the warrior's return. But the beginning was good and the last act very fine. He had a lovely dark girl as Helga. Here I send it. *Deirdre* is an exquisite whole on the stage. But I want to know how Yeats came to use the phrase 'Libyan heel'. It isn't Yeats at all, is it? But *The Playboy*.* Have you read and seen it? I daresay it is the greatest play of modern times. Of course I don't know. But I felt it to be utterly new and altogether fine. Goodbye now. In a hurry and I hope you are well again now. Write and tell me.

I am Emily and yours ever | Edward Thomas

To Gordon Bottomley

Week Green | Petersfield | 14 December 1909

My dear Gordon,

This is the new address. The rhythm of it is quite modern at any rate, though Garnett puts the house down to the period of King Stephen. We move in on Saturday and I have just packed all my books and take the children to town tomorrow to be rid of them for the move. We are in a pickle. I am dirty and my hands are all chipped and scraped and stiff. So I doubt if I can write. But I want to send you Masefield's book. I think *Nan* a very fine thing and so do you.

I was glad to have some news of you though it was bad. I guessed it would be. This must have been a deadly year for you. It has been a great weight to bear continuously and I hope for a crisp winter to clean the earth and help you. For two months nearly I have been better, chiefly because I have had to work hard and regularly in the new garden clay. I don't really care about it, but it had to be done and I kept at it day after day and it did me good almost against my will. I got a hard hand and my fatigues were more purely physical than usual. I had to do my reviewing badly and to do very little else. Still, one or two stories I worked at did not turn out badly. I used some old Welsh fragments of legends. You shall see them some day.* I always feel that when I treat these *external* things my approach is very literal and matter of fact, but I hope not. Perhaps I am not quite just to myself in finding myself very much on an everyday ordinary level except when in a mood of exaltation usually connected with nature and solitude. By comparison with others that I know—like de la Mare—I seem essentially like the other men in the train and I should like not to be. This is quite genuinely naive and will amuse you. It may be only because I am inarticulate and that I can usually only meet others on ground where I have no real interest—as politics, social and current literary affairs.

I am perhaps about to begin a book on poets and women. Originally it was to have been the influence of women on English poets. But that is too difficult: so it will be mainly the attitude of poets to individual women and the idea of woman and so on. Please send suggestions, warnings etc. as they come to your mind.

I have been dangling after publishers with all sorts of proposals but could not come to terms. This looked bad and I was willing to accept anything especially as our move means an increased expenditure and Helen talks of having another baby. In fact I have consented to do a guide—pure guide—to Hampshire and Wiltshire, but it is not settled and I shall cry off if I possibly can, though my expenses will be paid to cover some fine country and I should get much material by the way.* I am not sure that I could do it. The General Election will postpone my little book of sketches.* I am trying to cozen Dent into letting me do a country book with houses—cottages, farms etc.—as centres, and dealing more than ever with people. If he will let me—and let me bring in Wales as well—I could make a good book of my kind. I hope *The South Country* at its best was beyond *The Heart of England*. It had no structure and its joins were execrable, but I felt some of it was the truest I had achieved.

Ezra Pound's second book* was a miserable thing and I was guilty of a savage recantation after meeting the man at dinner. It was very treacherous and my severity was due to self-contempt as much as to dislike of his work.

Goodbye. I must go to bed out of this empty room.

Yours and Emily's ever | Edward Thomas

To C. F. Cazenove

Wick Green | Petersfield | 16 April 1910

Dear Cazenove,

I confess I don't see any grounds for hoping that a publisher can be beguiled; and as to paying money for the Homes after seeing specimens that is surely fantastical. I have always got money for books which no publisher would have accepted had he seen them beforehand.

There is also this to be considered. I might in the course of a year or two sell the greater part of this book to magazines etc. and that would be far more profitable than taking *less* than £50 for the whole. I did want £50 badly *at once*, but say £30 in six months time is no allurement.

To put it plainly, this book is fiction and you can't get money down for fiction by me. Much better try it with magazines, returning 'Lostormellyn' and 'Home'* (part of which has appeared in Wales).

Yours sincerely | Edward Thomas

To C. F. Cazenove

Wick Green | Petersfield | 28 July 1910

Dear Cazenove,

Thanks. I see Dent's point. He wants to have Thomas plus somebody else, preferably A. G. Bradley. I wish very much I could oblige, but I am pretty sure I can't. I will think over it though. Meantime is it any good proposing a book to deal in detail with one piece of country either in Wales or in England, describe it generally with some historical outlines and then take a town, some villages, some isolated houses with studies of the people etc.? The only thing is that I refuse to give it away openly by giving it a name, though I will give good fictitious names. Or I will make a leading character and set him walking and telling what he sees; *or* make the book his journal. If these do not seem to you worth trying I must have time to think it over, and shall be glad of any definite suggestions from Dent or yourself—very glad. Of course I would consent, if there was nothing else for it, to do a book on the Severn or the Towy; but it would be dishonest, because it is not worth my while to make it a solid definite book because it would be one that anybody else could do and would have nothing of me in it, which I am assuming is desirable; and to avoid doing this obvious thing I should find some tricky way out which would annoy Dent.

The best thing would be for him to let me make a walking tour over the south into the west, giving the book a clear hard backbone and building everything round that. I will, if he likes, mention by name the place I stay at every night and describe my route quite substantially though not giving the exact names of villages, hills, etc. It shall have a beginning, a middle and an end and there shall be as little no man's land as possible.

I am sorry I have mislaid Secker's letter. As soon as he answers I will send you some M.S.S. or bring it up on Tuesday next.

Yours sincerely | Edward Thomas

To Gordon Bottomley

Swansea | Monday [September 1910]

My dear Gordon,

I have just had a fortnight in Wales mostly in the wild part of Cardiganshire and am going home tomorrow. May I send you these proofs now and the preceding pages a few days later so as to save space in my bag going home? You will find yourself lowering your standard of English and of sense as you go along, or there will be nothing but corrections. It is a strange piece of work.* I put down all but everything just as it occurred to me during the few months I was doing it. How are you now? I have just had a post-card from Guthrie and he speaks as if you might be ill again, but I hope not. He probably needs a holiday very badly himself. If he calls on you, give him my love. I should go over there more often—as he does not come to me—if it were not for Mrs. Guthrie's sick looks and conversation solely about her ailments. Don't worry about these proofs. The thing is not worth it. But if you can look them over within 10 days or so, so much the better for me.

Helen and the new baby are still very well I hear. The baby's name is probably to be Helen Elizabeth Mevanwy (Myfanwy is the Welsh spelling but impossible in England). I liked Olwen best, but it is too near Bronwen. With my love to Emily and yourself.

Ever yours | Edward Thomas

To David Uzzell

Wick Green | Petersfield | 22 December 1910

Dear Dad,

I had not forgotten you and was beginning to think of writing again when your letter arrived. You did very well at Swindon this time and I was glad to see it. Now we want to see what is going to be *done*. I am glad to hear that you are all well or pretty well. Granny must find it a bit stiff sometimes going to get that cup of tea for Bill in the morning, so I am sending her five shillings to get something to ease it a bit on Christmas Day. I should like to be down there when the frosty weather comes, but most likely it will be March or April before I come that way.* I shall be walking from

Wantage to Avebury and shall probably break my journey at Chiseldon and come and look you up. So Bill is a sweep and Charley* a lamplighter, two of the best jobs a man could do but I suppose not the best paid. It is not often you meet a black man and a light man in one family like that; they ought to be very useful to one another.

Well, what weather we do have since you and I used to go walking. What summers they were. Here we are up as high as Barbary Castle and we feel the wind and rain.* But today it is fine and shining and there is a thrush singing beautiful down in the wood. I as usual, am writing a book, and if I live much longer and they put a list of my books on my tombstone I shall want one as big as one of the stones at Stonehenge.

I suppose you will never get me a nice oak stick, a root that would make a good knob. That is what I should like. I have got a good ash and a hazel and a blackthorn, but there's nothing like oak, a good tapering stick with a knob. If you have one on your estate send it along.

Remember me to Granny and Bill and Tom and Charley and wish them all a Merry Christmas and a happy New Year.

Yours sincerely | Edward Thomas

To W. H. Hudson

Wick Green | Petersfield | 8 March 1911

My dear Hudson,

I am very sorry not to have come after your leaving word with Garnett and so on. But I have been suffering from exhaustion lately and had a return of it just as I was going to take the Tube towards you. I always have a bout or two in Spring but this is worse perhaps owing to my change of diet.* Thank you for your letter. The Woburn Natural History sounds nearest to the right thing. After reading your letter—I had forgotten Thoreau's complaint about poetry—I felt that probably I was asking for better bread than is made of wheat. Most cultures being mainly urban, the wildish man does not write poetry except among nomadic or mountainous people as among the Arabs and the Celts.* I just glanced at Kuno Meyer's book and wish I had it. It contains some most beautiful things of a kind, I suppose Thoreau could not have known, unless he had seen Stephens' 'Literature of the Cymry' or one of the other early books on Celtic literature. But it is noticeable that the English poetry of the sea is very very poor between the earliest times and the 19th century. The Elizabethan poets appear to have regarded the sea chiefly as a division between lovers and a path for invaders, if not as a mere bulwark of England. The wildness that I want, and probably the want itself, is perhaps a reaction against luxury and refinement. It is not satisfying in Emily Bronte. It is too painful like the rapid beating of a bird's heart in the hand. Her wildness is too delicate and helpless.

I hope I shall catch you in town next time I am up or not long afterwards.

Yours ever | Edward Thomas

To Gordon Bottomley

Wick Green | Petersfield | 14 April 1911

My dear Gordon,

Thank you for your letter and Emily for hers. I wasn't at all hurt by not getting a letter, but was silent only because for sometime I have been in one of my worst moods and in fact seem hardly likely to get out of it. By the way don't put it down to vegetarianism (which I have complicated by much reducing the size and number of my meals). I don't think it would be risky for you. Fruits, vegetables (steamed if possible), good bread and butter and nuts and cream, seems sufficient whether in simple or elaborate dishes: in fact I enjoy the taste of my food much more now than ever. But I can't advocate anything I practise just now: I am in such a poor way. I only hope I am still suffering from the transition out of youth, and that someday I shall laugh at having taken myself so tragically—as many people say they have laughed. I am beginning to see myself a little clearly and to see what things are probable and what improbable in my life. But I don't think I had better go into this and I apologize for merely telling you enough to trouble you a little without perhaps seeing what is up—which of course I do not quite know. It is connected with my work too, the unpleasant tendency being the necessity of producing many books instead of a few and much reviewing. The *Chronicle* and *Morning Post* are taking away my reviewing. The books are mostly not worth telling you about. One—a collection of Celtic tales retold for schools—I have lately finished. The *Maeterlinck*, by the way, ought to be in proof soon and I shall be very glad if you are able to correct the proofs. Thank you for promising. When they come I will send them. Then there is the *Icknield Way* but so far I have only done book work on it.

I am very glad to have your news, especially that you like Criccieth and the country and the sea round about. I hope it is really doing you good. I should like to be there, but my travels for some time must be chiefly in connection with work, especially the Icknield Way (from East Anglia S.W. into Dorset).

I can't remember when I wrote last. But did I tell you Garnett and I were trying to get a small pension for Davies? You have perhaps heard Yeats and Conrad were to have pensions. Davies is not certain yet. We got an interesting lot of signatures, including Bridges. Gosse is helping to get something from the Royal Literary Fund.

I saw Ransome in town. They are thinking of a Chelsea house now, and I suppose they are pretty well off. But I find myself remote from them now, especially from him. I heard about Tabitha and the little Abercrombie. Did you see *Mary and the Bramble*?* Rather loose and eloquent, with nice feeling, I thought.

I am falling asleep after a lot of gardening in these warm lovely days. How are they with you? The garden is very crude, but the terrace and the flowers are already pretty. We have some rosemary—at least I have by my study window. But we hope for a sprig of yours. You should see my wallflowers, the yellow and the darker than blood. We are waiting for the cuckoo. When I see you next I have a Welsh cuckoo song to hum you. I hope that will not be far ahead. By the way, Guthrie was here a month ago. He and I hit it off less, I think. Except in his art he is inarticulate but not silent. We are all well and glad of the new weather I assure you. Goodbye. Give our love to Emily and thank her for writing and ask her to forgive my not writing back. She would not have thanked me had I done so when I ought.

Yours ever | Edward Thomas

To Harold Monro

Wick Green | Petersfield | 19 May 1911

My dear Monro,

I am glad to hear from you and especially to hear you are coming to England. If you do settle here I hope it will not be too far away. Houses are not quite undiscoverable in this neighbourhood, by the way, where you will still find Lupton next door to me, and he is married now.

I don't know what to say or what not to say about journalism. I suppose your friend* has a gift of writing and perhaps nothing very definite to exercise it—I mean no special subject or temper. With health and persistency such a man, if at all clever, soon makes £50, £100, £200 out of journalism in London. I have known very few and they have usually begun with literary and journalistic friends to suggest or introduce. But the usual beginning is to get reviewing on a Daily or weekly, or to write articles upon subjects or people of the day or of the day after. I got my first reviewing by calling without an introduction and finding an editor* friendly. Then I got to know people and ways and means developed. Everything was rather accidental in my case and I daresay often is, so that it is hard to recommend any course—I have never myself had any influence to use. I don't think I have ever ventured to introduce any one to an editor, partly because I have not been personally friendly to editors and my word would have little weight, partly because I should have been cutting my own throat. At present I am in a worse position than usual and am being threatened with the necessity of writing many more books and losing most of my reviewing. Low as reviewing is it is only for the day and can be shaken off, but continuous hack-writing of books seems to me worse, more damaging to freedom and reputation. This I mention because it may not be without bearing on your friend's case. I was without special knowledge, had only a sketchy acquaintance with a number of things and a youthful bookishness. Partly owing to my work, perhaps chiefly, I have lost the bookishness and my acquaintance with things remains sketchy. But I am no longer entirely youthful and both the dulness and the ripeness of maturity are against light adventure. Hence I am dropping out, I believe. Your friend may of course be much better equipped: he will almost certainly have more vitality. I don't like to advise. If he does come to London I should advise him to find a special subject or domain if he has not one already. He will have to do much that he is only slightly qualified for, but let him try to master a subject or a particular kind of writing. Then he will have something to keep his head above the mud of things. Also it is well when first looking for work to have a subject which you know rather particularly well, a language, a period of history or literature, or form of literature, the hobbies of royalty etc. Under cover of this one subject a young writer insinuates himself among editors and others who usually have no subject at all: they are not afraid of a man who asks only for books relating to the reign of William IV. But do not trust me. I have done hard work, it is true, and made a living, but I have never made my way. I was kindly treated as a very young man and as I say things seemed to come my way. Thus I have not a fair knowledge of the field, and I am suffering from this now and it may be inclined to take too gloomy a view. As you say, there is no regular entrance to journalism. But your friend can evidently write well enough. I should not think shorthand was necessary except to a regular newspaper man, a reporter and sub-editor. This cutting tells me only that he can do the usual things in a competent manner. If he wants to write paragraphs, interviews, leaderettes, I know nothing personally about that side of the trade, but could possibly introduce him to one or two that do. The necessities in every branch are the power of writing grammatically with ease (and still better, with plangent confidence), and persistency. I have been talking too generally, because I don't know enough to be particular. I can't answer your question as to 'what sort of work is most wanted now,' except that more and more the journalist's business seems to be to follow while seeming to lead, and to connect everything he does with the moment. But I have never done anything for the papers except reviews and a very few articles which represent the one out of a dozen of my own choice which was also theirs.

I hope you are not going to meddle much with journalism. I shall be glad to see your book, tho I have so many to read and write now that it needs an effort to regard a book as anything but an enemy, though a helpless one. I have three books in hand to be done before the year's end, have written two short ones already this year, and have just published one and am about to correct the proofs of another. Let me know your plans and if I can be of use in any particular I will try. At present, as you can guess, I cannot subscribe to your belief that good things are bad for one, if it has the corollary that unpleasant things are good. And yet I am not so sure, because after all, unpleasant as things seem to me now I have always believed myself to be choosing what was pleasantest and least troublesome at the moment; and with such a motive I suppose it is inevitable that nothing should come up to one's standard of pleasantness.

Yours sincerely | Edward Thomas

To Harold Monro

Wick Green | Petersfield | 19 July 1911

My dear Monro,

I wrote to you exactly a month ago but put off finishing the letter because I was expecting your poems* every day. When they came I still left the letter and now it was sufficiently faded and stale to be burnt. I am only sorry because I am not likely to write as long a one now, and I estimate (my own) letters by their length, because it seems a virtue to write a long letter when mere writing is repulsive. It is late for me to be writing about your poems. I have already reviewed them—with much more confidence than I feel, and also with much less attention to the *body* of the book than it deserved. The reason is that—possibly because it is new work—I have not discovered in the poems the unity of word and spirit which I always look for. In fact I feel that you might do equal and possibly greater justice to your view of things by a reasoned statement in prose. Whether I am right or not you can see that I could never get quite at home with it. I kept feeling that I wanted to reach your ideas but that your form was a veil, often an attractive one in itself, between me and your ideas. Not that you leave me or anyone else in any doubt as to many of your ideas, but that these are so absorbing that I resent anything which (however good in itself) hinders you from expressing them and me from understanding them fully. Directness is not an essential, I know. The great poets are not concerned to tell us everything straight out like a man in search of converts: nor do they make converts either. But

I do feel that in your case an increase of directness would be a gain. I feel it in 'God' and equally in 'Dream' and 'To the Desired'. They make me want even crudity and bluntness, especially when I come to a phrase like 'some faint delicious dream': I find myself trying to translate this into physical actuality and cannot. This may be pure perversity and I should not be surprised if you feel sure that it was.

As likely as not, this criticism is the outcome of weariness and dissatisfaction. I am just finishing a book; I finished one in June; and I am correcting the proofs of two others.* You were quite accurate in interpreting my last letter, and I am afraid nothing has happened to make me revise what I said. At this moment I could say it over again even more bitterly. There is now some chance that circumstances will drive us away from here, if indeed they are not so confusing that they will not compel us even to so unpleasant a solution but leave us merely uncertain. However, I hope we shall stay and if you come as a neighbour, so much the better. Houses are not very easy to find but some friends who were looking for one lately heard of several. I hope I shall see something of your friend if he comes to town.

Yours sincerely | Edward Thomas

To Edward Garnett

Wick Green | Petersfield | 16 September 1911

Dear Garnett,

I have not got on with the Shakespeare papers yet. Since I saw you I have not been well and I got away to Wales. But it did me little good and I have thought of a seavoyage. It occurs to me as just possible that you might be able to suggest an article or series connected with a voyage, say on a Welsh trading ship to the Mediterranean parts, perhaps as far as Constantinople. This may strike you as quite impossible for me and in any case impractable; and I am not at all confident myself. But if it could be managed I should be glad as well as surprised. Don't answer if it merely seems fantastic.

Yours | E Thomas

To Edward Garnett

4 October 1911 | Wick Green | Petersfield

Dear Garnett,

I am sorry to have troubled you so much for nothing (except knowledge of me), but I don't think I shall go away now.* It is not the war but closer things that prevent me—mainly, I believe, dislike of being thrown with new people; partly also the great unlikelihood of finding a publisher to offer me much for such a lean and shadowy outline as I could offer and partly that as things are at present I could not get away with any piece of mind. I am really very sorry to have cried 'Wolf!' in this way and hope it is not my last chance.

Yours ever | E Thomas.

I had already been offered a choice of Cardiff ships to the Black Sea or Port Said.

To Harry Hooton

c/o Mrs Wilkins | Victoria Street | Laugharne | Wednesday [December 1911]

My dear Harry,

Many thanks for a big batch of proofs* but I suppose the one preceding it was lost. Never mind. I have adopted most of your suggestions. By the way Ellesborough is near Wendover, Edlesborough near Dunstable. I am sorry to say I don't believe what you say about my writing.

I can't tell you how astonished I was when you said I was secretive. I go about telling everybody everything till people take no notice. I am sure I have not spared you. Perhaps you did not think it *was* everything. I have somehow lost my balance and can never recover it by diet or rule or any deliberate means, but only by some miracle from within or without. If I don't recover it and causes of worry continue I must go smash. Then I must remove some of the causes of worry. It is not easy as I must either have a remote study or a separate dwelling, I think. Greatest difficulty of all is a school we know something about and a master we can trust and low fees as well. Just going to *any grammar school* is abhorrent. Do you know any schoolmasters? Then I ought not to be over 60 miles from London.

Sometimes I feel wellish here, sometimes very bad; never well, I never can be well again without the miracle. But do not allow Helen to know this as I contrive to write to her at the better times.

Yours ever | ET.

Do any suggestions about expenditure occur to you? I may not like them but should like to know how it strikes you.

To Edward Garnett

Llaugharne* | 13 December 1911

My dear Garnett

My temperature being what you know it is I naturally can't thank you properly for your letter—and also for the book sent me by Dewar at your suggestion, of which I am now using the wrapper for notepaper. I should not be surprised if the camera proved a saviour as well as an instrument of pleasure and profit. Up till now I have had to put up with my own childish sketches to give me an idea of the relation of things seen etc. As a young brother* who is rather expert and knows my ways advised me not to develop the negatives myself I shall not do so, and will write to G.B.* at once, also asking him to send the camera to Petersfield as I leave here tomorrow. The fact is I finished *Borrow* on Tuesday and then suddenly found myself restless and tired and unable to stay on here for the present. So I am going to have a look at Swansea and Newport and Caerleon again and I may see you on my way home on Tuesday: I hope so and Hudson too.

If I had a few quiet months I could write a Welsh itinerary now, partly at any rate following Gerald,* as I have been a good deal in his steps at St. Clears, Whitland, Llawhaden, Haverfordwest, Camrose, Newgale, St. David's and Llanrhian, and I already know Caerleon, Newport, Neath, Swansea, Kidwelly and Caermarthen. Perhaps I shall fix myself somewhere on his northern route early next year and in a real Welsh district. Laugharne is mostly English in language and other ways, though all the surrounding villages except close to the coast on the West side speak Welsh and are only moderate at English.

I have had some splendid bright windy weather, but of course too mild. I am just beginning to master the geography here and also the gossip of Laugharne. But Borrow has absorbed me and I have scarcely written anything else. Sometimes a tune makes me think: 'Give me health and a day——,' and I leave it at that. Did you ever see Haverfordwest? A most fascinating dirtyish old town with steep narrow streets up a hill and with a castle and two fine towered churches on top at the brink of a tidal river with many-windowed store houses by the little quay, and some river mist, sawmill smoke, and a half moon before frost. I went twice and walked up and down as I never did before in a town. The one drawback was that I felt Muirhead Bone* ought to be there for a few years.—If I can possibly manage it I shall make some sketches out of this visit. I want to do a book on Swansea which I know better than any town but nobody wants it.*

It was kind of you to speak to Dewar.* Like everyone else—nearly everyone—he probably has a hundred people to please and doesn't please any single one very much. Look at Milne.* I am now competing for Xmas books with the Editor's little daughter and Arthur Waugh's schoolboy son and Tighe Hopkins' niece and so on, above all with Milne himself. Someday I shall do a book on Milne's prose. I am collecting specimens now.—Belloc did send me Borrow's letters after all but I don't know if he will print my remarks.

The reason I asked you about Borrow was that you scoffed me out of doing this book three years ago. You probably didn't mean as I took it and will probably remember nothing about it. I don't revive it out of unkindness but to show that miserable sinner in journalism as I am, I am not the hardened and unconscious sinner that my misdeeds seem to proclaim. I sin with a score of sins in these matters also. You sometimes rub it in as if I needed telling!

Please tell me of some celebrated monarch, poet, prostitute or other hero that I can write a book about. My own list includes none that publishers will look at. Seriously I should like to see what I could make of some non-literary man or woman.

Yours ever | E. Thomas

[R. A.] Scott-James' notice of Davies* was very good, and I hope you found something to like in the book. I think he is advancing with something stronger and more passionate as he gets sure of himself.

To Irene and Hugh McArthur

Wick Green | Petersfield | 31 December 1911

My dear Irene and Hugh,

My best thanks to you for a turkey where 'youth and beauty meet together.' I think it is a very good substitute for a rocking chair. The only disadvantage of it is that you can never point with satisfaction to it or its effects, after it has once been consumed, unless of course I came out in lumps or spots, or write verses, or good prose, or become a lover of animals, or take to dance and song. I did take to the dance last night. Helen and I went as a country couple to a fancy dress affair. There were a lot of very nice males and females under 20 who made up for my grotesqueness. I had on an old Sussex pedlar's smock, black hat and red ribbon with a bunch of corn, kneebreeches and grey stockings tied with black ribbons. Helen had a print dress bunched up behind to show a red petticoat and a lot of white stocking, and a sunbonnet on her head. We are now recovering, on a most beautiful morning of sun above a solid mist filling up the valley in rolls like an inverted sky exactly.

The children are away for a few days with the idle rich of Petersfield. So as we have 2 rabbits, you can suppose the turkey is really our own and can rely on a large part of it being turned into E.T. *N.B.* This is not original but from a poem of de la Mare's about how

All things that Miss T eats
Turn into Miss T.*

If it turns into anything really interesting I will let you know, or should it incapacitate me for such things, Helen will.

Yours ever with Helen's love | Edward Thomas.

To Gordon Bottomley

Stow on the Wold | Gloucestershire | 22 March 1912

My dear Gordon,

I was very glad indeed when your letter caught me up just as I was starting on a short walk. I had been thinking of you daily wondering whether to write, knowing well you must be ill. It didn't seem worth while as I was always either busy at *Pater* and good for nothing else or contending with my usual devils. I was not reborn in Wales. Work is the only thing though when I am at it I don't invariably realise it especially as it's always in a hurry. I roughly finished a book on Pater last Sunday: am keeping it by me to tone it down for a few weeks. I am going to write on Swinburne. Probably I told you. I brought away *Songs before Sunrise* but at the end of a day's walking can make nothing of it. I am travelling from Cirencester along the Fosse Way to Stratford Warwick and Coventry, where I am to spend a day or two. I did think of rushing up to see you, but the strike and increasing irregularity of trains seems to forbid it. If I don't come I will send you some of my works but they are very numerous now. I have just corrected proofs of *Norse Tales*. *Borrow*, *Hearn* and *Icknield Way* impend. *Celtic Tales* please Mervyn and Bronwen. They are exercises in English, only. I am only just learning how ill my notes have been making me write by all but destroying such natural rhythm as I have in me. Criticising Pater has helped the discovery. But it is too late now, in these anxious and busy times, to set about trying to write better than perhaps I was born to. You have some advantages over me after all. Fancy being able to write those verses for music. I think they have the just nakedness for words to be sung and I wish I could hear them. Tell me who was the foundress. Now if I had any *time*. No, I will not say what I might—but should not—do if I had time, which is impossible. However, when I have exhausted the books which publishers and I can seem to agree on,—and that will not be very far hence,—I may find myself with Time. Stow on the Wold is perfectly silent after a day of wind and rain, except the choir practising in the church over the way. It is a little stone town on a slope and summit of the Cotswolds and looks far away east over floods and red ploughland. I wish I were not so tired. I will keep this over another day's walking. Goodnight.

Chance has brought me to Stratford upon Avon where it is evident Shakespeare once lived and is not alive now. I shall leave it to the tradespeople tho I am too tired to walk beyond it tonight. I wonder what a man would do here who was not afflicted by the spectacle of trade? It has been a beautiful warm day but I have been walking on my nerves all the time and am fit for bed not letterwriting. 'Glory to Man in the Highest! for Man is the master of things!' says Swinburne. I shall have to discover what that amounts to. Can you recommend me to some sane admirer on whom I can sharpen my wits? Somehow I have fallen into a habit of abusing literature for not being what it was never meant to be, and it won't do me or the public any good I expect, especially as it probably originates in personal disgusts of an irrelevant kind which I ought to be getting over in silence and not in print. Coining everything into hasty words is I suppose the punishment as well as the living of a journalist. Is it lifelong, too?

I wish I had been listening to Rathbone and not a cheap and outworn gramophone. It would have been worth *my* money, Emily.

Goodbye, and please write as soon as you can.

I am yours and Emily's ever | Edward Thomas

To Walter de la Mare

Dillybrook Farm | Road nr Bath | 15 May 1912

My dear de la Mare,

Thank you. I have just looked through your book* and half glad half sorry, but more glad. Sorry to think there are so many poems in it I might have seen all these months: glad to think there are so many new ones to read. You won't suspect me of mere dull ingenious compliments when I confess I have only glanced at the book. The fact is I am writing Swinburne and can't get free just yet so I shall leave the book to fit in this evening. You won't mind hearing that Bax admired Miss Loo (and some that I believe you have left out, from the English Review) without being advised to. He lives 8 miles away and I spent Saturday night there. This is delicious country in the sun and now today in misty rain. There is may and nightingales at hand. I wish you could come. I can give you a bed and I believe I could manage Whitsun if you could. Tell me. Otherwise I may not be in town for another month. I am not sure, I am restless here now that I am writing, Many thanks for Saintsbury but to tell the truth I really can't read him, so I find now. The other book was G M Trevelyan's Garibaldi book or rather his 2 Italian books. If you could send them this week they would be useful, but don't trouble to send them later. When I come to town I shall be very glad to come to you if Dick doesn't mind. You aren't 40 already are you? No I wasn't too tired (for myself).

Hodgson will be pleased to see The Cherry Trees* again. I am jealous of you for being able to write such unprofitable things. Unprofitable even for me this time, for no one has sent it to me for review. I shall have pleasure without profit for the first time in reading you.

With my love to you all and tell me if perhaps you could come.

Yours ever | ET.

After all I stayed in in the rain and find I have read nearly all your book. You might as well ask me to write a poem myself as to write about them. Each one takes me a little deeper into a world I seem to know just for the moment as well as you—only not really knowing it I can not write. I think it is equal to 'Songs of Childhood' and 'Poems' together. It is as fresh as the first and it has the grain of the second book like gossamer over its blossom colours. I did not think one book could be so good. My favourite is 'the Dwelling Place', if I dare commit myself.

To Helen

Selsfield House | [East Grinstead] | 16 August 1912

Dearest one,

Here we are waiting for Ellis* to turn up. We have been over the garden with Mrs. Ellis and down the deep dark ghyll where they quarried the sandstone hundreds of years ago, now full of hazel and oak. The Ellises are thinking of adding a newer bit to their garden—a square deep hollow with sandmartin's nests and ragwort, suitable for an outdoor theatre, fives court etc. It is drizzling now, but there is a wood fire in the big open fireplace and Mervyn is deep in cushions and the *Chronicle*. Our lodgings last night were a great success. We had eggs and fruit for breakfast and only paid 5/– for everything. The people are named Wadey, and if I go to Slinfold* again I shall go there.

Ellis arrived at 6 and cut this short. Mervyn sat down and listened to us talking till dinner at 7.30 when he went to bed with a bath.

Well, about Friday, we were again in a district of parks tho we did not see so many grand entrances, iron gates, stone pillars surmounted by eagles or suits of armour with no men inside as at Petworth. First we went to see Shelley's house, Field Place, but only saw that it was there among trees near Broadbridge Heath, a small treeless roadside common halfway to Horsham, with reeds, and a pub nearby called the 'Dog and Bacon' and with a big sign of a dog up on a chair sniffing at some bacon that stands beside a mug of beer on a table—obviously the original of Worthington's 'What is it master likes so much' except that here the dog is facing right, which is harder to draw than left.

We didn't stay long in Horsham which has a square called Carfax as at Oxford. We kept some way on the Brighton road passing close to a beautiful lily mill pond at Whitesbridge in a dark hollow. We turned off at Manning's Heath, which is like Ashdown, a big region of oak and fir woods cloven by deep valleys, several containing big long ponds—one a Hammer Pond used in the ironworks when wood instead of coal supplied the furnaces and Sussex was almost as black as Staffordshire. Some of the Forest is high and bare and purple for acres with heather and their undulations against a background of wood are lovely. Our road was horseless for a long way, with barbed wire to keep us out of the heather stretches in the east but no hedge on the west where there was oak birch bracken and heather—heather only at the sunny edge. We sat and looked at the view, the barbed wire and our bicycles. Isn't Coolhurst a nice name? It is a house with a small park and entrance gates just South of Horsham. The nicest flower all the way was the wood betony at the edges of the woods. It looks so wise—a purple flower like basil, but darker, with dark leaves, rather stiff. The combination of oak birch bracken heather and harebell is one of the sweetest.

Then we got to a main road which took us to Crawley—an automobile-yellow town where we bought fruit and which we ate a few miles further on after going into Worth churchyard, a big rough place full of Brookers, Streeters, Ellis, Morris, Davis, Rice, etc., entombed among many trees of yew and lime etc. The church, which has a short Sussex spire and Saxon double windows, was shut. By where some men were cutting up larch wood in Worth Forest we ate our fruit and got to Ellis' at 3. Meantime my bicycle had gone wrong, and I now find I shall have to borrow Ellis' to finish the tour, as a cone in the back wheel is broken in half and it may be long before a new one comes from the maker.

Mervyn has gone to Cowden.* We sit and smoke and talk.

Thank you for your letter. I hope this is not too dull a return for it.

Goodbye. I am ever and wholly yours | Edwy

Please keep these letters.

To Helen

Coulsdon | 20 August 1912

Dearest one,

We got here to lunch at 1.45 from Sevenoaks, we found no letters and no proofs,* and nothing at Davies' either. Why?

I told you Mervyn went to Cowden on Saturday and had an afternoon's roach fishing with the de la Mares. They were too full up for the Ellises to come on Sunday. So we went alone expecting to be put up at the inn but they made shift and we slept in somebody's bed. We got there at 12.30 without rain but after the 2 o'clock lunch rain fell at intervals and saved us from a Rectory tea. We played pitch and toss etc. with the children, led by Hodgson. Tea followed on lunch and then after some languid fishing in a dry interval came dinner. The pond is a little one full of roach by the White Horse on Holtye Common, a gorsy common almost spoilt by golf. The de la Mare's house is a pleasant new one with varying views of Ashdown Forest, first a gentle meadowslope then a rising wooded ridge with a distant hilltop fir clump eastward and nearer woods more to the West. We talked comfortably about Futurists, animals etc. till near midnight. De la Mare was tired and irritable and full of work. *The Edinburgh Review* has asked him for a quarterly article on recent books. But what am I going to do?

Monday morning was wet when Hodgson left. But we started in sun at 11.15 and soon got among hopgardens and orchards at the Kent border and bought 3^d worth of apples and pears at a farm and ate them in the park of Penshurst Place for lunch. The church was shut. The old house and the smooth turf with sheep feeding round a clump of bracken was very pleasant. We sat against one of the limes that stand in lines on either side. Then we went into Tunbridge through Leigh, and I lost my temper because Mervyn wanted 'something to read' while I had some coffee—which I didn't have. We had a hilly ride up and down from Tunbridge mostly through well known country, resting at the Shipborne Inn which has seats in a verandah looking over the gorse and cows of Shipborne Common eastward.

Then through Ivy Hatch and Stone Street (you remember the 'Rose and Crown'?) to the beautiful shallow valley with beeches on the upper slopes on either side of the road which goes through it—called the Wilderness—to Seal and Sevenoaks. Davies had been expecting us for days, an anxious host. We had tea. Mervyn went out but did not recognize anything or anybody. He listened to us—Davies talking about his Welsh walk*—till dark and bed and our supper of fish and stewed plums and undrinkable coolish coffee. By 10.30 I was sleepy and just wrote telling [Godwin] Baynes I shouldn't join him at Caermarthen and then to bed. We had to go and see the Littles who were just back. It had rained all night and again at 8.30 after we had a stroll into Knole Park. They thought Mervyn looked strong and well. So he does. But we didn't communicate much. Little told me Morgan and his wife are legally separated. The Littles are friendly still with both. Morgan is much cut up: probably that accounts for his slackness in answering my proposal for a visit in May. We had a boring talk till 11 which left us little time to get here against a strong West wind. But we had no rain. We went along under the downs by Riverhead, Brasted, Westerham, Limpsfield Common, Oxted, and Godstone and then up across the Pilgrims Way northward over the downs by a Roman road to Caterham and Coulsdon common and windmill and ridiculously thin-spired church* round the end of Farthing Down by the big marlpit here. Janet [Hooton] is childless and servantless and herself goes away on Saturday. We did eat. Mervyn seems none the worse for his 21 miles against the wind before lunch. Now he is reading Ali Baba in an armchair.

The rain has come on again. We have been lucky all along in avoiding the showers. Mrs. Little would like to see you and would motor over if we were a little nearer.

Davies is amassing unread books and talks dully about his purchases and how after all it is surprising what a few standard books there are and 500 will be a sufficient library. The Marlowe I gave him is shaving paper becuse he has a *new copy* of the same edition. He has 2 Ben Jonsons if not 3, Whiston's *Josephus*, scores of Elizabethans, a hideous volume of British poets in double columns unreadable and never read, Ransome's *Book of Love*. He reads the [*Daily*] *Chronicle*. His portrait angs on the wall, a ghastly sight, like an indiarubber coloured horsey publican. He talks of taking his next oliday in Paris to see the orrible vice but is afraid of drugged wine so may put up with Jones.*

Please save my review of *Wuthering Heights* in today's *DC*.

The post goes at 4.35. I do hope I shall hear from you tonight and hear that D. [?] is gone. Goodbye. We send our love to you all.

I am all yours (there is not much left) | Edwy.

P.T.O. So far as I know I shall return Ellis' bicycle (which is a brute) on Thursday and return from there on Friday by train or (if it is ready) by bicycle. But you needn't send any of Thursday's letters to Selsfield House, as I shall be home, I hope, before dark on Friday. Please send proofs to Rusham Road if any come tomorrow as I daresay Julian* will look through them, though they will be too late for me. This delay won't please Secker and I can't imagine why you haven't sent them here as I asked you to.

To Clifford Bax

13 Rusham Road | Balham | SW | 19 September 1912

My dear Clifford,

Thank you for your letter and the pictures. If ever I feel I ought to indulge again in so long and happy a dream as I had at Broughton Gifford I shall come. I could not tell you without painful explanations and contrasts how happy your wife and you and Baynes made me for the whole of the time.* I hope I shall see you in town.

Did some letters come for me after I left and were they

forwarded here or to Wick Green, Petersfield? Don't trouble to answer if they did arrive and were forwarded.

Please tell your wife what I think she must know how much I enjoyed myself and how grateful I am.

Yours ever | Edward Thomas

I enjoyed Dermot O'Byrne* very much and shall make an opportunity of saying so.

To Gordon Bottomley

Wick Green | Petersfield | 31 October 1912

My dear Gordon,

Thank you for Emily's letter. Helen and I were thinking of you and Holmbury* just now so I must send you a word. The month has not been good for letters because I have always been either busy or anxious. Now, however, things are a little better and for the moment I see that I can keep going. We have nearly settled to move in the Spring—into a new labourer's cottage that will just hold us with half our furniture. I may keep my hilltop study but the chances are I shall fix myself alone in London for about half the year. It seems necessary partly to ensure work and partly to give Helen peace, since I am a mere nuisance and a considerable one when I am working and rather worse when I have no work to do. Just now I have got some reviewing again. What is more I have started a fiction!* It is a loose affair held together if at all by an oldish suburban home, half memory, half fancy, and a Welsh family (mostly memory) inhabiting it and collecting a number of men and boys including some I knew when I was from ten to fifteen. The scheme allows me to use all memories up to the age of 20 and so far I have indulged myself freely. I feel however that it will be better than isolated essays and sketches, each helping the other, and the same characters reappearing; and more honest than the other pseudo-continuous books I have written. I hope it will get finished or drafted before the year is out.

I look forward eagerly to hearing that you are at Holmbury. I recall the turnings out of the Portsmouth Road to Ockley and try to invent a place for you among the pine trees. De la Mare stayed once in Ockley I remember. He is a too busy man now, reading for

Heinemann and reviewing multifariously and never quite unpuckering in our scanty meetings. I shall try to get you and him to meet though, and you would like Locke Ellis too, who has a nice young rich wife and an old house near East Grinstead now and is amusing himself with a picture shop in the Adelphi. Clifford Bax is 100 miles away near Bath but just off to Siena. He is a local magnet [*sic*], cricketer, theosophist, and an amusing talker who knows poetry because he likes it. He will probably never write any. He edits an occultish quarterly—*Orpheus*—which Cecil French contributes to, and also his brother Arnold Bax, a most excellent pianist and composer, who writes verse and stories under the name of Dermot O'Byrne.

Goodbye and I hope to hear good news of you before long. You must have enjoyed the good parts of September and October. I only watched them. With our love to you and Emily

Ever yours | Edward Thomas

To Helen

Tuesday | 32 Rue des Vignes | Passy | Paris | 12 November 1912

Dearest one,

We got here last night at 11, I went to bed at 12 and slept till 7.30. Now I am waiting for breakfast. It has been easy and pleasant since Charing Cross except the 3½ hours in the train from Calais to Paris. We were 2 hours getting to Folkstone, passing the Weald, Elses Farm and many other similar farms and groups of 2 to 7 or 8 oasthouses with very white cowls. The white cliffs—or rather green hills peeled here and there to show dirty white in the twilight—disappeared in the manner of which you have read before. Everybody had got on the steamer in a hurry because it was cold and windy. About 9 were men and mostly English. Mrs Jones had a private cabin where Jones sat with her to ministrate. I walked about or leaned all the 2 hours and enjoyed every minute, until the sea and the sky became as black as the steamer smoke. The wind behind us was so strong that the smoke almost streamed out almost straight before us. But the sea was not very rough. I had no qualms. However I found it hard to walk straight. For the first time I saw a man standing leaning (against nothing) like this / instead of |. I suppose he was keeping perpendicular with the *sea* not the boat. At first I thought he was a magician, especially as he was a sailor with sea boots etc. The Calais light appears when we got ½ across. At first just an appearing and disappearing spark. Then it caused a slight mistiness round it, which grew. Then it could be seen to *sweep* the waves from right to left with a swift soft misty light, and go out, and then do the same again. At last the smooth sides of the waves began to gleam blackly in the light. We landed at Calais because Boulogne which we were supposed to enter was impossible in that sea.

The landing was nothing. You drew slowly up alongside and walked a few yards to a train. However we had to wait an hour and had dinner in the Terminier [*sic*] hotel, rather a scramble and not very good or interesting, very prompt and very expensive. Mrs Jones all the time headachy and floppy etc., but slept in the train. We talked a little and read a little. The drive here was through straight long streets of very high houses and nothing unEnglish except the chairs and tables on the pavements by cafes, but those (at 10.30 on such a night) were almost all empty. Very little traffic, about as much as Maida Vale at night. No horses. This an eight story block of flats, Jones' is all white painted, with glass doors, mirror over the marble fireplace, all bright and clear. Lots of food which I had the fortitude to refuse. I had a good night, thank God.

I did see Collins and got 2 books and leave to review Douglas's book, so I felt easier. He is very amiable, though I can't talk to him. He gave me the address of the Pall Mall Gazette man here whom I might see. I travelled with nothing but those 2 books and my toothbrush.

The coffee is being ground. It is the only noise, for we are on the inside of a small courtyard and can see only some scores of near windows mostly still darkened, and a blue sky above the pit. When you get that good servant and are free from lodgers for a week you ought to come. Mrs Jones asked and I would have telegraphed. Only I can't bear the children being entirely dependent on Maud. Is baby having fruit or for any other reason getting better?

It is not much use my writing impressions, as you know that means unreadable disconnected scraps of no use except to the owner (E.T.) and tending perhaps to spoil a broader and more genuine view.

This will be posted at noon in the hope of reaching you tomorrow. Tell me if it does. I write small because this paper is thick. Will use thinner next time.

Please keep the D.C. as I may not get it here.*

Goodbye. I am ever and wholly yours | Edwy

To Helen

Friday | 32 Rue des Vignes | Paris | 15 November 1912

Dearest,

Thank you for your letter (*not* enclosing Guthrie's). I wish you had come. But it isn't that I put the children before you but that I put the *comfort of my own imagination* before you. With you here, I should have had more confidence. However I have now bought several things, hired taxis, etc. You should have heard me asking for Castor Oil which the chemist did not know by that name—it is Huile de Ricin. Well I got it. I am sorry to say I need it. And I was yesterday disabled by an instep so full of ache that I could hardly put it to the ground. I am afraid this is connected with the wine and the increased amount of meat, and the condition of my stomach. So I am now eating only nuts, fruit, and bread and butter.

I went to the Luxembourg Gallery in the morning and looked chiefly at the statuary. It's quite a small gallery and yet crowded and too full for one to do more than pick out what one would like to steal. From there I walked to the river, found my way across it and up many streets to Jones' office. We had lunch. Mrs Jones met us after and she and I went to the Opera Comique and saw La Traviata. Well done, but stupid. I can't get over the stupidity of acting and singing together. But there was a dance of five minutes. About 12 slender girls doing a very simple high kicking, low bending in and out dance, with pretty oriental costumes to the knee, tied like a towel so as to display the behind, scarlet stockings, and shoes, and green drawers occasionally visible. They had small really pretty faces and hair down and smiled without any of the hideous effects of paint on which English choruses often show.

$3\frac{1}{2}$ hours of it with my sore foot never forgettable was too much. We had tea and went back at 6 when I read till 8 o'clock dinner. Jones not returning till 9. In the evening we talked about Hootons etc, about poverty and boasting of poverty when you can't boast of anything else. Jones played the pianola till nearly 12. Then I slept till 7.30. I sleep very well in these darkened rooms. Every window in Paris has thin shutters which are locked at night against thieves.

I have the same objection to the tiny cottage as you and should be glad to try the Powell's if you like, especially if you could do without a servant. Also I am certain it need not prevent you from going away as often as you do now. Have you heard more from the Russels or Powells?

I think it was Miss *Wilson* had the waterproof. And did you get the address; and will you give it me?

Mrs Anthony hasn't written, though I wrote and perhaps you did. Nor has Rhys, in fact only 2 out of 8 people I wrote to before starting and De la Mare wrote on Monday to Rusham Road, offering Monday and Thursday—had mislaid my letter—was too much rushed—said nothing else. As I had sent a postcard from here explaining why I didn't appear if he had suggested it, there was nothing to be said. I am sorry to lose him, but I am sure I can't keep him by making all the efforts to bring off meetings myself, while he does nothing.

The weather continues grey and drizzly and coldish, as it is with you apparently. Today I shall only be able to get about in cabs and train. I shall go to the Louvre, I think, and look about for some presents. I have now seen the streets almost as crowded and noisy as London and less under control. They keep to the *right* too which adds to difficulties. The crowd is mostly men and women. Very few girls 17–22 because they don't get about much and never alone. It makes a lot of difference. Of course you see young servants, but not many. The servants here go about in the streets bareheaded. I suppose because I haven't been about after dark much, I haven't seen any recognisable prostitutes.

My hosts are extremely kind. They will do or obtain anything I want at home or elsewhere and show no uneasiness at my ways. This afternoon Mrs Jones will take me to a place where I may find a birthday present for Father and something for Mother perhaps.

By the way will you send my evening dress and the best white shirt you can find (from the bottom of the chest) to Rusham Road in case I don't go to Rhys and can get to the Nation. Send if off in good time on Monday with the white scarf you will see in the chest, and put any gold studs you can find with the shirt. If however all the shirts are limp I must borrow from Julian.

Goodbye, and thank you for everything, for typewriting* for example. I hope you are not having to force yourself to write so sweetly to me. I hope all is well. I am ever and wholly yours | Edwy

Saturday (16.11.12) P.S. Will you keep my Paris letters because I have been very careless with notes.

To Edward Garnett

Wick Green | Petersfield | 6 February 1913

My dear Garnett,

I am sending you my MS* today. Is the thread too slender and too impudent? Do you even perceive a thread? I had hopes the book was better than any probable collection of essays, but quite see the possibility that artistically the pretence of being more than a collection of essays may spoil it. I think of writing a preface stating that all the characters but one are from life and offering prizes for identification. My idea was to be pseudonymous—calling myself Arthur Froxfield.

Yours ever | Edward Thomas

To Eleanor Farjeon

Wick Green | [Midsummer] 1913

My dear Eleanor,

Are you better now? I hope you are. If not and in any case you may find something in Davies's last book*—not nearly so much as usual, though—to like. Can you choose your own time at the week end? Could you come down on Monday afternoon and stay the night? My Mother will be here on Sunday and things always go a little stiffly with her—she is diffident and sad and not clever.

I don't want postcards from you, except that they would put me at my ease, especially in these days when to write more than a page means attempting the impossible and wearying myself and uselessly afflicting others with some part of my little yet endless tale. It has got to its dullest and its worst pages now. The point is I have got to help myself and have been steadily spoiling myself for the job for I don't know how long. I am very incontinent to say these things. If I had never said them to anyone I should have been someone else and somewhere else. You see the central evil is self-consciousness carried so far beyond selfishness as selfishness is beyond self denial, (not very scientific comparison) and now amounting to a disease, and all I have got to fight it with is the knowledge that in truth I am not the isolated selfconsidering brain which I have come to seem—the *knowledge* that I am something more, but not the belief that I can reopen the connection between the brain and the rest.

I think perhaps having said that much I ought to say Don't speak to me about it, because it is endless and no good is to be done by talking or writing about it. And yet I am letting this go. Well, all my thoughts are of myself, alas, except the scraps I can give to my 8 novels, now almost done with. And I keep afflicting myself by imagining all the distasteful work as if it were a great impossible mountain just ahead. Please forgive me and try not to give any thought to this flat grey shore which surprises the tide by being inaccessible to it.

I haven't even read Hodgson's poem,* yet, tho it is by me. Tell me when you are coming to talk about Keats not me—did I tell you I had accepted rotten terms to do a rotten little book on Keats. I am rather thinking of going away to work and be alone and not afflict 5 persons at once.

Goodbye | Edward Thomas

To Harry Hooton

Steep | Petersfield | 24 September 1913

My dear Harry,

I was glad to get news of you and sorry it didn't suit you to have me just then. We all got back together last week on Tuesday, Helen very well and pleased with her Swiss holiday with Irene.* As I had had one or two of the children always with me for a month I had done little work and so had to settle down to something here at once. There was little enough that *had* to be done. Work is less and less. But there is still that dubious book on *Ecstasy** which I have wanted to abandon the more I thought of it. However I must get the £20 so I am beginning it—have begun it—this very day. Can't you say something suggestive or provocative? I don't know what I shall do after it's finished. I badly need some plan or framework to enable me to use my enormous collection of travel notes of the last few years and yet cannot succeed in finding one. If my fiction,* which will be out in a month, has any success I may get an impulse. So far I am pulling at a dead weight, with so much neglect or worse to contend against. It is cheaper here,* not cheap enough though for my income, to use a euphemism. Am I just to wait and do work I can in a quietly dispirited state? I get wonderfully near deciding that it shall not go on indefinitely, tho I don't see how to round it off. When shall we meet? Not very soon I fear because I can't often get a weekend and the next but one I have allowed to get engaged and I can't take another for some time. Tell me if it is ever possible for you to meet me in town for an evening or lunch. Are the Joneses well and Mrs. Jones in particular?

We are well. I work up at my study morning and evening and finish up down here, not doing much here however, because the mere smallness is vexatious. The garden proves manageable and looks well already. Send a word sometime and give my love to Janet.

Yours ever | E.T.

P.S. If I cycle or walk to town on Friday week, Oct. 3, and can manage to get to you, could you have me for that night? I would let you know some days before.

To Eleanor Farjeon

Steep | [October] 1913

My dear Eleanor,

I am reading two novels a day for the next few and last few days, every page of them, and can think of little else. But I do thank you for what you say about 'Light and Twilight'. Not time alone prevents me from quite facing the question how far the 'Stile' and others represent something which 3 years have shut a door on. But I don't think doors do shut—not quite fast. I remember how I used to think at 17 or so of games I had as it seemed accidentally given up but as it fell out, for ever, and used to try to get back and thought I could, yet didn't. This new difficulty is the same. I don't think in either case I am the same person. If I have time I shall prove that I am a very similar one. But there have been noticeable vanishings, I was going to say not natural ones, which would be absurd, because it is my nature that allows uncongenial work, anxiety etc. to destroy or change so much and so fast, so that during the last few weeks I have been like a misty wet dull flat shore, like that at Flansham when the sea seemed to have gone away for ever, and I haven't believed in another tide. I know now that what I thought a new strength about 2 months ago was only the quiet of weakness consummated.

However, I have work for some time ahead and I suppose I shall do it. You will be glad to hear that Heinemann accepts the Proverbs* and I shall soon be trying St. Nicholas etc. with them, as the book must wait till the Autumn of 1914. The illustrator is not yet chosen.

When I have a little leisure I will look up some of my unpublished papers and send them. Don't forget your story, tho at the moment I could not look at it or anything outside the novels I have to consider for a 'Times' article.

Yours ever | Edward Thomas

PS. Don't mention this 'Times' article as it is a very trying test on which a lot may depend and I only accepted it in the hope of better things from there later. It has to be done at great pressure too.

To Walter de la Mare

Steep | Petersfield | 26 October 1913

My dear de la Mare,

Thank you. Then I will come on Tuesday as soon after 7 as I can. I am sorry to hear you are not to do the Fairytales, for of course those terms are absurd. But won't you do them in any case? You would most likely find places for some if not all in the 'English Review' etc. If you can do them, you should. When they are done you will perhaps make better terms, or not need better, if you have sold them serially. I wish you would do them.

I am longing for something to do to prove to myself that I can do—something.

There is a new hitch over the Proverbs. Heinemann's agreement said payment on publication. I had suggested and now repeat payment on my final revision and completion of the M.S., that is in a few days after getting it back. I do hope this won't upset everything.

Do you really think *Pater* good? The only review I have had was a malevolent contemptuous (unreasonable) one in the 'Saturday'. I am afraid it's formless and does not admit as it ought to that Pater is good of his kind, and wastes too much time in trying to prove the kind bad.

No. Nothing more from the 'Times'.* But there is a chance of an outdoor book to do—that about the part of Wales I know best—which sounds too good to be possible.

Yours ever | E.T.

To Robert Frost

at Selsfield House | East Grinstead | 17 December 1913

Dear Frost* (if you don't mind),

I shall be glad to see you again and Flint for the first time on Monday next at St George's at 4. You remember the place in St Martin's Lane where we first met. Top floor. I think Davies and Hodgson will be there.

Yours sincerely | E Thomas

To C. F. Cazenove

Selsfield House | East Grinstead | 18 December 1913

Dear Cazenove,

If Waugh won't have any of the 99 things I've suggested lately I can hardly add a 100th. I suppose you have put Shelley to him; and Living Poets; and a book on South Wales people and places.

There is a history of the Feeling for Nature in English Life and Literature to be written. Would that tempt him?

Then there is that book on Shakespeare I offered Dent. You remember it? To give a background of the literature, social life and natural life, folk lore, and legend, and mythical natural history, and show how Shakespeare's pictures of nature and country life sprang from it, with of course his own particular contribution. Also I could do Cobbett as I did Borrow.

What I most like is the Shelley; next the Shakespeare, next the Living Poets: that is of literary books. I should prefer an outdoor book unrelated to writers, and particularly a Welsh one—the Castles of Wales or the Rivers of Wales. Let me do the Heart of Wales, Cader Idris and Plynlimmon and the sources of the rivers, Teify, Towy, Tawe, Wye and Severn.

Yours sincerely | E Thomas

To Gwili

At Selsfield House | East Grinstead | Sussex | 7 January 1914

My dear Gwili,

I am glad to hear from you especially as you mention a chance of seeing you. You speak of the 24th and 26th. Now when will you be free on those days? I think it quite likely I shall be in London on one or the other. Could you have tea or lunch with me on either day, meeting me at 1 or 4.30 at the entrance to the National *Portrait* Gallery? If not, tell me when you are free and I will see what I can manage.

I hadn't heard you were in the States.* The idea of going out there with you is attractive but not as lecturer. I wish it were possible, because otherwise I could not afford it. Things go worse and worse. My books are not now even very well reviewed and as usual nobody buys them—except my *Celtic Stories** which is being adopted by schools in Australia in largish numbers. But it is very little use going over again the latest chapters of my life. Yours, if harder, are not used for afflicting others. But there comes an end with or without a full stop.

I am very glad indeed George* is going to Amanford as a headmaster.

We are all pretty well. Father complains a good deal but does as much as usual. Mother does not complain and also does at least as much as usual, but is getting old. My wife is well, the children very well except (at the moment only) the baby, who is now $3\frac{1}{4}$.

There is nothing nowadays equal to nutting by the Gwili, but I wish you the best of what there is.

Yours ever | Edward Thomas

To Robert Frost

at 11, Luxemburg Gardens | Brook Green W. | 30 January 1914

My dear Frost,

Many thanks for your poem. I have just finished it and liked it a good deal except the last line. I should like to know why you do not print it as dialogue with the speaker's names. Is it self denial and a desire to cut off every chance of emphasis even by stage directions etc.?

Are you to be in town next week? I shall be at St George's on Tuesday at 4. But I might manage tea or lunch some other day if it suits you better—before Friday. I am here for another week or so before going into the country. I don't quite know where I shall go, but if you happen to know any really cheap lodgings in your part of the country will you tell me?

Yours | Edward Thomas

To Clifford Bax

Steep | Petersfield | 19 February 1914

My dear Clifford,

I was so sorry to run away from you in that hurried flustered fashion.* What I was fumbling to apologise for was treating you like an inn, in spite of the fact that there is no such inn in the world any more than there is such a landlady as Olga. But at least you had done nothing to make me feel guilty: so as I felt it I think I must have been. Forgive me and believe me nevertheless devotedly Olga's and yours and do not say anything about this cheque which is meant to pay for my butter and honey and washing for about three complete weeks.

Will you send the parcel that should have come to Steep where I arrive tomorrow.

Now may the gods and goddesses and fauns and nymphs and fairies and domestic servants and managers of theatres bless you and Olga continually and so bless

Yours ever | Edward Thomas

To Robert Frost

Steep | Petersfield | 19 February 1914

My dear Frost,*

It could not be done. And I have accumulated a press of little things to be done before I begin and am flustered in the extreme. When I am next up in London I will let you know and we must have lunch together somewhere quiet, though I will look at my map and consider the roads between us. But first I must see if I really can write something. I wish you were nearer so that we could see one another easily and our children.

Yours ever | Edward Thomas

To Eleanor Farjeon

[Steep | March] 1914

My dear Eleanor,

We are all sorry you will not be here on Friday and Saturday and twice sorry because you will not be able to do anything you want to except within a 3 mile radius. But as you say and as we say you must make up with an extra week end. Also I hope you will get to Wisbech all right. Should you still be in London and we have more than the inevitable night in town on our way to Wales I will let you know. Meanwhile we are most busy, gardening, writing, typewriting for me from morning till 1 a.m. and on the whole it suits me, tho I feel thin at times. The ground is almost just right and I have got all the roots in, and peas and beans (a first sowing). Now for the potatoes and artichokes.

Maitland disappeared the first fine day. He is a bit of a superman, I fancy, or else he was very well indeed.

I have looked through the typescript now, and it is very good (your part I mean). I almost wish you were wrong oftener than just to put Moonshers for Moonrakers: it would have suggested you enjoyed yourself between whiles. Of course I did laugh and I do not pretend not to, do I? I depict not what I *was* but what I see when I look back. I don't think I could do what I *was*.

There's a tune a lady has sent me for 'O'er the moor among the heather' and I wanted to hear from you what it sounds like.

Now I must try to clean my hands and have tea and get up to the study again and write about Meredith's Homes and Haunts.* Work does not come tumbling in, not by any means. In fact if I were not so busy I should be seeing reasons for being pretty sick.

Goodbye and I hope you will get well and tell us so. This is the third blessed day and you ought to be out at any rate. All send our love to you.

Yours ever | Edward Thomas

To Gwili

Steep | Petersfield | 8 April 1914

My dear Gwili,

We* will come to Tirydail on Tuesday evening, and hope to find lodgings ready for us. Will you please be kind enough to order brown bread to be got for us, and also some bananas and dates if possible. But only I shall want supper when we arrive. I hope you can manage to join us on an excursion to Careg Cennen on Wednesday morning. I expect to meet Thomas Seccombe there, and I am sure you will like to meet him. If you write again please address me at

13 Rusham Road Balham London SW

as we shall be there on Monday.

I am sorry to be fussy but will you ask our landlady at Amanford to bake some slices of brown bread *very hard* in the oven? I detest baker's bread soft or even toasted. We should like also some very fat bacon for breakfast, the fattest in the land.

Yours ever | Edward Thomas

To Robert Frost

Steep | 19 May 1914

My dear Frost,

I wish I could write a letter. But every day I write a short Welsh sketch and a review and read a bit and weed a bit and every evening type something, not to speak of touching the fiction still sporadically. And then there is the weather to enjoy or (here comes the laugh) to imagine how it should be enjoyed. Today I was out from 12 till sunset bicycling to the pine country by Ascot and back. But it all fleets and one cannot lock up at evening the cake one ate during the day. There must be a world where that is done. I hope you and I will meet in it. I hardly expect it of New Hampshire more than of Old.—I was glad Hudson turned out as I hoped he would. I understand those 3 approaches. If only you were to be in town and he too and he well and not afflicted by his sick wife and age coming on I would take you to see him. He is, if anything, more than his books. Don't get at me about my T.P. article,* which wasn't all that even I could do, but a series of extracts from an essay I shan't do. You could do one now. And you really should start doing a book on speech and literature, or you will find me mistaking your ideas for mine and doing it myself. You can't prevent me from making use of them: I do so daily and want to begin over again with them and wring all the necks of my rhetoric—the geese. However, my *Pater* would show you I had got on to the scent already.

Your second note pleased me. I shall perhaps come soon. My wife and I are to have a week or so very probably early in July. We *have* to get in several calls. If we can we will come to Ledington. I assume there would be room (for 2 whole days).

Did Davies appear? He had left town when I was there last.—I go up next about June 5.

Bronwen is suffering from flat feet and a stoop. She enjoys the new school and the gymnastics. But we miss her. She won't be home till August. Now about August, could we *all* get into the Chandler's for a month and would they have us and at what price? The only difficulty would be a room for me to work in. For work I must. Will you consider? We shall try to let this cottage.

I don't hear when your book is coming. I tried to get T.P. to let me write on it but they won't.

I wonder whether you can imagine me taking to verse. If you can I might get over the feeling that it is impossible—which at once obliges your good nature to say 'I can'. In any case I must have my 'writer's melancholy' though I can quite agree with you that I might spare some of it to the deficient. On the other hand even with registered post, telegraph &c. and all modern conveniences I doubt if I could transmit it.

I am pleased with myself for hitting on 'Mowing' and 'The Tuft of Flowers'. For I forgot the names of those you meant me particularly to read, these I suppose being amongst them. You see that conceit consorts with writer's melancholy.

I go on writing something every day. Sometimes brief unstrained impressions of things lately seen, like a drover with 6 newly shorn sheep in a line across a cool woody road on market morning and me looking back to envy him and him looking back at me for some reason which I can't speculate on. Is this North of Bostonism?

Goodbye and I hope you are all well. Mervyn has been writing to Lesley I see. I hope he will go North of Boston before it is too late—North of Boston and West of Me.

Yours ever | Edward Thomas.

To Robert Frost

Steep | 6 June 1914

My dear Frost,

Let Lesley keep it certainly. That is all there is to say really. I am so plagued with work, burning my candle at 3 ends. Every night late I read one of your poems.* I enjoy them but if I did what I liked I wouldn't read them now. It is not fair at all. I just see how they *could* be enjoyed—which reminds me that I *did* enjoy 'The Generations of Men'. Now for the same reason I can't come next week, not till about the 25th when we will both come. I have curtailed everything: am only just going up to Bottomley's to keep my promise *and* to work. So I shall be here until the 16th I expect.—Yes I quite see about using the 'naked tones', not the mere words, of certain profoundly characteristic instinctive rhythms. And No, you don't bore me. Only I feel a fraud in that I have unconsciously rather imitated your interest in the matter.—I didn't see the *Times* notice, and am sorry for one thing to hear of it, because it shows the book is out, and yet I have not got it from anywhere. I kept badgering Adcock for it. De la Mare might have done it in the *Times*—unless it was done in the columns where books are acknowledged.

By the way unless the letter was sent to her in London Bronwen hasn't had a letter from Ledington.

I have dropped that fiction, so that's two truncated M.S.S. in a year. I should feel vain at doing unprofitable things if I hadn't added up my earnings the other night. Something has got to happen. I keep saying, Why worry about a process that may terminate a kind of life which I keep saying, couldn't be worse?

I will let you know later what day exactly we shall come. Oh, and £3.3s. is satisfactory. I will not say We shall come but I feel sure we shall.

Yours ever | E.T.

To C. F. Cazenove

Steep | Petersfield | 28 July 1914

Dear Cazenove,

I didn't mean to neglect your kind letter but to see you last week. But I could not manage it and the book has kept me up to the neck ever since. I don't think there is anything I can say. I believe you are right. Only the kind of work I have had to do has paralysed me for original work except in short bursts, supposing I ever could have done more. Perhaps you can do something with the collection of sketches.* Call it 'Thick and Clear', perhaps.

I hope to send in the M.S. of Homes and Haunts* early next week. Then my family and I are all going for the rest of August (from the 6th) to

c/o Mr Chandler | Ledington | nr Ledbury Herefordshire

where I shall be glad of any news and a cheque from Methuen. The book will be difficult to estimate but will run to over 80,000.

Yours sincerely | Edward Thomas

To Eleanor Farjeon

c/o Mrs Chandler | Ledington | Ledbury | 14 August 1914

My dear Eleanor,

Thank you for your two letters and a postscript. At anyrate the p.s. was deserved. But talk is worse for letters than writing is. It is bad for writing too. At least its *immediate* effect is bad on *mine*. And talk and strolling and odd games of cricket fill most days; or I might have written—you know if I should. Things are quietly disturbing away here where there are few papers, those late. Mr Chandler is a soldier of 44 who saw 21 years' service and has this morning been sent for to Hereford. It may be that Frost and I will do some of the work he will leave behind. But if not, other things have postponed our Welsh trip. We can't go now in any case till after Baba's birthday. And Abercrombie is to join us. It might be Tuesday. That would perhaps mean not returning till the 22nd. Would you like to know definitely, or would you come in any case on the 20th.? We are doing rather moderately here. The boys are bored. Peter* is here—he helps to raise the standard of what boys may do, I suppose. Bronwen is alright. Baby is, too, tho she had a very bad fall from a swing a few days ago and I thought she was going to lose a birthday. Helen is not up to very much, and I don't help. One thing and another leaves me very irritable indeed. The quarters are too close. I want to get away to Wales and should like a full week, but travelling has new inconveniences and things cost more than ever here, so I don't know what they'll be at inns. I haven't thought of serving my country, or of putting one leg round my neck and singing those songs that Clifford and Olga [Bax] and Bertie and Joan [Farjeon] like so much, but don't say so. I did think of turning plain reporter and giving unvarnished reports* of country conversations about the war. But Frost discourages. In any case varnish is the thing. Do you read Harold Begbie for example? But this sounds as if I imagined myself a James Thomson or Richard Middleton who was going to die unrecognised and got some consolation from the imagining.

The one advantage of waiting a week to write to you is that Joan appears to have escaped the water bailiff. Of course if I could have done anything I would. But witty replies to water bailiffs are not my long suit.

Baby is grizzling upstairs. The Frosts are all over the house seeing Mr Chandler off. Peter's chair creaks as he reads the Baroness Orczy and Mervyn sounds completely satisfied with the old Strand Magazines. But it is a very fine hot day. God is in *His* heaven all right, obviously and ostentatiously. Mr Chandler will be in *his* in Hereford. Goodbye. I am sorry this letter turns out so. Please remember me to Clifford or is he serving our country?

Yours ever | Edward Thomas

To Helen

Swansea | 9 October 1914

Are these letters boring and tiring you? I admit I leave out (unintentionally) what I can't put down in a note-taking spirit. Still it is better than notes—I make practically none these days. I remember the best things afterwards. I remember for instance how yesterday the cloudy day stilled and cooled and misted more then so that as early as 4.30 beyond Bath the starlings were concentrated all whistling in a tree as if it were evening and winter. I remember too how beautiful the hills round Swansea looked as my train was coming in—very black and velvety and the innumerable variously spaced lights all of them very crystalline: of course I could not see the buildings to which the lights belonged nor the trees or stones on the hill, just black and crystal.

[*Two days later—from Ryton*]*

I was meditating a poem about the gypsies by the roadside, their gramophone and cosy lighted tent so near wind and stars, the children searching for coal in the refuse of the old mine, and me faintly enjoying them. I thought how feeble and aesthetic my admiration of the mountain was, when I knew nothing of life on them, shepherds and stonequarrymen and ministers etc which I can only faintly imagine with a bellyful of ham. However I missed my tea and was very glad of broth cheese and damson tart at this house at 8 when I got in and then I wrote all this. I have been considering all the roads over the mountain to Brecon and can't decide yet. Perhaps the weather will decide.

I am to do the War Poetry article* for Monro. That is all the news. Frost is better and expecting to be home soon and the Abercrombies are gone. Goodnight. It is 10.30

To Helen

Ryton | Dymock | 17 October 1914

[*Continuation of a serial letter from Ryton*]

Saturday now, my boil has decreased, so that I am fairly well content except that I want to be home—yet would be content to wait—would enjoy the waiting as a sort of luxury of expectation, only I should like to be doing my share of the work while you are not so fit. Don't try to do the garden. Let me finish it, there's a dear. And if you feel at all hurt by my postponing return, forgive me, and forgive me saying how I enjoy these quiet soft still days. No rain this morning, but a low soft dark and pale sky and the thresher going. I went out first thing, having lit the fires, and picked apples from under a bent old apple tree on a sort of natural wall (perhaps a path went under it once, or they dug sand there) over in the corner of the greenfodder field where the cottage is with the walnut one side and the dead cherry tree the other. Rather a nice corner with this steep grassy wall, where the field runs up into a pasture above it. The tree has dropped heaps of apples as big as a child's fist, some nearly all rosy dark, the best streaked with blood red dots and dashes. The path doesn't go there, but the cottage people don't touch the apples, wonder at our eating them. Over the rising field above the path takes you up and you see the valley of the Leadon flowing under the strangest low hill covered with small crooked bushy trenches that look so pretty cutting across the road here at right angles to it and to the firry hill. The river is followed by willows that are now lovely silver fountains among the yellow and ruddy trees. The elms are dark green mixed with bright yellow insertions. We went over yesterday to Dymock that way and got your letter with The Times.

We will go to the Luptons, but I don't think we had better have that bureau, do you think?

Will you make note of any country people's war remarks that might be useful for my article? Please. Mrs Farmer (Lesley* was there yesterday) says its the Kayser's 'hambition' to eat his Xmas dinner in London; but 'if the Germans try to beat us the United States will join us.'

Frost is not very well, very nervous and not wanting to eat. Mrs Frost is tired. But the children are well. She doesn't intend to come to us now, I believe.

There's still lavender and borage blossoming in this garden and lots of evening primrose over the neglected parts where the children light bonfires that smoke eastwards over the stubble and pheasants. Rooks are always going over with jackdaws shouting among them like boys among men. They are ploughing in the mustard in one field, turning the light brown soil over the plants in their prime of greenness with yellow flowers just coming. Yesterday they killed a pig while we were at dinner. Soon he went by wagging and quaking still warm in a barrow. Later we saw his corpse pale cold and hairless as an egg like Julia's leg, stretched full length belly upwards for further operations. All the time the thresher goes.

I expect I shall be back on Monday. I post this on Saturday afternoon. | Edwy

To Robert Frost

Steep | 31 October 1914

My dear Frost,

I would rather have had a bad ear than that letter. But now I have the bad ear, too. 'I cannot pipe to skies so dull and grey'. I only hope that you wrote immediately after Gibson's call and in the worst pangs of it. When I wrote like that you replied that you wished I was near enough to be kicked. Well, I wish I were near enough to kick you, but have no faith in that kind of school. Did you want or expect a letter sooner? I should only have told you I was surprised to find you again like me, and I was inclined to write anything. But I find that when I write a moan people keep silent for a fortnight or so either because they think you will by then have forgotten or because they don't think it 'requires an answer'. It is no use telling you I could feel the same about a book (tho I don't know how it feels to have written 'North of Boston') and with as little reasonable ground. I imagine that few writers so early become assured of the understanding and admiration of such a variety of readers. But also I don't imagine that because a man has reasonable ground for some contentment at times, therefore he ought to be content at times, though he probably will be.

I didn't suspect all this wisdom when I began to write or I would have waited. What I really wrote for was to ask you to send me the M.S. of the Proverbs

c/o Clifford Bax | 1 Bishop's Avenue | East Finchley | London N.W.

I am to meet an artist there on Wednesday who wants to try illustrating them. But if you don't send it off on Tuesday or Wednesday address it to Steep.

I have now got the 4th volume (since September) of M.S. poems to read and pronounce on for fond unknown bard. Would this bring the warm blood to your cheek? In each case I have written hostile unanswered opinions without the least belief they are right or useful.

My only fun out of reading has been from Wilfrid Blunt's Collected Poems.* There is a man in them very easy to disengage. Do you know him?

I have just made myself almost ill with thinking hard for an hour,—going up to my study and sitting there,—that I ought to enlist next week in town. Now I am so weak I wouldn't show anything but my ear to any doctor. I am just going to do that.

I go on writing, unlike all the patriots, or rather as the patriots feel they oughtn't to.

What about the poems you wrote after we left? Send them if you feel inclined.

There is something wrong and artificial about this letter without more than one dot at a time. I am sorry. I shall be glad to have one from you with or without dots.

Our love to you all | Yours ever | E.T.

To W. H. Hudson

c/o Robert Frost | Ryton | Dymock | Gloucester | 26 November 1914

My dear Hudson,

I came over here yesterday morning with your letter fresh in my pocket. I was very glad to have it and especially to hear you had been working in spite of everything. But I am extremely sorry to hear Mrs. Hudson is suffering so. I hope it is a transient attack. How beautiful the sea must be these frosty mornings after a wet night, such as we had yesterday. I walked in to Alton by Colemore and East Tisted while the frost was melting and was lucky to get a lift with a farmer going to Basingstoke Market, such a neat fine man of 72 who came from near Ryde which he pronounced Hryde. He talked of getting a small motor but said his wife wouldn't ride in it if he drove. The wood-pigeons are just getting thick about us.

About Garnett—I have no idea what he went for,* but heard he looked ill. David, I heard him say earlier, had been dissuaded from enlisting. I must write to Mrs. Garnett. I have now got the Parliamentary Recruiting Committee's form to fill in or not and hesitate because I would sooner enlist in London with a friend (if possible) than be pitchforked anywhere suddenly. It is an insoluble problem till one has some really strong impulse one way and one doesn't get that by thinking about it. But a young soldier I was talking to in the train agreed that no man could face the war if he could foresee his own part in the fighting. The difference between people is that they try or do not try in various degrees—often against their will—to foresee it. He was bringing home 2 canaries from Pekin for his mother. Yet he had in his pocket the reply form of a telegram which she had sent inquiring about him.

It is odd that [Wilfrid] Blunt should bother to think which is his best poem. I thought better of a bull-fighter than that. But, however good it may not be, it does show a man of a particular kind and so do all his few real poems. He is a kind of miniature Byron who will perhaps never have the luck to get his personality and other activities added on to his poems so that you can't distinguish them.

I haven't any work now. That is why I have travelled over here. But I don't find the war shuts me up. In fact it has given me time to please myself with some unprofitable writing,* and up to now I have not been hard hit as many are. Davies was with us last week-end. He complains a little about the reduced lighting in London and even grumbled at the dark in country roads, forgetting they never were lit. Otherwise the war hasn't much touched him. I hear he (like everyone else) wrote a bad war poem. I wish someone would send me Hardy's new poems.* By the way, I should like you to see 'The Stonechat' in a volume of poems by Geoffrey Young. I thought one of the best of all pure bird poems, the bird on a wet stone pure and simple up on a heath. I will try to remember to type it for you.

With kindest regards to Mrs. Hudson

Yours ever | E. Thomas

To C. F. Cazenove

Steep | Petersfield | 2 December 1914

Dear Cazenove,

Do you think there is a publisher for a book, I thought of a short one, on the idea of *England* from earliest times, as shown in writers of all kinds, kings, statesman, poets, private persons down to our own day, as popular as I can make it? And in any case, wouldn't Harrison perhaps like either an article on the subject or on what England means to a man to-day, drawing both on my own experience and on what I have heard said by a variety of people since the war began? I should like to do both and could begin at once.

Yours sincerely | Edward Thomas

To Robert Forst

Steep | 15 December 1914

Dear Frost,

I am glad you spotted 'wings' light word'.* I knew it was wrong and also that many would like it: also 'odd men'—a touch nearing facetiousness in it. I've got rid of both now. But I am in it and no mistake. I have an idea and am full enough but that my bad habits and customs and duties of writing will make it rather easy to write when I've no business to. At the same time I find myself engrossed and conscious of a possible perfection as I never was in prose. Also I'm very impatient of my prose, and of reviews and of review books. And yet I have been uncommonly cheerful mostly. I have been rather pleased with some of the pieces, of course, but it's not wholly that. Still, I won't begin thanking you just yet, tho if you like I will put it down now that you are the only begetter right enough.

I should like to see the man who was upset by you rhyming 'come' and 'dumb'. I should also like to write about you in the 'Forum'. But they wouldn't want me to, I feel quite sure. Only I will write to them just to see.

You speak of your 'few remaining weeks here'. But that doesn't mean any early move, does it, whether you only leave Ryton or go back home. Scott sails tomorrow. He was willing to take Mervyn out and tutor him. He was to be learning blacksmithery and would teach Mervyn (if Mervyn would learn). But Mervyn hasn't gone, didn't much want to, while the proposal was a little too sudden tho I had the feeling it might be God's idea to get Mervyn away from me for ever that way.

Mervyn is to have Peter for company this Christmas probably. We are expecting him instead of the Dutch boy.

My works come pouring in on you now. Tell me all you dare *about them*. I have been shy of blank verse tho (or because) I like it best. But the rhymes have dictated themselves decidedly except in one case.

I gather that Marsh is more or less engrossed now and reckoned not to be approachable, but I don't know whether to believe it. In town I saw de la Mare and that is what he said. But he and I have withdrawn from one another I fancy. At least I know I am never myself so long as I am with him. Now I have put it to Monro that he might show 'North of Boston' to E.M. We'll see.

I wish you were a day's walk away or were really at anchor.

Yours ever | E.T.

To Harold Monro

Steep | Tuesday [after 15 December 1914]

My dear Monro,

Many thanks for saying it.* I am sorry because I feel utterly sure they are me. I expect obstacles and I get them. It was chiefly to save myself what I think unnecessary pain that I asked for no explanations. One blow was better. I assume the verses expressed nothing clearly that you cared about, as that is the only ground for not liking written work. But don't let us talk about it. I have to be at the Museum next week, far too busy for my liking. If I have time I will suggest an evening.

Yours ever | Edward Thomas

To Margaret Townsend

Steep | Petersfield | 14 February 1915

My dear Auntie,

Thank you for Kenneth Morris's book.* I am very fond of the Mabinogion, and it is obvious that he is too. But I can't help thinking it is a mistake to retell the stories with the colouring of an interpretation which he cannot think adequate or final. I should have thought so had I been merely told of his method. On reading the result I think so still more. As they stand the old stories are works of art in which, as in every work of art, the writer accepts many things he could not explain and feels no need of explaining. If he did feel the need he would make a work of philosophy or natural history, not a work of art. And I think K. Morris has just made the compromise which is neither one thing nor the other. I feel sorry to say this about a friend of yours who likes my books.

I have been thinking to write many times since the New Year, because I have had a great deal of leisure, owing to a bad sprained ankle which isn't well yet after 6 weeks. It has kept me mostly in this small house and made me rather a burden to others as well as myself. It was none the better that I had very little work to do. Tonight I am thinking of you because Mervyn sailed for New York yesterday with American friends in the 'Saint Paul'. He is going to make a long stay with an English friend—formerly headmaster of the preparatory school here—Mr. Russell Scott, at East Alstead, near Keene, in New Hampshire. There he is to have lessons and to try his hand at a forge which Mr. Scott is learning to use. But it was chiefly to get him away from the easy, sheltered and wearying life of home and school, where he was dependent and irresponsible to excess. We hope he may develope more freely there and perhaps get clearer as to what he is going to do. He might stay some years: the plan at present is for six months.

I am going to London on Tuesday to work at the Museum. I shall stay with Mother. Father, I think, is still away on a round of visits in Wales. Mother had a bad cough when I saw her a fortnight ago. She spent a day or two here. I wish she lived in the country and could see more people that she liked. At this moment Helen and the Baby are there. Helen went to Liverpool with Mervyn and is off for a fortnight's holiday with friends tomorrow. Bronwen and I are at home keeping house for one another. She is very good company, so cheerful and careful and willing. Nothing comes amiss to her, and she is very happy at school and at home. She is not at all clever. Nor is Mervyn. Baby seems to be much cleverer than either and more independent, but I suppose the youngest often seems so: she is very short-sighted, by the way, and has to wear spectacles: it makes her very timid of heights, at least I think it is that, she does not know what is below when she walks on a bank above a steep wooded slope.

I don't know what to say about things in England now, except as they concern me. Naturally my work is gone and what I write is of less interest than ever. If the war should end before summer is over and I should feel it was fair to Helen and the children, I think of going to New Hampshire myself. My American friends, the Frosts, are taking a farm and want me to come and try farm life. They actually think I might be able to farm myself. Goodbye. I hope you are well.

Your affectionate Edwy

To John Freeman

Coventry | 8 March 1915

My dear Freeman,

The 20th then and early. I believe the 8.55 still runs and another something before 11 (getting in at 1.15) but make sure about this just before the day as there are so many changes nowadays. If I could produce a nightingale on March 20 do you think I should bother about being a bard. I wish I could. Now if it were a very very pretty March 20 the Lord might produce a chiffchaff or a thrush's egg, but since I hurt my ankle I have seen nothing, and it isn't a real ankle yet by a long way.

The Anthology* is substantially done. It grows slowly now while I am waiting for the Oxford Press reader's judgment. (He is J. C. Smith, who edited Spenser's *Faerie Queene*). All that typing and turning over pages knocked all the rapture about as far off as the nearest nightingales. Then came a beastly Index and a beastly book on Babylon (to review). Now I've had more at the Museum and still have a day of it left. Then I hope to put myself in an attitude worthy of the Muse's indulgence more. Whether the habit of writing will make me command it more often than I deserve it, and whether that will be fatal to success, *I* can't say. My pseudonym is just a family name, Edward Eastaway. I never thought of Gibson. It would have been a lark. So far I have heard no news. By the way what I have done so far have been like quintessences of the best part of my prose books—not much sharper or more intense, but I hope a little: since the first take off they haven't been Frosty very much or so I imagine and I have tried as often as possible to avoid the facilities offered by blank verse and I try not to be long—I even have an ambition to keep under 12 lines (but rarely succeed).

I've not dipped into *New Numbers** yet. Drinkwater is hopeless. Gibson, for me, almost equally so. Abercrombie, I fancy, applies the lash, and I wonder whether he always did. I used to think he was naturally a spirited steed. I am always anxious to like him.

We haven't yet heard from Mervyn. His ship arrived 12 days ago so we might do soon.

By the way I got Doughty for my Anthology. He was very nice.

Yours ever | E.T.

To Edward Garnett

Steep | 17 March 1915

My dear Garnett,

Your letter gave me a lot of pleasure this morning when few other things could because I had tired myself to death with two days cycling (to the sea and back) in this tempting and tiring weather—which is my reason for writing only a short note. I am fit for nothing at all really. I am glad to find you preferring certain things—like 'Old Man' and the 'Cuckoo' and 'Goodnight'—and sorry to find your preferring them to certain others like 'The Sign-post'. But the great satisfaction is you obviously find them *like me*. I had fears lest I had got up in the air in this untried medium. So long as I haven't I am satisfied. Of course I must make mistakes and your preferences help me to see where they lie, though I shall risk some of them again—e.g. what you find petty in incident. Dimness and lack of concreteness I shall certainly do my best against. I hate them too much in others to tolerate them in myself—when I see them.

It was almost as pleasant to know you like Frost.* The reviews he got here were one by Abercrombie in the *Nation*, one by Hueffer in the *Outlook*, and a number by me in the *New Weekly* etc. In America he got only an echo or two of these. He had been at American editors ten years in vain. But may I suggest it might damage him there if you rubbed the Americans' noses in their own dirt? I know he thought so. Most English reviewers were blinded by theories they had as to what poetry should look like. They did not see how true he was, and how pure in his own style. I think the 'Hired Man', the 'Wood Pile', the 'Black Cottage' and one or two others—such as 'Home Burial'—masterpieces. I send his first book.* Much of it is very early indeed. Look, however, at 'Mowing' and 'The Tuft of Flowers' (pp. 34 and 25). Hudson didn't return *North of Boston*, or not to me. I will send him some of my verses.

The reason of my wire is that I am only sending out verses at present under a pseudonym, and have already done so to the *Nation*, *Times* and *English Review*. I don't want people to be confused by what they know or think of me already, although I know I shall also lose the advantage of some friendly prejudice.

And I should be glad if you would not mention my verses to friends.

Frost is descended from early English (Devonshire) settlers, with a Scotch mother. He has farmed for some years and has gone back to farm. He has also been a teacher of English and paedagogy.—There are some of his latest verses in the last number of *Poetry and Drama*.

Yours ever | Edward Thomas

To W. H. Hudson

Steep | Petersfield | 23 March 1915

My dear Hudson,

I believe that a man who likes poetry and says honestly what he likes is about as rare as a good critic, and I am really not sure if the two are not one. At any rate apart from one or two such men I don't know where to look for the critic, so that as far as getting into his hands and having his opinion go, I am not in a hurry to be published. So far as I know reviewers there are kind and complimentary ones, there are enemies, and there are idiots besides. They have the power to tickle or sting for a moment, but nothing more. They ('we' I should say) have to show how much cleverer they are than the reviewed. It is so much easier to do this with offence. I would rather never do it again, and I am certainly not anxious to be the victim of it as a versifier. I had quite enough ups and downs reading your letter first, though I was really very glad of it all. I was glad you liked 'After Rain' and 'The Signpost'. (I will type 'The Signpost' and 'Beauty' for you gladly) and glad to have your reasons for not wholly liking some others. I must think about the sensation at the end of 'May 20'.* I think perhaps it must come out. But about 'Merry' in 'The Manor Farm', I rather think I will stick to it. If one can feel what one has written, and not what one *meant*. I feel here as if the *merry* England asleep at Prior's Dean added to the sleepiness and enriched it somehow.

I am sending them about and getting them back. Probably I shall soon tire and be glad to consign them to a printed book.

If I had been coming up today I would have telegraphed. But I thought I would wait till next week. It is very good gardening weather and has been for a week now, and in fact good for everything except walking far. It has got very languid after a little rain following on nights of frost and days of sun. I shall be at the Mt. Blanc,* so far as I can tell, next Tuesday, or at 3 Henrietta St.* at 1: if you are to be, I will be. And I hope you will be better.

Looking back it seems possible you might think I had found your letter too critical. But really I would very much rather know that you like or don't wholly like a thing, than that somebody else thinks it a pity I ever read Frost, etc.

Yours ever | E. Thomas

To Robert Frost

Steep | 3 May 1915

My dear Robert,

I got a letter from you on Friday, the one I have been gladdest to yet, and not only because you said you liked 'Lob'. I was glad to hear of you going off to Stowe 'tomorrow'. You are enjoying this period, but it is silly of me to tell you so. If you weren't you ought to be, because you are not writing about Marlborough. But we have one piece of luck. Two pairs of nightingales have come to us. One sings in our back hedge nearly all day and night. My only regret when I first heard it was that you hadn't stayed another Spring and heard it too. I hope the Gods don't think I'm the sort of poet who will be content with a nightingale, though. You don't think they could have made that mistake do you? What does it mean?—I get quite annoyed with people complaining of the weather as soon as it greys a little. Am I really ripe for being all sound content, or what? 2nd piece of luck (still embryonic) is that Scott-James has some connection with an American literary journal called The Bellman and is recommending them things by me, beginning with a remark on Rupert Brooke. You heard perhaps that he died on April 23rd of sunstroke on the way to the Dardanelles? All the papers are full of his 'beauty' and an eloquent last sonnet beginning 'If I should die'. He was eloquent. Men never spoke ill of him.

But you have some poems by you fit to send out, haven't you? These editors mustn't go sour with waiting.

I find I can't write. Re-reading Rupert Brooke* and putting a few things together about him have rather messed me up and there's Marlborough behind and Marlborough before. I shall have to go up to London for the last time next week—for the last bout at the Museum, I mean. Bronwen is now at school again. I shall take Baba up and leave Helen to contrive some spring cleaning. I tell you—I should like another April week in Gloucestershire with you like that one last year. You are the only person I can be idle with. That's natural history, not eloquence. If you were there I might even break away from the Duke for 3 days, but it would be hard.

Are the children at school now? Or are you still 'neglecting' them? God bless them all. By the way, there was a beautiful return of sun yesterday after a misty moisty morning, and everything smelt wet and warm and cuckoos called, and I found myself with nothing to say but 'God bless it'. I laughed a little as I came over the field, thinking about the 'it' in 'God bless it'.

Yours and Elinor's ever | Edward Thomas

Don't send back that parson's letter and of course keep the poems. (I haven't quite stopped even yet.)

P.S. Here is Ellis very elderly and masterly about my verses, not finding one to say he likes, but seeing the 'elements of poetry'. The rhythm is too rough and not obvious enough. He wants to talk them over. I don't. Well, I feel sure I'm old enough not to know better, though I don't profess to know how good or bad it may be.

I have now gone the round of pretty well all the verse-writers I know. Ellis was kind enough to find mine 'eminently the stuff of which poetry is made' &c. Thinking he might make a book of them I did at last send a selection to Monro. He didn't like it. He muttered something about conception and execution as if they were different things. But I had requested him not to trouble to give reasons why he liked or didn't like them.

If you have a farm by now these remarks will easily sink into perspective. But I am thinned out by all this reading and smoking.

My love to you all

Yours ever | Edward Thomas

*To Harry Hooton**

Steep | Petersfield | 19 May 1915

My dear Harry,

Thank you for the two poems. You have brought on yourself all these others now. Tell me which you like, if you like any, as I hope you may; and tell me anything that strikes you in reading them, either general or particular. I don't suppose anyone's warning or advice will have any direct active effect. But I want to know an honest reader's opinion because I seem to be committed to a new path that does not promise money and I want any confirmation I can get that it promises at any rate some advance in effectiveness. I had got past poetical prose and my new feeling is that here I can use my experience and what I am and what I know with less hindrance than in prose, less gross notebook stuff and mere description and explanation.

I have begun to write *Marlborough* now and can do nothing else, but if you and Janet come down any time after this weekend I shall be game for a walk or two, and you can take a stick away.

Yours ever | Edward Thomas

To Robert Frost

Steep | Petersfield | 13 June 1915

My dear Robert,

Your two letters came together Friday night. When I saw the Franconia postmark on the smaller I guessed it was the second and that you were there. I hope very much you still are and will be almost as long as you would like to be. My next hope is that I shall see you there. But this is a funny world, as I think you said before I did. 'Rum job, painting', Turner used to say when Ruskin had poured out a can of words. I wish I hadn't to say more about poetry. I wished it on Friday night particuarly as I had to spoil the effect of your letter by writing 1000 words about Rupert Brooke's posthumous book—not daring to say that those sonnets about him enlisting (?) are probably not very personal but a nervous attempt to connect with himself the very widespread idea that self sacrifice is the highest self indulgence. You know. And I don't dispute it. Only I doubt if he knew it or would he have troubled to drag in the fact that enlisting cleared him of

All the little emptiness of love?

Well, I daren't say so, not having enlisted or fought the keeper. But I ought to write about 'The Road not Taken'.* I ought to search for the poem first among your letters. But I shan't yet. I am pretty tired. I must own though that it wasn't a very honest remark that of mine. For whether it was that I was deaf or that you didn't quite speak in the verses I got the idea somewhat apart from the words. That is to say I thought I did,—the fact being that I got the idea as much as if I had skimmed the words, which I don't think I did. So at the time I was content to deceive you by referring to the poem when it was really to that idea not yet in the form of poetry which existed in my head after reading. The word 'staggering' I expect did no more than express (or conceal) the fact that the simple words and unemphatic rhythms were not such as I was accustomed to expect great things, things I like, from. It staggered me to think that perhaps I had always missed what made poetry poetry if it was here. I wanted to think it was here. I don't know what an honest man would have said under the circumstances. Well, I won't go about with a lantern just yet, though I am going to have a devil of a lot of leisure which I shall do no better with. The Marlborough got practically finished yesterday morning—26 days writing. I am going to cycle for a few days probably up to Haines at Gloucester (through Swindon) and perhaps on to Coventry. And yet I hate spending the money. We get scared now, with things 25% dearer than they were and work so much more than 25% scarcer. I take no steps. I try to imagine what I should do if I got to New York or Boston. For I can't deceive myself into imagining I should be a new man. I know I shouldn't meet any one nearly half way if I didn't feel something of a friend in him and I know I should seldom feel that. Perhaps I should not be much easier there than in London where if I want work I can only ask for it uncomfortably or hang about without asking for it as if I had forgotten what I came for, but it wasn't for nothing. 10 years ago an editor having to say the first word said 'Well Mr. Thomas what can I do for you?' and I could only say 'That is what I came to see'. He laughed. It was almost clever in me then, but I can't *enfant prodigue* it now. So I pester my friends or did when I had such. I suppose one does get help to some extent by being helpless, but when one doesn't—it is as if one had pride after all.

Still, I am thinking about America as my only chance (apart from Paradise). Tell me when would be the best time to begin. Are people back in town in September? I suppose I ought to take what introductions I can get. You will tell me if there is any way of living cheaply and yet not being in the wilderness. But what will your distance be from Boston and what the fare?

I am glad to hear about your 3rd edition. You must get something out of it. And then I want to hear that the *Atlantic* is hospitable. There is nothing in Garnett's article to turn your head. It is extraordinary only because it is sensible and goes straight to your substance and psychology. It surprises Sidgwick because he is used to seeing bards praised by a set of epithets and abstract substantives. It should be out in July I suppose.

Honest man (Marlborough used to think he was honest), I have found 'Two Roads'. It is as I thought. Not then having begun to write I did not know that is how it would be done. It was just its newness, not like Shelley or de la Mare or anyone. I don't pretend not to have a regular road and footpath system as well as doing some trespassing. On looking at it again I complain only of a certain periphrastic looseness in 'the passing there had gone to them both about the same'. Also I hope that so far you have not found that you had to sigh on realising it had made all the difference, though it had. You don't wish you had been Drinkwater. Another trifle—the lack of stops I believe put me off a little. There. If I say more I shall get into those nooks you think I like. It is all very well for you poets in a wood to say you choose, but you don't. If you do, ergo I am no poet. I didn't choose my sex yet I was simpler then. And so I can't 'leave off' going in after myself tho some day I may. I didn't know when I left you at Newent I was going to begin trying to write poetry. I had proved it was impossible. Have you got your lecture written out or typed and can I see it? I am glad they asked you and got you to Boston.

I tell you those two letters were the best thing I have had since you were here. Odd, but they made me discontented too with what I knew I was going to do (and wasn't going to do) with the 2 or 3 days leisure. I have now—the book near done and my youngest brother here to keep me off it and fine weather to go about.

To think of your doubting Davies knew what shame was! I never knew anyone at all who so often got himself into positions that made him feel uncomfortable. Did I ever tell you that when he lived near us he used to carry home his groceries in the lining of his overcoat, and Helen asked him once what he would do if they began to leak out as he went down the street. He said he would let them lie and pretend not to notice. He would have been ashamed to be seen admitting (1) that he did his own shopping and (2) that he carried things in the lining of his overcoat. Of course you need not believe it. As to the bed, either a married couple had slept in it or a single man in distress.—He has just gone into his 4th London lodging already.

I read 'The road not taken' to Helen just now and she liked it entirely and agreed with me how naturally symbolical it was. You won't go and exaggerate what I say about that one phrase.

This moment a letter from Haines telling me I am free to drop in on him next week as I hope to do. The weather keeps so fine though that each day it seems must be the last—just like last year.

People are getting pretty black about the war, realising they have not got the Germans beaten yet. It is said however that we are really through the Dardanelles and the price of wheat is falling. It is said to be kept back to prevent rowdyism in the rejoicing.

Good luck to you at Franconia and all our loves to you six.

Yours ever | E. Thomas

To Edward Garnett

c/o J. W. Haines | Hillview Road | Hucclecote | Glos | 24 June 1915

My dear Garnett,

Thank you for writing at once. I got your letter when I arrived here from Malmesbury last night. But I can't really answer till I have been able to think a little more. I can only say now that at first sight you seem to ask me to try to turn over a new leaf and be someone else. I can't help dreading people both in anticipation and when I am among them and my only way of holding my own is the instinctive one of turning on what you call coldness and a superior manner. That is why I hesitated about America. I felt sure that unless I could make a friend or two I could do no good.—Nor do I think that any amount of distress could turn me into a lecturer. It would weary you if I tried to explain: I don't justify.—But these are first thoughts and I am tired rather.

As to the Civil List,* will you ask Hudson? I believe others might speak to Lloyd George. I hate the idea of *urging* it, but I am urged and I know that somehow or another I must find some sort of safety however low. Anything rather than a continuation of the insecurity of the last three years. Anything (I must add before you say it) rather than make a bold bid. Anything (I suppose) rather than be independent.

However I think I shall go over to America in a couple of months and see what I can make myself do.

I shall write again. I stay here till Saturday or Sunday, then go on to Bablake School Coventry and so back home, I should think through Oxford.

I have had four marvellous fine long days on end through Salisbury Shaftesbury Avebury Wootton Bassett Tetbury and Malmesbury here.

Yours ever | Edward Thomas

I hope I shall see you before you go. Good luck to David.*

To his parents

Steep | 9 July 1915

Dear Father and Mother,

I have got on a step in the half decision I came to while I was with you of enlisting. I saw a sergeant of the Artists Rifles at their H.Q. to-day. They are virtually an Officers Training Corps now. If I joined I should be for a week or two in London, and able (I believe) to stay with you. Then I should spend a month or two in Richmond Park in camp and then a similar period of training at H.Q. in France. If I were then considered fit for a commission I should be at liberty to apply for one. But if I got one it would not (on account of my age) be for service, at first at any rate, if at all, in the trenches, but for training men in England. I have practically come to the decision to go up next week and offer myself to the doctor. The alternative is the Sportsman's Battalion of the Royal

Fusiliers, but there (I am told) I might find a rowdy set, no better company than the ordinary crowd of privates, whereas the Artists would be largely professional men. Of course there are still some things to consider, but Helen is willing, and I believe my savings and pay would if necessary cover her expenses during as long an absence as two years. She does not want to go to the Ellises and for the present she and the two girls would stay on here. If I am accepted next week I can have several days for putting my things in order.

I hope this will not seem to you very unreasonable. The conditions being as I say you will have little cause for anxiety unless some unforeseeable changes take place . . .

Duckworths offer me £10 in advance for the *Proverbs*. It is something but I have not accepted it yet.

I am inquiring how if at all my insurance policies will be affected.

The *English Review* rejects my poem. Perhaps if I am in khaki they will be more genial. I am not troubled. I never felt easier in my mind except for a fear that the doctor will not pass me.

Every your loving son | Edwy

To J. W. Haines

Steep | Petersfield | 15 August 1915

My dear Haines,

I don't know if one has the right to be plain unless one is sure one doesn't mind others using the right. But I shall be plain and say that reading your poems makes me feel that you do not express yourself in verse. As it seems to me rhyme and metre compel you to paraphrase what you would have said or sometimes not said at all, had you not formed the habit; and after it all, what you individually feel or think remains unexpressed, at most faintly suggested to a sympathetic reader, if I may dare to call myself one on top of this. The subject is endless. You can't judge yourself. You know your intentions. You know the experiences out of which your poems spring. You can't separate the poems from those intentions and experiences. I don't know how many of us can. I don't pretend to be able to myself, but I do feel sure that I am right in your case, though I may not have put it plainly. I might be plainer at greater length and to no purpose. I can't expect to convince you. I don't know why I should want to convince you. In fact, as I hinted at first, I doubt whether I have the right to say what I have said, and I ask to be forgiven if I seem to intrude as a reviewer into private life. For I know how I should feel if I got this letter myself. But I could not lie out and out. It would have been even more unpleasant to beat about the bush and leave you to guess at my meaning than it is to speak like this. I can't imagine if it would have been more unpleasant to you. I would lie to an idiot. I would beat about the bush to an old fool. There are other categories where I should feel powerless to say what I thought, but I must not attempt to dictate to you how you should treat my plainness.

Yours ever | E. Thomas

To Robert Frost

'A' Company Artists Rifles | Hare Hall Camp Romford Essex | 6 December 1915

My dear Robert,

It seems an age since I wrote and longer since I heard from you. Now it is a wet evening and every one is playing cards and it is easy to begin a letter. We have begun real work again,* each of us taking 10 or 12 men out for 5 days on end and trying to teach them the elements of map-reading, field sketching, the use of compass and protractor, and making a map on the ground with and without the compass. We get a fresh set every week of 5 working days. The pay is still 1/– a day, but one learns a lot, and if I decide to take a commission the experience will have been valuable. Whether I decide depends on how I like this work and how useful I find myself. As I probably told you, everyone advises me to stick at it, at least for some months.

We don't take a class on Saturday so I have got off two Friday nights in succession, returning Sunday night. So I had a whole Saturday at Steep the week before last and did some gardening, chopped some wood, lit a fire in my study. Last Friday night I got to Coventry to talk to Hodson about Mervyn. Mervyn is to live there and attend the school for 2 terms. After that Hodson may get a commission in the Artillery. He took a course in the Cambridge Officers Training Corps last Summer vacation.

We are now hoping to hear that Mervyn's fare has reached him at East Alstead. If it has he says he will sail in the St. Louis on December 10 and I can't tell you how we look forward to seeing him. Of course we don't know yet here what Xmas leave we shall have. But I hope for 3 days. I have never had more than 2 days at home on end since I joined 5 months ago, and that only twice.

Yesterday afternoon I saw de la Mare. Did I tell you Garnett had promised to see if he could get me something from the Civil List. (Davies by the way is getting his £50 doubled, they say). Well, Garnett went off to the Italian front with an ambulance party, and I imagine he forgot me. So I put my tongue in my cheek and asked de la Mare if he could put things in motion. Perhaps he will. I am first making sure that Garnett hasn't done anything.

Have you seen the 2nd Georgian Anthology? I had a faint chance of getting in. At least Bottomley wanted to show some of my things to Marsh. But they have kept in Monro. The only things I really much like were de la Mare's and perhaps Davies'. Bottomley may be all right. The new man Ledwidge isn't any good, is he? Abercrombie of course is a poet. I don't know. I couldn't really spend any time on the volume after looking to see if there was anything new in it and except Ledwidge, there wasn't. But I suppose what I think doesn't matter at all considering I read less than any man in the hut. I don't want to read anything. On the other hand as soon as I get really free with nothing close before me to do I incline to write. I have written two things here or rather 3, but one was just (a) rhyming one.—I am always just a little more outside things than most of the others and without being made to feel so at all acutely. They aren't surprised whether I come in or stay out of a group.

It won't be long before Christmas when this reaches you. I hope you are all going to be together and well and glad to be there on Christmas day. We shall be thinking about you. It must somehow fall out that we don't have to live on letters very long. Give my love to Elinor and all the children.

Yours ever | Edward Thomas

To Helen

Thursday | Hare Hall | Gidea Park Romford | 24 February 1916

Dearest,

Fancy your thinking those verses* had anything to do with you. Fancy your thinking, too, that I should let you see them if they were. They are not to a woman at all. You know precisely all that I know of any woman I have cared a little for. They are as a matter of fact to father. So now, unless you choose to think I am deceiving you (which I don't think I ever did), you can be at ease again.

Silly old thing to jump so to conclusions. You might as well have concluded the verses to Mother were for you. As to the other verses about love you know that my usual belief is that I don't and can't love and haven't done for something near 20 years. You know too that you don't think my nature really compatible with love, being so clear and critical. You know how unlike I am to you, and you know that you love, so how can I? That is if you count love as any one feeling and not something varying infinitely with the variety of people.

Thank Bronwen for her letter and give her a large kiss.

We are all fairly deep in snow today. I got one snowball in the ear but luckily only on the flesh of the ear. There was a lot of snowballing. But we were indoors all day conducting an exam, which is very tiring. Tomorrow we don't know what we shall do. We have done with one lot; it will be a bad day to begin with another.

Goodbye now. I saw Father and Mother for an hour or so. I tried my tunic on, but I could get no change out of the compass man. I was back here again at 8.30.

I am all yours | Edwy

To Lascelles Abercrombie

'D' Coy | Artists Rifles | 15 Hut | Harehall | Romford | 2 March 1916

My dear Abercrombie,

I can't tell you how your letter pleased me. It pleased me more than it could have done with any other man's name at the end. That is a fact. I am all the more pleased because of course I still wonder whether the things* can be any good, beginning so late as I did and after such a bad preparation of journalism. You make me almost sure. But in any case I believe I shall go on, and I shall be curious to see the good company I am to keep. I want to be Eastaway because I should be sick of the nice things as well as the nasty things such a lot of reviewers would say if they had my name to go on.

As to the Anthology* it was an impudent afterthought at 11.30 to put some Eastaway in, just to see what happened. Nothing did till you wrote, that I know of.

I usually enjoy this life a good deal. My job is largely a schoolmaster's and I have to do some unaccustomed things, such as lecturing, but it is all useful. My wife and the children are all well at home. I am glad to hear yours are, especially to hear your wife is not ill. Will you remember me to her? I wish we were to meet again soon. But my leaves are short and few. At present they are all stopped by a case of measles in the hut.

Yours sincerely | Edward Thomas

To Robert Frost

Hare Hall Camp | 5 March 1916

My dear Robert,

No one can have Patience who pursues Glory, so you will have to toss up with Eleanor which vice you shall claim in public.

Well, I was hoping your silence meant you had something better to do than write letters. When they told me you would contribute to the Annual* I thought it likely. Now I am glad to hear it is so, but sorry to have to wait for the Annual before seeing the poems. I don't know if you got them, but I have sent several from time to time. Your not mentioning them made me think I had missed fire. I have written so many I suppose I am always missing fire.

I have done nothing like your lecture at Lawrence.* As soon as I stand up and look at 30 men I can do nothing but crawl backwards and forwards between the four points I can still remember under the strain. It will mean a long war if I am to improve. You ask if I think it is going to be a long war. I don't think, but I do expect a lot of unexpected things and am not beginning really to look forward to any change. I hardly go beyond assuming that the war will end.

We have been through a time of change here lately. In fact we may not be out of it yet. I was not sure if the reconstruction would leave me out and compel me to take a commission. Today it seems most likely we shall go on as we were. Even so, if I have to wait much longer for promotion I shall be inclined to throw this job up. I have been restless lately. Partly the annoyance of my promotion being delayed. Partly the rain and the long hours indoors. Partly my 10 days chill. Then there has been measles in the camp for 6 weeks and now we have it and are isolated and denied our leave this week, which included my birthday* when I meant to be at Steep.

This should only improve what you condemn as my fastidious taste in souls. Yet soul is a word I feel I can't have used for years and years. Anyhow here I have to like people because they are more my sort than the others, although I realise at certain times they are not my sort at all and will vanish away after the war. What almost completes the illusion is that I can't help talking to them as if they were friends.

Partly what made me restless, was the desire to write, without the power. It lasted 5 or 6 weeks, till yesterday I rhymed some.*

Your talking of epic and play rather stirred me. I shall be careful not to *indulge* in a spring run of lyrics. I had better try again to make other people speak. I suppose I take it easily, especially now when it is partly an indulgence.—I wish you would send some of yours without bargaining.

Well; the long and short of it seems to be that I am what I am, in spite of my hopes of last July. The only thing is perhaps I didn't quite know what I was. This less active life you see gives me more time and inclination to ruminate. Also it is Sunday, always a dreary ruminating day if spent in camp. We got a walk, three of us, one a schoolmaster, the other a game-breeder who knows about horses and dogs and ferrets. We heard the first blackbird, walked 8 or 10 miles straight across country (the advantage of our uniform—we go just where we like): ate and drank (stout) by a fire at a big quiet inn—not a man to drink left in the village, and drew a panorama—a landscape for military purposes, drawn exactly with the help of a compass and a protractor, which is an amusement I have quite taken to—they say I am a neo-realist at it.

Abercrombie wrote a nice letter about some of my verses he had seen. Nobody's compliments would *flatter* me so much or more.

I can't go on with this now because everything is upside down. We don't know who or where or what we are. We five don't want to be split up and scattered. On the other hand we may each be made independent and put in charge of a company and so get rapid promotion.

Goodbye. They are all well at home, and Mervyn at Coventry. I was to have gone home for my birthday last week. Eleanor Farjeon was there. Now I have a chance of going this week end. My presents are waiting for me. But one of the best things I had on the day was your letter—a lucky accident. Give my love to them all and I hope I shall see them before I am still another year older.

Yours ever | Edward Thomas

To Robert Frost

Hare Hall Camp | 16 March 1916

My dear Robert,

Your letter of February 29 only reached me yesterday. It referred to some verses I had sent—dismal ones, I gather. Perhaps one was called 'Rain', a form of excrescence you hoped it was when you said 'Work all that off in poetry and I shan't complain'. Well, I never know. I was glad to know of a letter reaching you. I had begun to fear perhaps my letters didn't reach you. Lately I was able to write again. But I got home on Saturday and left them there. If I can find the rough draft here I will copy one out.

Things are still difficult here. There has been a complete re-organization. We do not know how it will affect us ultimately. So far it has meant that we only instruct the company (D) to which we have been attached since Xmas, whereas we used to instruct the whole battalion of 4 companies in turn. Our sergeant has gone and left us, so the corporal who would have been my junior is now in charge of us and may get made a sergeant and leave me still as I was. We are very busy. I lecture twice a day. Nearly all the work is indoors, and the weather is changing at last. The snow has melted. The sun is very warm. The rooks in the camp trees are nesting. They wake us at 5.30. We turn out for physical drill at 6.30. I have made myself fire-lighter now. We are ~~5~~ 4 non-commissioned officers in our hut and N.C.O.'s* are not supposed to do anything menial, which is hard on the other men, there being usually only one N.C.O. in a hut of 25 or 30. So to appease them I light the 2 stoves while they are still in bed, and so far the Lord has been on my side and my fires are wonderful. That is where my modesty fails, you perceive.

Yes, I knew it was a year ago you went away, and two since Tyler's Green;—and one before what? But Ledington, my dear Robert, in April, in June, in August.

It *is* warm today. We have a day with no work (but plenty to consider) and 2 of us are left in the parlour of 'The Shepherd and Dog' 2 miles from camp, a public house rather like that one at Tyler's Green or Penn. I am writing this and the other man, who is an artist, is trying to draw me.* The taproom is very noisy, but here there is only a fire and 3 billiard balls on a table and us. He is the man through whom I fell into disgrace. I haven't outlived it yet. But now there is a chance my senior may go to anther company and leave me in charge of D. The worst of it is he and I are very good pals and if we are in different companies we can't see nearly so much of one another. This means a lot because most of the men around are going to be officers soon and fresh ones will arrive and take their places and then still another set arrive.

You might have sent me Flint's address. I hardly know where to find it unless through Monro.

I heard from de la Mare lately. He has been talking to Newbolt about a pension for me. Newbolt he says isn't very hopeful.

When I was at home I picked out 40 poems and sent them to Bottomley to pick out as many as he likes to fill 15 or 20 pages.

The news nowadays is pretty good. It looks as if we could stand any battering the Germans inflict and as if we might yet give them a battering they could not stand. There is a prophecy abroad that it will be over by July 17. Helen says Why not by her birthday which is a few days earlier? She would be more pleased than I. She has had enough of the war and of comparative solitude.

Well, we had to leave the inn (being soldiers) at 2.30. We drew a panorama (you must see some some day) and got back to the usual thing, with the news that my brother has got his 2nd stripe on his sleeve, i.e. is a full corporal. These reminders that I am going to be passed over all the time don't please me, especially at the end of a soft moist warm day, the first such day since last April. But I am yours ever

Edward Thomas

To Helen

Saturday | Gidea Park | [late April 1916]

Dearest,

I too was wishing I could be with you, just because I wanted to see you and be with you. I was very much alone. Everyone was away or on duty and I had the whole day to myself except that I saw Wheatley a little in the morning and then late this afternoon, he being in a job that kept him in camp. I was free after pay at 10 for the day. I set out with a meal in my haversack for a long walk, but didn't go more than 6 miles all day. I sat down a good deal both in the fields and at an inn, and passed or was passed by the same pair of lovers 3 or 4 times. It was very pleasant too, warm and cloudy. I wrote some lines too and rewrote them. As I have the job of Battalion Orderly Corporal tomorrow I got back at 7 to clean up.

Thank you for the form, I can't fill it all up till I am home next, which I hope will be on Saturday but possibly I might have to wait till Whitsun. Unfortunately the returns I have made for the Income Tax won't prove much as they apply only to the year ending two months after I joined. But I will make the best show I can. Also I find my deposit is a good deal larger than I thought.

I have no dream girls, dearest. Don't you imagine it.

Yesterday we were at last compelled to do field engineering with the rest of the company. We have got out of it for 10 weeks or so, but in future we are always to do it. The first day was not bad as we had to do some panoramas from the trenches the battalion has made. So we were on our own. Later on we shall just have to do the ordinary trench-making. I don't mind—in fact I like—that sort of thing; but it is annoying only to work with the Company at odd times when we don't fit in. However I shall really be glad to do everything that everybody does.

Sunday

It is now 10.15 a.m. and really mostly my duties are done. I have been up 5 hours already. It is a most lovely hot day, a pity to waste the remaining 10 hours smoking about the camp. Benson has just come off guard and is trying to sleep. Nash is on guard today. Wheatley will come occasionally and say things like 'why do people want to kill one another on such a fine day?' He is really a dear. Vernon is Battalion Orderly Sergeant today. We work mostly together.

Pearce goes to Chelsea tomorrow to be smartened up by a 3 weeks drill course with the Guards. I wish I could have the same.

Now the day has nearly gone. It has been rather boring, but I got out with Benson and Wheatley on to the golf links. In fact I am sitting there now finishing this for the 6.30 post.

God bless you three | Edwy

To Robert Frost

Hare Hall Camp | 21 May 1916

My dear Robert,

This last letter of yours (dated May 1) with the poem 'Not to keep' mends all, though it was opened (and untouched) by the censor. I hadn't been able to write to you for some weeks simply because I didn't know where to join on. I began to fear the censor had been a Hodgson patriot and found something rotten in me or my verses. However, all's well—we don't care a b—do we? to use 2 phrases which an Irishman in our hut used to make seem so witty. He had a face like an archaic Greek god's that people had trodden on for 1000 years. Now he has gone to France to see if he can still be witty.

'Not to keep' is all right. It is no disadvantage to you to be 40. Of course one would prefer to be able to run a mile in 5 minutes and jump a spiked fence, but actually I find less to grumble at out loud than 10 years ago: I suppose I am more bent on making the best of what I have got instead of airing the fact that I deserve so much more. Yet I feel old—I felt old seeing Bottomley's 'Lear'.* Gibson's 'Hoofs', and Rupert Brooke's 'Lithuania', yesterday afternoon. Bottomley's play, for example. It was all the result of thinking, not an explanation for what might very likely be a fact. He had to make Goneril run a knife through a rabbit's eyes. Well, I firmly believe that if he had imagination he would have kept such a thing dark supposing he could go the length of imagining it. As it was, it sounded just a thought out cruelty, worse far than cruelty itself with passion behind it. Of course he pretended there was passion. There wasn't. Brooke was better though he was only painting with Russian paints. I quite admired the simple souls who couldn't help laughing.—I mean I felt old because I believed I saw how it was done though I don't suppose I could do it myself as well or better if at all.

Nobody recognises me now. Sturge Moore, E. Marsh, and R. C. Trevelyan stood a yard off and I didn't trouble to awake them to stupid recognition. Bottomley and his wife I just had a word with. I was with a young artist named Paul Nash who has just joined us as a map reader. He is a change from the 2 schoolmasters I see most of . . . He is wonderful at finding birds' nests. There is another artist, too, aged 24, a Welshman, absolutely a perfect Welshman, kind, simple, yet all extremes and rather unreal and incredible except in his admirations—he admires his wife and Rembrandt for example. I am really lucky to have such a crowd of people always round and these 2 or 3 nearer: you might guess from 'Home' how much nearer.

Though I am Corporal P. E. Thomas I am not growing so efficient as all that. We don't get a chance. We idle away for days together for lack of organisation. Shall I copy out the speech our captain made to the men who were leaving us to go to be finished at the cadet school? 'Pay attention. Stand easy. I just want to say a few words to you men who are going to the school. I wish you all success. I hope you won't get into any trouble at all. Take care to mind your Ps and Qs, and do everything top-hole'. He is a kind huge man with no memory, very fond of the country. The other day in the fields he said 'Company attention! Oh, look at that rabbit'. I wish we could win a little sooner. Then I could come and see you barn-storming. Also I could perhaps begin to earn some money. They are going to relieve some soldiers to the extent of £2 a week, but only those who joined *after* last August 15. So I don't count. They had to put some limit. Perhaps they thought the waiters had more to give up. Or they want to encourage the last. Don't you worry, though, about money. Something may happen.

A pension or grant is still just possible, tho de la Mare says—improbable:—I am not old enough is his explanation. Also I may possibly get a job which will take me out into the fighting line yet not with the worst risks and give me more money—as an officer. Of course anything may happen now. Things are continually being shaken up and one drops through a hole or not. You make sure of your farm. If I did want money I would ask you, but I have £100 of War Loan left.

Yes, I wear 2 stripes or chevrons on my upper arm now—not on the skin, but the sleeve.

Haines writes occasionally with news of the great and lately a persuasion to review Doughty's last, which I did. I can't get to see him. He is too far for my short leaves. I go home every time. Mervyn was there last time. He hasn't got on with Hodson and we are all uncertain what to do. I am thinking of asking acquaintances in Wales if he could go into steel works there. He isn't much changed and still shows only his apathy. The others are well. As I was walking home with Helen and Baba last week, Baba asked whether Mrs. —'s baby was a boy or a girl? 'A boy'. 'Everyone has boys'. But I said boys were wanted to replace the dead. 'You don't think I haven't heard that before, my lad, do you?' she said to me. She is acquisitive and not generous, but she gets her own way without annoying much. I have some new songs for her from camp, and rather more for you.

Goodbye and my love to all of you. Elinor is well, isn't she? Don't forget to send any photographs you have of all or any of you and the farm ground.

Yours ever | Edward Thomas

You should have seen Monro in the vestibule of the theatre selling Bottomley's 'Lear', standing up straight and just pursuing the women with the whites of his eyes.

To Robert Frost

13 Rusham Road | Balham | London SW | 9 September 1916

My dear Robert,

Three days ago came your letter dated August 15. So I have still a hope that mine (with some M.S.) sent about the end of July reached you just after you wrote. I have not been a good letter writer. But you know the reason. I have had no peace of mind since May. I have been busier and I have had more to think about. Now I have been 2 weeks in the Artillery learning about guns and wearing spurs &c. I think when I wrote I was down with vaccination. And I still am. I suppose it is the vaccination. I was run down. I was not careful. I got a poisoned hand. I am still poor and feeble and it is very nearly all I can do to keep on with the work here, tho it is not hard physically. I learn to aim at invisible targets, to know the parts of a gun, the gun drill &c., the telephone by which we shall communicate, the work of an observation officer who watches the result of his battery's fire &c.

Mervyn has started in lodgings at Walthamstow and is cheerful about it. Bronwen is with an aunt a few miles from here. Baba is at Steep with the John Freemans' who have our cottage there. Helen is walking with one of her sisters up in the Lake district. Meanwhile we are supposed to be moving to our new cottage in a week or two. I think there will be some delay. Helen runs away so comfortably from affairs, and I am not free to manage them now.

I see a few people now I am in barracks in London. [R. A.] Scott-James is a cadet with me. The Farjeons are not far off. Nor is Davies, but I never see him. Ellis and John Freeman I have seen. Garnett is still to see. We have missed one another a number of times since I enlisted.

I am likely to be at this preliminary training a month yet. It might only be 2 weeks but I am slow at it and likely not to go with the first batch to Wiltshire where we do more advanced work. I might get my commission next month. More likely it will be later. There is so much to learn and we are a big crowd with rather few instructors. Many of the men are more apt than I am—engineers, surveyors, schoolmasters. It is not like camp life. I make no friends. We are treated rather better and have fewer duties and responsibilities, fewer demands on one another, than in camp. The result is I am rather impatient to go out and be shot at. That is all I want, to do something if I am discovered to be any use, but in any case to be made to run risks, to be put through it. I have been saying to myself lately that I don't really care a fig what happens. But perhaps I do.—I am cut off. All the anchors are up. I have no friends now. Two I had in camp, but one is just going out to France and the other is still in camp and is not likely to come my way for some time; and both are 12 years younger than I am, and away from camp not likely to be so much like friends. I have a cold. I have no strength. So that beginning all over again comes harder.

I may go and see Haines some week end, but I don't feel equal to anything but idling here at my Mother's for 24 hours at the week ends. My mother was operated on for cataract 6 weeks ago and they seem to think she will not get her sight back in that eye.

This is dismal reading. But I don't want money. Didn't I tell you the Government had been persuaded to grant me £300? They would not give me a pension. That £300 might last till the end of the war. But those 50 faggots* didn't. We took to cooking with them in the Summer out of doors and that spoilt my verses on the subject so far as they were a prophecy. It is no use me saying how much I wish I were destined to come and live at your farm. You know I think of it often. But of course the future is less explorable than usual and I don't take it (the future) quite seriously. I find myself thinking as if there wasn't going to be no future. This isn't perversity. I say I find myself doing so. On the other hand it may be I am just as wrong as when I wrote about those 50 faggots. I thought then that one simply had to wait a very long time. I wonder is it *pleasanter* to be Rupert Brookish. Anyhow it is impossible, and I suppose I enjoy this frame of mind as much as I can enjoy anything (beyond my dinner) at present.

Monday the 11th

This frame of mind is lasting too long. The fact is—my cold is worse and I am sick at not being really equal to my work. Once I get into the country I shall be all right.

I don't believe I can do much yet at 'The Old Cloak'.* You can't imagine the degree of my disinclination for books. Sometimes I say I will read Shakespeare's sonnets again and I do, or half do, but never more than that. I should love to do it with you. I thought of what love poems could go in—could Burns's 'Whistle and I'll come to you, my lad'? There are the songs in the very earliest Elizabethan dramatists. There's a deal of Chaucer, Shakespeare, Cowper, Wordsworth and the ballads: some Crabbe: one poem apiece out of Prior and several minor 18th Century people: a few of Blake's. But I daren't begin to look at books: I must keep all my *conscious attention* for my work.

Mervyn looked none the worse yesterday for his 9 hours a day standing up in the factory. He is in lodgings till we make our move.

I have just been seeing off one of the 2 men I knew best at the Artists. He is just getting his commission and will be out long before me. I had some time to spare and called for Davies but he was out. He is only ½ a mile away. He is bringing out a big selection of his poems and is looking for a great man to do the introduction.

A small new publisher* I know is thinking of publishing my verses, of course under the name of Edward Eastaway, and I believe 2 are to be included in a new anthology of 'cheerful' poems at the Oxford press which Smith has a hand in. He is in town but I haven't met him yet.

Goodbye and try to imagine me more like a soldier than this letter sounds. My love to you all and I hope Carol is much better.

Yours ever | Edward Thomas

Use this London address till you know the new one, not Steep any more.

To J. W. Haines

13 Rusham Road | Balham | London SW | 15 September 1916

My dear Haines,

I may go to Trowbridge on Friday. Then perhaps I get over to you. From all I hear about the barracks there I shall be glad to escape, but I don't know yet what the leave amounts to. I will write again. Up to now I have been so unwell with a cold following on a very rundown condition after vaccination that I have made no use of my weekends.

I like reading over your comments on my verses. 'Roads' I think one of the best. Helen of the Roads is simply a Welsh Goddess connected with Roads. Many of the Roman Roads in Wales are called 'Sarn Helen' or Helen's Causeway. She comes in the Dream of Maxen in the Mabinogion. Then I like the 'Unknown' and refuse to believe it is clever, tho I admit it is a bit quicker than the rest. 'After You Speak' I believe is alright and 'The Weasel'. Nobody has cared much for 'The Ash Grove'. 'How at once should I know' is perhaps natural history. The poems to the children are I hope among the best. I wonder how they will look in a book? There is a chance of their appearing before very long. Also a fair selection is to appear in Trevelyan's 'Annual' (Constable).

Wilfrid Childe I seem to remember in the Oxford Poems of 1910–1912, or whatever it was. But I don't remember his books at all. I don't see any books new or old now.

I shall be glad to get out of London though I can see friends there. I am going down to Steep now with my wife—the first bit of the country I have seen it will be since I left Romford a month ago.

The new work is difficult, especially as I am unfit and the instuctors are bad [improvised]. We have 7 weeks more at Trowbridge and then may be gazetted. I want to go out badly now.

I heard from Frost at last. He has been reading publically for a fund in aid of the wounded in France. He has been writing but did not send anything. He said nothing about his family. Carol has been ill I know. It was a more cheerful letter than I have had.

My love to you all three,

Yours ever | Edward Thomas

To Robert Frost

High Beech nr. Loughton Essex | 19 October 1916

My dear Robert,

This morning the postman brought your letter of September 28. I am home helping to get things straight in our new cottage. It is right alone in the forest among beech trees and fern and deer, though it only costs 10d. to reach London. Luckily I had a week's leave thrust on me just at the time when I could be of some use. We have had fine weather, too, luckily and have had some short walks, Helen, Bronwen and I—Mervyn being still in lodgings 6 miles off, and Baba with an aunt, waiting till the house is ready for them.

Since I wrote last I have been shifted to Trowbridge Artillery Barracks and have had 3 weeks hard work there. I am waiting for the result of my 2nd examination. If I pass, I shall be an officer in another month. My going out depends on whether they are in great need of men when I am ready, also on my passing the final medical test. If I go it seems likely it will be to a not very big gun, so that I shall be far enough up to see everything. There may be a week's leave before that and there may not, in any case not enough to come to see you even if that were allowed, which I doubt. If you were to come over here I don't think you would meet much annoyance, if any. People say things you would not like to hear, but the chances are a hundred to one you would not hear them. There is certainly no strong feeling. What feeling there is only unlucky chance or your own putting it to the test could bring out. I don't like to think of your coming and my not being free to see you. I have short week ends of 24 hours—giving me less than 24 hours at home. In a month's time I may have a number of days of freedom, but I can count on nothing.

I have just written the 2nd thing* since I left London a month ago. If I can type the 2 you shall see them. I am wondering if any of these last few sets of verses have pleased you at all.—Haines liked some I showed him. I was there for 24 hours a fortnight ago and had a walk up Cooper's Hill and picked blackberries. He was the same as ever, and relieved at his (apparently final) exemption. I think he was going to write to you then. He showed me 'Hyla Brook' and another piece of yours which I enjoyed very much. I like nearly everything of yours better at a 2nd reading and best after that. Truce.

About my collection of verses, the publisher remains silent a month. I wrote off at once today to ask whether he could decide and if he will publish I will do my best to hunt up duplicates and send them out to you in good time for a possible American publisher. I shall be pleased if you succeed and not feel it a scrap if you don't. As if I could refuse to give you a chance of doing me good!

It would take me too long to be sure what I think of Rupert. I can tell you this—that I received £3 for his first 'Poems' the other day and £2 for 'New Numbers' (because of him). So I can't think entirely ill of him. No. I don't think ill of him. I think he succeeded in being youthful and yet intelligible and interesting (not only pathologically) more than most poets since Shelley. But thought gave him (and me) indigestion. He couldn't mix his thought or the result of it with his feeling. He could only think about his feeling. Radically, I think he lacked power of expression. He was a rhetorician, dressing things up better than they needed. And I suspect he knew too well both what he was after and what he achieved. I think perhaps a man ought to be capable of always being surprised on being confronted with what he really is—as I am nowadays when I confront a full size mirror in a good light instead of a cracked bit of one in a dark barrack room. Scores of men, by the way, shave outside the window, just looking at the glass with the dawn behind them. My disguises increase, what with spurs on my heels and hair on my upper lip.

Bronwen is at my elbow reading 'A Girl of the Limberlost'. Garnett, whom I saw yesterday, for the first time since I enlisted, was praising 'The Spoon River Anthology'. Can he be right? I only glanced at it once, and I concluded that it must be liked for the things *written about* in it, not for what it expressed. Isn't it done too much on purpose?

Noyes is reciting to the public, not to a drawing room. He was too valuable to be made a soldier. Monro has gone off to camp somewhere, but not so Miss . . . aski* [*sic*]

You would like one of our sergeant-major instructors who asked a man coiling a rope the wrong way—from right to left—'Were you a snake-charmer before you joined?' We have some ripe regular specimens at the barracks. By the way, have you had any news of Chandler? I asked Haines, but he didn't know. Flint, I suppose, has been gathered up by now.

Now I will try to type those verses. Goodbye. Helen and Bronwen and I send you all our love. Bronwen, by the way, wrote to Irma in August, addressing her at Bethlehem. I wonder with what luck.

Yours ever | Edward Thomas

To Helen

13 Rusham Road | Balham SW | 20 October 1916

Dearest,

Here are the verses which should make up pretty well, with those I put in the oak chest, the set Ingpen* has. If they don't, put together, make up the same set; the only thing is to take out of Ingpen's set those which are not in yours, unless you can find them in the pink case. Then send yours to Frost, registering them. Or else send Ingpen's to Frost, taking careful note of what are missing from yours, so that I can replace them later. That is the better plan, I think. Remember, of course, to cut out anything that is on Gordon's list.* If there is anything in *my* set that is *not* in Ingpen's, add it to Ingpen's and make a note of it as something to be added to the duplicate before it goes to Ingpen for publication. That is, if Ingpen is to publish. *Don't send to Frost before I tell you that the thing is settled.*

Mother is better still. She tells me Bronwen has a ring, so I will simply combine with you if you are getting her something useful. I can't get anything in Trowbridge beyond an Artillery badge. I got a good haversack, so don't you worry. If you get a pipe, get it at the Stores. One of the dark red French briars would be the best, and don't think of paying more than 5/– or 6/–. It should not be mounted.

It is late now. All is well—if only I have got through the exam. Goodbye

Edwy

I hope my letter card and the £1 enclosed in it reached you. It was a risky thing to do.

A note from Mary says Baba is very well.* They have been expecting you or a letter.

To Robert Frost

High Beech | 31 December 1916

My dear Robert,

I had your letter and your poem 'France, France'* yesterday. I like the poem very much, because it betrays exactly what you *would* say and what you feel about saying that much. It expresses just those hesitations you or I would have at asking others to act as we think it is their cue to act. Well, I am soon going to know more about it. I am not at home as the address suggests, but am on the eve of a whole week's continuous shooting. It begins tomorrow. Then at the end of the week or soon after I shall have my last leave. After all we are going to have smaller guns than we thought and we shall be nearer the front line a good bit and are beginning to make insincere jokes about observing from the front line which of course we shall have to do. I think I told you we were a quite mixed crowd of officers in this battery. As soon as we begin to depend on one another we shall no doubt make the best of one another. I am getting on, I think, better than when I was in my pupilage. The 2 senior officers have been out before. Four of us are new. I am 3 years older than the Commanding Officer and twice as old as the youngest. I mustn't say much more.

I was home for Christmas by an unexpected piece of luck. We were very happy with housework and wood gathering in the forest and a few walks. We had snow and sunshine on Christmas day. Mervyn's holiday coincided with mine. Some of the time I spent at my Mother's house and in London buying the remainder of my things for the front. I am very well provided.

I wish I had your book.* Haines has, but I don't want to borrow his. Mine still hasn't been fixed up. I wonder have you had your duplicate of the M.S. which I sent over a month ago? It looks now as if I should not see the proofs. Bottomley or John Freeman will do it for me.

It is nearly all work here now and in the evenings, if I haven't something to do with my maps for reading, I am either out walking or indoors talking. When I am alone—as I am during the evening just now because the officer who shares my room is away—I hardly know what to do. I can't write now and still less can I read. I have rhymed but I have burnt my rhymes and feel proud of it. Only on Saturday and Sunday have we a chance of walking in daylight. Twice I have seen Conrad who lives 12 miles away. But now we can't travel by train without special reasons. I tried to begin 'The Shaving of Shagpat' just now, but could not get past the 3rd page. I could read Frost, I think. Send me another letter, though I expect it will find me over the sea. Goodbye all, and my love.

Yours ever | Edward Thomas

To his parents

Dainville | 10 February 1917

Dear Father and Mother,

We have reached our position. It has been by such easy stages that now the real thing is no worse than Codford. Our actual billets are a mile from the guns and they are really comfortable and warm. My servant, a country carpenter from Oxford, is very handy and zealous and we have—or I have—nothing to complain of. I have just had a day in the trenches looking from Observation Posts and examining the country with map, compass and field-glass. I found the work interesting and I could tumble to it easily. Nor did I mind being in dangerous places. In fact I just had a good day in beautiful cold weather and was privately very pleased to have done my first day of the real thing.

We are on a main road at the edge of a village on fairly high ground close to a cathedral town. We are being shelled, but not in very great danger. The noise of shells arriving (or departing from our own batteries) does not trouble me and I am really contented with everything except the entire absence of letters. So far no letters have reached 244 Battery since it left Codford. Now that we are settled we ought to get them soon.

I am sorry to say the men are never warm at night and nothing can be done to improve their condition. Also the food is not very abundant and is practically just meat and bread and tea. They say everything at present is sacrificed to ammunition. Even bread is scarce and the men have mostly hard biscuit—which suits me personally very well. The other officers mostly want a lot of extras and unfortunately the expense is borne equally by all.

There is nothing I want except that I wish you would order *The Times* to be sent to '244 Siege Battery, B.E.F., France'. If you do send a parcel please include tracing paper or better still some blue tracing linen.

If you send any eatables I should like cake and butter.

All is well. This part of the line is not very busy at present—chiefly artillery work. I saw only one dead man, killed by a sniper to-day. The infantry are doing nothing.

I wish I knew you were all well. My love to every one

Edwy

To Robert Frost

244 Siege Battery BEF France | 11 February 1917 and a Sunday they tell me

My dear Robert,

I left England a fortnight ago and have now crawled with the battery up to our position. I can't tell you where it is, but we are well up in high open country. We are on a great main road in a farmhouse facing the enemy who are about 2 miles away, so that their shells rattle our windows but so far only fall a little behind us or to one side. It is near the end of a 3 week's frost. The country is covered with snow which silences everything but the guns. We have slept—chiefly in uncomfortable places till now. Here we lack nothing except letters from home. It takes some time before a new unit begins to receive its letters. I have enjoyed it very nearly all. Except shaving in a freezing tent. I don't think I really knew what travel was like till we left England.

Yesterday, our 2nd day, I spent in the trenches examining some observation posts to see what could be seen of the enemy from them. It was really the best day I have had since I began. We had some shells very near us, but were not sniped at. I could see the German lines very clear but not a movement anywhere, nothing but posts sticking out of the snow with barbed wire, bare trees broken and dead and half ruined houses. The only living men we met at bends in trenches, eating or carrying food or smoking. One dead man lay under a railway arch so stiff and neat (with a covering of sacking) that I only slowly remembered he was dead. I got back, tired and warm and red. I hope I shall never enjoy anything less. But I shall. Times are comparatively quiet just here. We shall be busy soon and we shall not be alone. I am now just off with a working party to prepare our Gun positions which are at the edge of a cathedral town a mile or two along the road we look out on. We are to fight in an orchard there in sight of the cathedral.

It is night now and cold again, Machine guns rattle and guns go 'crump' in front of us. Inside a gramophone plays the rottenest songs imaginable, jaunty unreal dirty things. We get on well enough but we are a rum company. There is a Scotch philosopher,* an impossible unmilitary creature who looks far more dismal than he really can be—I like him to talk to, but he is too glaringly timid and apologetic and helpless to live with. The others are all commonplace people under 26 years old who are never serious and could not bear anyone else to be serious. We just have to be dirty together. I also cannot be sincere with them. Two are boys of 19 and make me think of the boys I might have had for company. One of the two aged about 24 is rather a fine specimen of the old English soldiers, always bright and smart and capable, crude but goodhearted and frivolous and yet thorough at their work. He has been 10 years in the army. All his talk is in sort of proverbs or cant sayings and bits of comic songs, coarse metaphors—practically all quotations.

But I am seldom really tired of them. I suppose I am getting to like what they are, and their lack of seriousness is no deception and is just their method of expression.

I used to read some of the Sonnets while we were at Havre, but not on these last few days of travel. 'Mountain Interval' also is waiting.

My love to you all,

Yours ever | (2/Lt) Edward Thomas

To his parents

Dainville | 13 February 1917

Dear Father and Mother,

This is only a note written partly because I have nothing to do this morning—so far as I know yet—and I have a slight chill (everyone else has already had it) and do not feel inclined to go out. It is very fine though. The thaw has begun without the rain which would have infallibly come with it in England. I suppose we may see something green soon besides the artificial overhead covering for the guns which they have made green even in winter for some reason or other.

Since I told you I had been out on a trench reconnaissance we have had little to do except superintend the digging which prepares for taking up our new position. But the Captain has just said we may be going to shoot this afternoon and certainly tomorrow. This does not mean we are in our position but that we have temporarily taken over from another battery just behind our billets and are going to work their guns till further notice.

Our own guns and stores, as a matter of fact, have not come on to us yet, and apparently they are not going to be ours any longer but to go to the battery we replace, the worst of it is that half my own private kit is with the stores and it may be a very long time before we receive it. So could you also send me a little mending wool for my socks? My servant washes for me and can mend too and I can therefore do with less underclothing than I anticipated.

We thought to move to-day but this latest news that we fire with another battery's guns probably means that we stay on in these billets for a time. The new position is only a mile or so away and half the men are billeted near by to be near their work.

I like this country, open and rolling, with villages up on the slopes above the streams—like the one behind us with its church spire smashed but otherwise not badly damaged. The villages closer up to the trenches of course are all battered about and only a few old natives hang on in their homes.

My hands are all burning and chapped, I suspect through wearing gloves, which I never used to do. If you could send me something to rub on them it would be a boon.

I sleep and live in a biggish room with whitewashd walls, tiled floor and a window looking on the road, and a stove and a mirror opposite the door. Four of us sleep here and all eat here—the other two sleep in a dug-out just over the road. We have a dirty kitchen adjoining where our cook prepares good but monotonous meals. The walls are hung with our field-glasses, helmets, water-bottles, towels, sticks, and coats when we are indoors; and round the walls stand our boots, suit-cases, washing things and some stores, also two bombs left behind by a trench mortar battery. The mirror and stove are quite genteel. Otherwise things are a bit grimy. Over the door remains a photographed group of old French people in their best clothes—the family occupies the rest of the house but is almost invisible. The men are in a barn behind. Also on the walls hang our orders and reports of operations from H.Q. We have one small round table for eating, writing and map work. At this moment—nearly 11 a.m.—the crumbs from breakfast remain mixed with a spoon and fork. One other officer is writing like me, the rest are out. Now the servant has come in to clear the crumbs. I suppose my thinking about them set him moving towards them.

The water from the well is quite good for drinking. We have white wine occasionally at 1fr.50c. a bottle. I am in charge of the men and mess accounts, but not having our mess kit here things are a bit hand to mouth so far.

There was a great cannonade on the Ancre, I should think, away to the south of us, the night before last, but I expect you know more about what it means than we do. We see papers irregularly and hardly look at the dates on them.

I wonder if you would mind keeping my letters, so that I might some day, if I wished, use them as a supplement to my diary?*

Give my love to my brothers and everyone.

Ever your loving son | Edwy

To Eleanor Farjeon

Dainville | 13 February 1917

My dear Eleanor,

This is my idlest morning. It is sunny and mild, but I have got the chill that everyone has had in turn and I shall not go out till I must, which will probably be this afternoon, for we have a shoot on then. My servant is a gem. He is a carpenter from Oxford named Taylor, rather slow but extraordinarily good-humoured, and thoughtful and ingenious. He washes and darns for me and pillages wood to keep our stove going and in between he keeps up a slow stream of nice rustic remarks. He won't lose anything if he can help it. He is the most devoted thing I have met since we lost our dog. He mutters 'They put upon good nature, don't they, Sir' but though I tell him not to listen to anyone but me he goes on being put upon without complaint. This is a fine hilly country with trees only on the roads and in a few woods. The villages lie along the slopes above the streams, with tiled roofs and mud in brick walls, and churches with towers and short spires something like Sussex, but often shell-bitten. There are hardly any hedges. You see nothing yet but snow and field telephone posts and barbed wire entanglements. No cattle out, no sheep. Then the straight main road lined with young trees leads past our window to the town and the cathedral. There we are to be in an orchard on the outskirts. Looking out of the window we see our dug-outs just across the road, beyond that a short slope of snow and posts and the trees lining a road on another hill a mile off. It is a somewhat dangerous position, but all the shells fall fairly well behind us, being aimed at a battery some hundreds of yards away. They had one of their guns hit yesterday, but the men were all in cover and no one was hurt. You could bury several horses in the shell holes. It is not what is called a healthy spot, but as these buildings are isolated they are hardly worth making a target of and only an accident will demolish them. It is nice to have sun without rain, but it would not matter which the weather was if I had no chill and my boots were a good old pair that didn't make me feel as if my feet were artificial wood. There is not much traffic on the road, but small parties do use it and despatch riders and a farm cart or two go along. I haven't had the curiosity to go into town yet and have only seen the cathedral with fieldglasses. Partly it is the lack of perfectly comfortable boots. Partly, of course, one does not stroll here, but only moves with an object. Do you know I have not had a letter—nor has anyone—since leaving England, so that I am more egotistic than usual, as I am the only person that I really know exists, apart from these strangers round me. We are strangers who just talk insincerely and humorously when we are not talking shop. But we have come to a modus vivendi. T[horburn] and I get on when it is pure talk between us two, but he is intolerable to live with, being dismal, timid and clumsy. I should like to know you were well and what you were doing. I suppose letters will begin some day. And how are your nieces, and do you ever see Maitland? I have to admit I have joined the majority against T—. He is the most unpleasant presence imaginable in our midst. He was born with the most dismal face and voice ever was, and no doubt he is not happy in this frivolous coarse crowd. But then he has never mixed with men and never learns day by day and is never helpful except with a horrible suffering sad look and manner as if this were the last day. We can perhaps forgive it but we can't forget it. He hurts us and we hurt him—only his hurting us is no satisfaction to him as our hurting him is to us. I used to think I was dismal till now.—And perhaps I sound like it still, so I will be off. In fact I have just found it is 12 and not 11, I have to take a party along at 12.30.

Yours ever | Edward Thomas

To Helen

Arras | 27 February 1917

Dearest,

Only a word now. It is a fine sunny morning, but so was yesterday and they made full use of it. The guns here covered an infantry raid and you could not hear a word for over an hour. Then German prisoners began to arrive. Later on hostile shells began to arrive, but they were hardly so alarming as they didn't make anything like the same din. In the afternoon I had to go out to see if a certain position was visible to the enemy. This was the first time I was really under fire. About four shells burst 150 yards away, little ones and then in the street fell a shower of machine gun bullets. I confess I felt shy, but I went on with my field glass and compass as far as possible as if nothing had happened. This makes the heart beat but no more than if I were going to pay a call on a stranger.

I try to console myself by reflecting that you cannot escape either by running or by standing still. There is no safe place and consequently why worry? And I don't worry. What did disturb me was an English 18 pounder firing when I had only gone 3 yards past the muzzle. They do that sort of thing. The order comes to fire and they fire, damn them. But I slept very well last night. This morning is quiet again, though it is beautifully fine.

I haven't settled to my fate here yet. I shall wait for a good opportunity of letting the Colonel know I want to get back.

They are trying to drive an English plane back with shrapnel just overhead. It looks dangerous but neither the Huns nor we hit a plane once in 10,000 rounds, I believe.

I've nothing to do this morning except try to settle a billeting question for 244. I shall walk up there this afternoon or evening if I can. It is several days since I heard from you. I have to borrow an envelope now, but of course I shall buy some when I think of it—don't you get them. A writing block was really a thing I need not have sent for.

244 is still not fixed in its own position. Half are preparing it, the other half firing with another battery's guns.

They are a nice lot of officers here, better than 244's, only I being temporary or uncertain I don't get on as well as if I were going (for all I know) to remain. Still no thrushes singing here, only chaffinches.

I've rather a rotten servant here, never has hot water, has a watch that is sometimes half an hour wrong, and never understands anything I say.

I have only once heard from Mother. Her parcel has not arrived. I wonder does she worry much. I hope not.

You have had Eleanor there by this time and lost her too. But it becomes harder for me to think about things at home and somehow, although this life does not absorb me, I think, yet, I can't think of anything else. I don't hanker after anything I don't miss anything. I am not even conscious of waiting. I am just quietly in exile, a sort of half or quarter man—at Romford I was half or *three* quarter man. Only sometimes I hear the things I really care for, far off as if at the end of a telephone. What I really should like is more hard physical exercise. I am rather often bored though and for fairly long periods. I am rather like a dog doing what it doesn't want to do—as Belloc said of me years ago when I was going about with him on various errands of his before we could settle down to lunch together. The fact is it is a sort of interval in reality, a protracted railway waiting room. Yet of course not always merely that.

I won't post this today.

I have just walked up to 244 and found no one in but letters from you and Irene both written after she had been to see you. I don't think I will write much more. I have just seen an English plane shot down and set afire by a German; another fell near here almost at the same time and also one yesterday. The machine gun bullets came down and cut a telephone wire close by. It has turned dull and chilly and I feel damnably like early spring. The pilot of the plane managed to right it soon and came down in a spiral, though flopping—I did not go to see his fate—he was well within our lines, so was the other.

I hope Mervyn will join an OTC. It could be a good thing in many ways. The war isn't over yet even if the Germans are evacuating some dirty ground, and Mervyn would be much more likely to get a commission if he had been to an OTC.

But I am depressed. Lots of food and too little exercise and spring. Tea will do me good and they will make some soon, if the others don't come in.

We were sitting round the fire this evening talking about the way things are done in the Army, and I was saying we should suddenly have to signal (?) important orders to the batteries to fire instead of preparing them for probable targets—when in comes an urgent message ordering 244 and also another battery we know nothing about to open fire tomorrow. Good Lord, I hope we win the war. It will prove God is on our side.

There was a good deal of shelling at dinner and after which we kept out with talk and gramophone—

But now the rum is being opened. I have had a good talk with Berrington—he has just had a batch of *New Ages*:. All is well really.

All and always yours | Edwy

To Eleanor Farjeon

Arras | March 1 | St. David's Day 1917

My dear Eleanor,

The ginger came. All of 244 had a good dip into it and there was still some left in the tin. It was very good and it was still more good of you to send it. Thank you. Next day Helen wrote to say you were really coming to High Beech at last. I am expecting to hear now that you did. Well, I expect to return to 244 in a day or two. They know I don't want to stay here and a successor is being interviewed today, so that I shall soon cease to be a glorified lackey or humble adjutant to an old Indian colonel perplexed in the extreme. It has been a useful experience. I have got used to the telephone and I have seen how things are done and not done at Headquarters. Incidentally too I have been in the midst of quite a noisy artillery give and take. You can't imagine the noise this makes in a city. I don't pretend to like it. Sometimes I found myself fancying that if only the enemy pointed the gun like this —— instead of like this —— he would land a shell on the dinner table and send us to a quieter place. However he didn't. 244 is just going into action with its own guns and I wish I were there. Soon I believe I shall be. I haven't heard of your R.F.C. man Haslam yet. The R.F.C. was unlucky here 2 days ago. They had 4 planes brought down and officers killed. I saw 2 of them, one with the tank burning white as it flopped down. The 'old Hun' as the Colonel always calls him is 'confoundedly cheeky' with his planes in these parts. We are wondering now if the enemy is going to retire from this front. It will be strange walking about in a ghostly village* which was the first I saw of the enemy's ground, a silent still village of ruined houses and closegrown tall trees stark and dark lining a road above the trenches. It was worse than any deserted brickworks or mine. It looked in another world from ours, even from the scarred world in which I stood. In a curious way its very name now always calls up the thing I saw and the way I felt as I saw it. The name resembles a name in Malory, especially in its English pronunciation and this also gives a certain tone to the effect it had. I see it lining the brow of a gradual hill halfway up which is the English line with the German above it. The houses and trees dense and then to right and left only trees growing thinner till at last the ridge sweeping away is bare for some miles. But this is E.T.'s vein. Goodbye. Keep well and write soon.

Yours ever | Edward Thomas

To Robert Frost

Arras | 6 March 1917

My dear Robert,

I still don't hear from you, but I had better write when I can. One never knows. I have now been living 2 weeks in a city that is only 2400 yds from the enemy, is shelled every day and night and is likely to be heavily bombarded some day. Of course the number of shells that fall is larger than the number of casualties although the place is crowded and falling masonry helps the shells, but this does not really appeal to anything but the brains that may be knocked out by them. Nor is it consoling to know that the enemy has put shells into the orchard where the battery is and all round it without injuring anybody. However it may console those who are not out here.

For these 2 weeks I have been detached from my battery to work at headquarters, which has meant getting to know something of how battle is conducted, and also going about with maps and visiting observation posts, some of which give a view of No Man's Land like a broad river very clear and close. We went out yesterday morning to see the Gordons cross to raid the enemy but it was snowing and we only saw snow and something moving and countless shell bursts beyond. Our artillery made a roof over our heads of shells singing and shuffling along in shoals.—I return to the battery, a mile away, very soon now.

We are having many fine days, bright and warm even at times, and we begin to see larks as well as aeroplanes. I wish we did not see so many of the enemy's. Every clear day we are continually hearing the whistle blowing the alarm. It incenses the artillery very much as the planes spot us and then tell their batteries how to hit us.

I have not a great deal to do as a rule. Long hours of waiting, nothing that has to be done and yet not free to do what I want, in fact not consciously wanting anything except, I suppose, the end. Wisdom perhaps trickles in, perhaps not. There is nobody I like much, that is the worst of it. I don't want friends. I don't think I should like to have friends out here. I am sure I shouldn't. But I want companions and I hardly expect to find them. This may not be final. There are plenty of likable people. There is also one very intelligent man here, the Signalling Officer, an architect before the war, a hard clever pungent fellow who knows the New Age, Georgian Poetry (and doesn't like it) &c. He didn't seem to know 'Mountain Interval' or the author.

A letter from de la Mare came yesterday. So he has seen you. He says you don't look as well as you ought to. Whatever he said would be little or nothing, so I needn't complain that he said nothing. He said he wished we could have a talk. Fancy being polite to me out here. Well, there is nothing I want to forget so far. Is that right?

I have time to spare but I can't talk. You don't answer, and I am inhibiting introspection except when I wake up and hear the shelling and wonder whether I ought to move my bed away from the window to the inner side where there is more masonry—more to resist and more to fall on me. But it is no use thinking like this. I am half awake when I do. Besides I have hardly learnt yet to distinguish between shells going out and shells coming in—my worst alarm was really shells going out. So far it excites but doesn't disturb, or at any rate doesn't upset and unfit.

I hear my book* is coming out soon. Did the duplicate verses ever reach you? You have never said so. But don't think I mind. I should like to be a poet, just as I should like to live, but I know as much about my chances in either case, and I don't really trouble about either. Only I want to come back more or less complete. Goodbye. My dearest love to you all.

Yours ever | Edward Thomas

To Walter de la Mare

Group 35 Heavy Artillery | Arras | 9 March 1917

My dear de la Mare,

I expect you had a letter from me soon after you wrote. At least I posted one about 3 weeks ago. Letters take a long time coming, always a week. I will write to you now in case I have less time or no time later, which is very possible. I am just moving back to my Battery after nearly 3 weeks at the Heavy Artillery Group head quarters, which has been rather an idle time but has shown me quite as much as I want to see of the way things are run. It has been idle but not exactly snug as we are only 2400 yards from the Hun and in a city which he shells daily. I think I shall prefer being shelled in a position where we are doing something direct in retaliation and not just map work. We are in a big rather pretentious modern house, with only one shell hole in it. The town hall and cathedral are all holes. It is cold, because it is big and because fuel is very scarce. I shiver all day indoors, but luckily what work I do is often out of doors and though I can't *feel* that my chances of escape are very good I contrive to enjoy many things. I think I enjoy the people least of all. But that may be cleared up when the Z arrives, whenever that is to be. The Battery is in an orchard outside the town. We may see the apple blossom, but I doubt that. Nobody is very hopeful. I think myself that things may go on at this rate for more than a year. The rate may be changed, but not if the Hun can help it and his retirement looks very inconvenient in every way.

I wish you had said more about Frost.* One is absolutely friendless here. Everybody has something to conceal and he does so by pretending to be like everybody else. All the talk is shop or worse. It is all tedious and uncomfortable except at odd moments. But then so is life anywhere, I suppose. It is all very different from the newspapers, and very much like what one would expect. Cold, dirt, fatigue, uncertainty, and the accidental beautiful or amusing thing. If only one ~~didn't expect~~ wasn't thought to think it was something else. But then this is the case anywhere, not only out here.

I heard Lovat Fraser was married, but didn't hear to whom, though I understood that was interesting. Hodgson I have heard nothing of. Hooton wrote me a jocular letter the other day which did not make me feel jocular. A machine gun up the street is hammering away at nails for coffins, but I never see the dead in more than a canvas bag. There is 'some stuff coming in' this afternoon—i.e. *some* enemy shells are falling in the street. It is snowing and dull, or there would be still more firing. What there is must be blind—without observation.

Goodbye | Yours ever | Edward Thomas

To Eleanor Farjeon

[Ronville] | 13 March 1917*

My dear Eleanor,

It seems hopeless to wait any longer for your parcels. I don't understand it unless one of our officers who has one every week from Fortnum and Mason took mine by mistake. I know he had two in one week. But if so it can't be rectified now. As a matter of fact these things all get pooled in the mess, except that I refuse to pool my apples. I am back with 244 now and much prefer it. I am out more and have a greater variety of things to do, including using my voice in the open air. We have had one or two more lovely days, mild and clear too. Yesterday a west wind blew and the rooks at their nests made things more like normal. Today actually I heard a blackbird trying, but it has turned into a cold dull day with no particular charm. The orchard is all mud now except one corner where snowdrops are flowering. It was time I left Headquarters. In the shelling yesterday shrapnel came into the office and killed the old serjeant major who had been wanting to get back to his poultry—the war had snatched him away from it. The town has been a very hot place these last few days. I only hope I shall fare no worse than I have done. I wish I enjoyed it more or rather thought about it less both during and after. Still I got some amusement out of it. For example some of the small enemy shell make a fine thin shrill whistling and I found myself mistaking the wind in the hairs of my ears for a shell approaching last night! The men as a rule are very good. They have a great advantage in being so much more matey than we are. They are always in twos or threes and we are usually alone when any difficulty appears. For example, I spent the day and night before yesterday at an O.P. with 5 men, telephonists, under me, not in the Observation Post but just handy. We were shelled and I was either alone up in the O.P. or equally alone down in the cellar with them where we eat and sleep. I didn't much mind, but I couldn't sleep after it. However the early morning was most beautiful, till the infantry made a raid and the artillery made a barrage for them.

Did I tell you Frost found an American publisher for my verses? Probably Helen told you. But I expect it was too late for anything to be done. De la Mare did see Frost. I heard from de la Mare, but he told me nothing really. All he said of Frost was that he looked very well and that he talked about me.

I have a cottage now. At least the Battery has. It stands at the edge of the orchard. One room is our office where I am now, with the maps. Another contains signalling stores, and the third is the sergeant major's office and sleeping apartment. There are rose bushes in the wall and a cherry tree in front. It is old and thin and only has a ground floor with beams overhead and dirty old wallpaper and still a few photographs of inhabitants. The old woman of the house comes round now and then to look in her cupboards for something.

There are signs we shall be very 'active' before long. I shan't be able to write much then, I expect. But I hope you will. It seems an age since I heard, though perhaps I still owe you a letter.

Now I must go out and get the men on to work after their dinner. There is always digging and finishing off to be done and today I have to see that it is done. It is too dull for much shooting yet.——But we have just had to shoot at a hostile battery as night came on. Now all is quiet. The enemy sent a few rounds back later, and you would have enjoyed seeing Horton's face beam as he laughed: 'Hark! Ack-ack!: The Bosh has got his rag out. We have got his rag out for him, right enough.' Horton is the regular who was a ranker, the only thorough soldier among us officers. He is now a Captain and 2nd in command. He is a sort of cockney blood with quite a curl above the middle of his forrid. As soon as he talks about anything where he can't use cant phrases and street proverbs and tags from music halls he is the most awful fool—but he is not in the least a fool.

Your letter has come by the way, when I had written half of this. It was a great joy, even to your remarks about my hour, because they reminded me of times I never think of alone but can enjoy with you for a moment. I am not pretending I am no longer E.T. but that I am not the author of *Horae Solitariae* although I quite admit he is a near relative.

I hope Hooper* will have a long time in England and a good time.

I was interrupted to do a shoot and in the excitement your letter has disappeared mysteriously. I had only read it once.

700 [sales] is quite good for your verse and I am not surprised Duckworth was agreeable when you discussed the 2nd [edition]. We shall be bards together. But it is nice to be where nobody knows I am a bard—nice for a change to be where they don't suspect I ever had more than 2 inches of mouse coloured hair.

They are very busy, hustling round to repair a gun and I can't write again yet, so I will send this with good wishes for your garden. The old French woman who owns this place is also busy carting dung and if possible I will watch you two racing towards harvest. Goodbye.

Yours ever | Edward Thomas

To his parents

244 Siege Battery | 22 March 1917

Dear Father and Mother,

As things have been happening here lately I had better let you know all is well. I have been out for 24 hours in our new front line trenches—an Artillery officer always has to be there now—observing the ground and reporting flashes of hostile guns at night. It was a very interesting and very tiring experience as I had no shelter and had not been prepared for a night at all. It taught me a good deal about cold and dirt and mud and how the infantry live and also how to tell the sound of shells that are not going to harm you, which saves you from much useless anxiety. To be relieved at breakfast time was a pleasure that overcame everything and to see the town in the sun as I came down into it was most beautiful. I slept 16 hours after a wash and a meal and now I am on duty again. The one thing I could have had and did not was my map case to protect my map from rain and mud . . .

We do not know enough yet about the recent movements to be elated. It means a lot of change and may only mean a new war in a new country. I am sure you are hopeful, Father, and I can only say I am willing to believe the best when I hear it.

I have been reading Beach Thomas* on the ruins of Peronne, etc. I am very glad it is not my job and at the same time sure I could do it infinitely better. Julian is probably right in saying that he gets his stuff supplied to him and writes through his hat. It is a pleasure not to have to write through one's hat.

The infantry in the trenches were very amusing company and the way they settle down and make the best of an impossible situation is just as wonderful as I have always heard. They grow all they want as fast as mustard and cress and keep smiling. Good bye and my love to all.

Ever your loving son | Edwy

To his son

244 Siege Battery | 23 March 1917

My dear Mervyn,

I brought back a letter from you in the mail bags today and also a new battery for my torch. Thank you very much. Do you know I have been so careful that the first one is not exhausted yet. It must have been a very good one. It is most useful in crossing this dark street when crowded with lorries or columns of horses and limbers and on all sorts of occasions.

I was so glad to hear from you and how much you were earning for Mother as well as yourself. At the same time I am more anxious for you to learn than to earn at present and I hope you will soon be moved to a new shop. You haven't found an O.T.C. yet, have you? I wish you could, though I hope you will not have to go further than that for a long time. I don't think war would trouble you. I see lots of infantrymen no bigger or older than you. There was one machine gunner doing duty over the parapet the other night when I was in the very very front trench. He had to stand up there behind his gun watching for an hour. Then he was relieved and made some tea for me and himself and turned into his comic little shanty and slept till the next relief. He looked ever so much older as well as dirtier when morning came. He was a very nice bright Scotch boy. Well, I expect you could do just the same. His officer was the same age and very much like him so that I think he had to look unduly severe to show the distinction.

I am glad you have got a good bicycle. Am I to buy the old one back from you when I come back? If so, you might oil it and keep it dry somewhere. It could hang up out of the way on the kitchen wall. I should like to ride over to Jesse's* with you in the summer.

I wonder could you climb that chimney?* There were iron rings all the way up and I knew one was loose, but I didn't know which. One bad feature was that you were always hanging out a bit, because the chimney tapered. It has been hit three times but only with small stuff. Now I suppose it is likely to survive as the enemy is farther off. The crossroads round it became known as Windy Corner because everybody 'got the wind up' as he came near it. Thousands had to go that way and yet very few were injured and only about two killed. Isn't it wonderful how some men get hit and some don't. But it is the same with trees and houses, so that I don't see why it makes some people 'believe in God'. It is a good thing to believe. I think brave people all believe something and I daresay they are not so likely to be killed as those who don't believe and are not so brave.

You would have laughed to hear the machine gunners talking to one another and chaffing the infantrymen as they came along the trench tired and dirty.

The men all think we are fast winning the war now. I wonder if we are. I hope so. Of course I am not a bit tired of it. I want to do six months anyhow, but I don't care how much so long as I come back again.

It is going to be Spring soon. Are you glad? Are you often happy and usually contented, and if not contented, not often in despair? Try never to let despair at anyrate make you idle or careless. But be as idle and careless as you can when you are happy and the chance comes. If you are troubled, remember that you can do what perhaps nobody else will be able to do for Mother and Bronwen and Baba: only don't let that make you anxious either. All will come well if you keep honest and kind.

Upon my word, this sounds like a sermon and I do hate sermons, of which it is not true to say that it is more blessed to give than to receive, but it is more easy to give a sermon than to receive.

Do you have time to read now? I only read for ten minutes in bed, Shakespeare's sonnets, with a pipe which I smoke about a quarter through and then put out the light and forget the flash of guns across the street and the rattle of the windows, everything except the thud of a shell in the marsh behind, but that seems to have stopped now. Goodnight.

Ever your loving | Daddy

To Helen

Arras | 24 March 1917

Dearest,

I was in that ghastly village today. The Major and I went up at 7.30 to observe; through the village was the quickest way. I never thought it would be so bad. It is nothing but dunes of piled up brick and stone with here and there a jagged piece of wall, except that the little summerhouse placed under the trees that I told Baba about is more or less perfect. The only place one could recognize was the churchyard. Scores of tombstones were quite undamaged. All the trees were splintered and snapped and dead until you got to the outskirts. The trench we observed from ran along inside a garden hedge with a cherry in it. No Man's Land below the village was simply churned up dead filthy ground with tangled rusty barbed wire over it. The roads running through it had been very little damaged: one the actual trench cut through it. But the trees alongside were torn and broken and stripped. It was funny to come along a road and find that bit of ruin of a burnt house that I expected to have to observe from when we first came here. Then you wound round to it by deep trenches. They had begun to strengthen it for an O.P. and given it a fancy name. The well alone survives that is useful.—As the telephone was wrong we could not do a shoot from the O.P. so we came down again and went to our new position. On the way we saw a Bosh fight two of our planes. He set one on fire and chased the other off. The one on fire had a great red tail of flame, yet the pilot kept it under control for a minute or more till I suppose he was on fire and then suddenly it reeled and dropped in a string of tawdry fragments.

Our new position—fancy—was an old chalk pit* in which a

young copse of birch, hazel etc. has established itself. Our dug out is already here, dug by the battery we are evicting. It is almost a beautiful spot still and I am sitting warm in the sun on a heap of chalk with my back to the wall of the pit which is large and shallow. Fancy, an old chalk pit with moss and even a rabbit left in spite of the paths trodden almost all over it. It is beautiful and sunny and warm though cold in the shade. The chalk is dazzling. The sallow catkins are soft dark white. All I have to do is to see that the men prepare the gun platforms in the right way, and put two men on to digging a latrine.—I am always devilish particular about that.

There are a few long large white clouds mostly low in the sky and several sausage balloons up and still some of our planes peppered all round with black Bosh smoke bursts.

I ate some oatcakes for lunch just now. They were delicious, hard and sweet.

The writing pads were quite all right, though no longer so necessary after Oscar had sent me half a dozen of these refills, which by the way are not very convenient except for short notes.

So you have found the village.* We are not quite so far out as that, but between two villages and a little to this side. Both these villages are still shelled, but this particular place has never been shelled yet, so though I hear a big shell every now and then flop 200 or 300 yards away it feels entirely peaceful. But I can't get over the fact that there is no thrush singing in it. There is only a robin. I don't hear thrush ever. All the bright pale or ruddy stems in the copse and the moss underneath and the chalk showing through reminds me of Hampshire. The stone that the village whose name you know is built of is just like the Berryfield Cottage stone.

I heard from Sergeant Pearce yesterday. There is no mapping in the battalion at all now, so he is working in the office where they deal with plans and billetings etc. for the Artists. He doesn't seem to mind it. He says he drives over with his wife to the village we used to walk to. Robins' sight had got worse (he injured his eye about a year ago) and he has apparently been discharged. I wonder what became of Mason. I keep forgetting or neglecting to write to Vernon. As to Benson, I forget the number of his battalion.

The wheat is very green in some of the fields a little behind us and they are ploughing near our orchard. I hope the old woman will get back to her cottage and apple trees and currant bushes and snowdrops and aconites and live happily ever after.

It is very idle of me to sit here writing, but the men are all at work and I can't help them except by appearing at intervals and suggesting something obvious that ought to be done. They will like the new position. It is full of dug outs as it might have been of rabbit holes, a perfect little village of dug outs, scattered about the copse alongside and in front of the guns. The copse is very little pulled about either. It is much like one of those chalk pits in Lupton's field only much larger. I shall soon go back to tea.

Now I have had tea and oatcakes and honey and also a cake from Burzard's Mrs Freeman sent me. I am having an agreeably idle evening, but then I am up with the lark tomorrow for 24 hours at the O.P. No letters today and tomorrow I shan't get them if there are any. Never mind. All is well.

I am all and always yours | Edwy

The latest is that perhaps we shan't go in to the chalk pit. The general is always changing his mind.

To his mother and younger brother

Beaurains | 30 March 1917

Dear Mother,

I will write you another letter to-night because I have nothing to do but be in the battery till the Major and Captain come back from dinner. One has always to be here and to-night is my turn. To-morrow I shall be too busy and probably too cold to write, and the day after I hope I shall be resting. We are still preparing. Nothing much is happening yet, though the firing seldom ceases. However, to-day has been a better day, with plenty to do and after much cold rain plenty of sunshine to do it in as the evening came on. Which somehow reminds me I ought to be writing to Julian, which I should have done had I not your parcel and your letter to-day to thank you for. The parcel came safe and was welcome as ever. A plain cake would be very nice whenever you can send it. The chocolate etc. will be most useful on days when I am up at the O.P. and do not want to have to carry more food than is necessary. Your letter and Eleanor's and Helen's give me a very clear picture of their visit with Myfanwy to Rusham Road . . . Now I will write to Julian.

My dear Julian I am sorry I have not written specially to you till I had one to answer and that I have had for a week now. There is not much really to tell you that I can tell you or that it would be permissible or profitable to tell you till it is all over. We are having a dirty long picnic, you know, with many surprising and uncomfortable things in it. Just here we are likely to be dirtier and more uncomfortable than ever before very long, compared with which my cold feet at this moment, and the smell of an oil stove, will be as honey and cream, which by the way I still taste now and then. In fact I never had so many nice things to eat or ate them with less compunction. I hope this does not excite your envy too much. You have had a rotten time* with no amelioration, I suspect. I hope it is over and that things are going to pan out not unpleasantly, though they cannot go as you would choose, of course. That goes without saying. I wonder will you find out for yourself some equilibrium in this mix-up, the war and of course everything else. War, of course, is not altogther different from peace, except that one may be blown to bits and have to blow others to bits. Physical discomfort is sometimes so great that it seems a new thing, but of course it is not. You remember cycling in the rain towards Salisbury.* It really is seldom quite a different thing than that. Of course, one seems very little one's own master, but then one seldom does seem so. Death looms, but however it comes it is unexpected, whether from appendicitis or bullet. An alternation of comfort and discomfort is always a man's lot. So is an alternation of pleasure or happiness or intense interest with tedium or dissatisfaction or misery. I have suffered more from January to March in other years than in this. That is the plain fact. I will not go into it any more. I hope I do not seem to be boasting. I am too often idle and inefficient and afraid to want to boast.

I cannot talk about books. I should have liked to see the Annual.* I heard Desmond MacCarthy approved of Eastaway and I wanted to see the said Eastaway in print. Perhaps I shall before very long.

I never see anybody I know. The only man here I can really talk to is most of the time a most confounded nuisance, because he can never play the part of an Artillery Officer but is always a melancholy Scotch philosopher bred mostly in solitude under his mother's roof. Well, well, what a thing it is, as the old man* at Swindon used to say. I should be glad to be back again. Give my love to Maud and the baby and everyone.

P.S. I was just going to tell you not to take too seriously my request for Epsom Salts when the order was given 'Battery. Action.' and now we are giving 167 rounds at a hostile battery over there in the dark.

Ever your loving son | Edwy

To his mother

Beaurains | 1 April 1917

Dear Mother,

I wrote to Father this morning and hardly mentioned your parcels, because I was tired out. I went to bed directly after but could not sleep. I do not feel so sleepy now. The parcels were very welcome and everything in them . . . The Epsom salts rather amused me because really I am very well and only feel otherwise when I am bored with a job of doing nothing in one place all day . . .

The day has kept fine on the whole and if it were a little warmer it would be good Easter weather, fresh, and bright. Only I feel cold after sitting out all night as stout as a market woman with so many clothes on. My servant is washing for me out in the yard and the clothes are blowing on the line just beside the motor car which shines in the sun. The aeroplanes are buzzing overhead and as I sit by an open wood fire it is more like a scene in a small country inn at home than anything else except that one of our guns rattles all the windows every now and then. We get good fires here with the boards and beams of ruined houses all round us. The servants will burn anything if you let them and I have just been lecturing mine on the evil of burning things that still serve the purpose for which they were made. The waste is indescribable. It would be interesting to compare the way the Germans spend their substance. The deep dug-outs they make are far beyond ours in strength and workmanship. We make them just as much as they do but we make wretched things skimped in work and materials so far as I have seen. The thing that is to shelter us in the battle is being made now in a hurry anyhow without any expert advice except that of a thatcher from Norfolk.

I am glad you had some violets. I have not seen any, nor primroses, nor celandines, not even a dandelion . . . It will be nice to have the kind of Easter weather it is good to sow seeds in. Nice for us, too. Goodbye.

Ever your loving son | Edwy

To Helen

Arras | 1 April 1917

Dearest,

Now the night is over I will tell you all about it before I go to bed, if I do go! I feel so cheerful for several reasons of which I will give you two. Firstly, I found a letter from you waiting for me when I returned at 7 a.m. Secondly, I found the car waiting for me as soon as I was clear of B.,* which was most cheering to a tired and overladen officer and four telephonists still more overladen.

Well, I didn't have much of the fire. I just waited to hear that the working party was only going to carry up the stuff, which they did, and to do the work today or some other time soon. I had to decide to let them carry the heavy stuff (too heavy for them to carry through a sticky trench) along the crest which was being swept by machine guns from time to time. Which they did and luckily came to no harm. I went off to the cellar, leaving two telephonists to take their instrument off the wire and see that the wire on to the cellar was all right. The cellar was full of smoke, except the lowest two feet of it, so that we (the two other telephonists and I) had to crouch or lie. Then shells began to fall in the direction of the O.P. In two hours the other telephonists had not arrived. I thought they had lost their way in the moonlight among the wire and ruins and trenches of B. or had been wounded—or perhaps the working party had had a casualty. So I sent back the other two telephonists to see if they had left the O.P. I had thought myself rather clever—or rather I was very much relieved—to find my way in the moonlight. There was also the complication that I had now been two hours away from the telephone, whereas I am always bound to be on hand. In about an hour the two returned to say the delay was caused by the shelling which had broken down the trench leading to the cellar and that they could not find the wire and that therefore two were staying on at the O.P. with the instrument. I ought to have gone back at once. Instead of which I dozed for one hour or two, dreaming of being court-martialled, till up I got and had a quiet journey. The moon had gone and left all the stars and not a cloud. I was sure of my way by the Plough. But it was dirty and tiring, for I had on vest | shirt | two waistcoats | tunic | one Tommy's leather waistcoat | British warm | and waterproof.

Only two or three shells came over and I found the telephonists dozing and there in a clay corner we dozed and smoked till daybreak. More heavy shells arrived well away from us. They moan and then savagely stop moaning as they strike the ground with a flap. They are 5.9s or Five Nines as we call them.—I had not been wanted on the telephone so all is well. Day broke clear and white and a lark rose at 5.15. Blackbirds began to sing at 6 and a yellowhammer. I got up and slopped through the trench and looked at the view over to the Hun, a perfect simple view of three ridges, with a village and line of trees on the first, a clump on the second and clumps and lines on the furthest, all looking almost purple and brown like heather in the dawn. Easter Sunday—a lovely clear high dawn. Then I returned and sat and ate chocolate till the relieving party arrived at 6.30. I had a talk with the officer about the dugout and then off, so glad to be relieved and down through the ghastly street with a mule cart in it waiting for a shell to come over, and at the bottom the other two telephonists from the cellar. Half a mile further on past No Man's Land and that jagged ruin that I expected to observe from, with a well by it, known as the Burnt House, which now has the first five crosses of a Military Cemetery by it, I saw the motor car and we all joyrode back here. I washed, shaved and had a slow breakfast after reading your letter. At breakfast I read one from Ivy [Ransome], such an artificial one, full of description, as if she thought that was what I should like.

Now everybody has breakfasted. There has been a shower and the sun has returned but among the clouds. I am not very sleepy yet, but just enjoying having nothing to do which is supposed to be the privilege of the day after the O.P.—that is in these peaceful days. You are having a fine Easter, I hope, as we are, though not a warm one yet. I like hearing of your days with Baba and Bronwen and Joy, and of Mervyn's ride with Ernest, and intended ride to

Jesse's. But here is Rubin saying he gets bored stiff if he is alone. Never mind. I liked hearing about your bath too and your working and the children eating. Rubin has set the gramophone to 'In Cellar Cool'. But everything, gramophone or not, out here forbids memories such as you have been writing. Memories I have but they are mixed up with my thoughts and feelings in B. or when I hear the blackbirds or when the old dog bangs the table leg with his tail or lies with his brains wasting in his skull. You must not therefore expect me to say anything outright. It is not my way, is it?

Now I must write and remind Mother she has sent only the inessential part of my mapcase, the waterproof cover for it.

A happy Easter! Goodbye | Edwy

To Robert Frost

Beaurains | 2 April 1917

My dear Robert,

I heard that the mails have been lost several times lately at sea. I thought I had better make another shot at you. This is another penultimate letter. Things are closely impending now and will have happened before you get this and you will know all about it then, so I will not try to tell you what they are, especially as I could not get them past the censor.

I have seen some new things since I wrote last and had much and worse things to endure which do not become less terrible in anticipation but are less terrible once I am in the midst of them. Jagged gables at dawn when you are cold and tired out look a thousand times worse from their connection with a certain kind of enemy shell that has made them look like that, so that every time I see them I half think I hear the moan of the approaching and hovering shell and the black grisly flap that it seems to make as it bursts. I see and hear more than I did because changed conditions compel us to go up to the very front among the infantry to do our observation and we spend nights without shelter in the mud chiefly in waiting for morning and the arrival of the relief. It is a 24 hours job and takes more to recover from. But it is far as yet from being unendurable. The unendurable thing was having to climb up the inside of a chimney that was being shelled. I gave up. It was impossible and I knew it. Yet I went up to the beastly place and had 4 shell bursts very close. I decided that I would go back. As a matter of fact I had no light and no information about the method of getting up so that all the screwing up I had given myself would in any case have been futile. It was just another experience like the gamekeeper,*—but it was far less on my mind, because the practical result of my failure was nil and I now see far more from the ground level than I could have seen then from 200 feet up the factory chimney.

Otherwise I have done all the things so far asked of me without making any mess and I have mingled satisfaction with dissatisfaction in about the usual proportion, comfort and discomfort. There are so many things to enjoy and if I remember rightly not more to regret than say a year or ten years ago. I think I get surer of some primitive things that one has got to get sure of, about oneself and other people, and I think this is not due simply to being older. In short, I am glad I came out and I think less about return than I thought I should—partly no doubt I inhibit the idea of return. I only think by flashes of the things at home that I used to enjoy and should again. I enjoy many of them out here when the sun shines and at early morning and late afternoon. I doubt if anybody here thinks less of home than I do and yet I doubt if anybody loves it more.

But why should I be explaining myself at such length and not leave you to do the explaining?

We have shifted lately from the edge of a small city* out to a still more ruinous village. The planks and beams of the ruins keep us warm in a house that has not had an actual hit except by fragments. We live in comparative comfort, eat luxuriously from parcels sent from London or brought up from places well behind the lines, and sleep dry and warm as a rule. We expect soon to have to live in damp clay pits for safety. There are some random shots but as a rule you know when to expect trouble, and you can feel quite safe close to a place that is clearly dangerous. We work or make others work practically all day with no rests or holidays, but often we have a quiet evening and can talk or write letters or listen to the gramophone playing 'John Peel' and worse things far. People are mostly friendly and warm, however uncongenial. I am more than ten years older than 4 of the other 5 officers. They are 19, 20,

25, 26 and 33 years old. Those of 25 and up regard me as very old. I don't know if the two boys do—I get on better with them: in a sort of way we are fond of one another—I like to see them come in of a night back from some job and I believe they like to see me. What more should anyone want? I revert for 10 minutes every night by reading Shakespeare's Tragedies in bed with a pipe before I blow the candle out. Otherwise I do nothing that I used to do except eat and sleep: I mean when I am not alone. Funny world. What a thing it is. And I hear nothing of you. Yet you are no more like an American in a book than you were 2½ years ago. You are doing the unchanged things that I cannot or dare not think of except in flashes. I don't have memories except such as are involved in the impressions as I see or hear things about me. But if I went on writing like this I should make you think I was as damnably introspective as ever and practised the art too. Goodnight to you and Elinor and all. Remember I am in 244 Siege Battery, B.E.F., France and am and shall remain 2nd Lieut. Edward Thomas | Yours ever

To his mother

5 April 1917

Dear Mother,

We are now in the thick of it, though not quite in the middle. This is the second day, and a beautiful day it is, sunny and misty, the sun sometimes failing behind the mist and coming through again quite warm, which I have enjoyed as I sat out on the bank between No. 3 and No. 4 guns while we fired. Yesterday was cold and slippery and dirty and I got clean tired out by the end when I was relieved at 9.30 p.m. after beginning at 5.30 a.m. I moved into the battery position to a dug-out I have been strengthening, because any day the Hun might see the wisdom of laying our street flat with the ground. It is a little damp in the dug-out but wonderfully quiet except when our No.1 and No.2 guns fire straight over it. All the other artillery only makes the air flap heavily all night. It is nice to wake up practically out of doors and hear the wrens in the copse. For the dug-out is dug out of a bank and not down into the ground, so that the light of day reaches it, and it has the advantage of lying across the line of fire of our own and the enemy's guns, with the entrance not facing either.

I live for the moment in trousers concealed by rubber boots almost to the waist. This shortens the time of dressing and undressing by a quarter of an hour, as I have no boots or breeches to lace up. Otherwise I remain civilised and clean so far.

I have just seen quite a respectable review* of the *Annual* in the *Times* and I hear there will be one in the *New Statesman* . . .

As things are at present arranged I may see exciting things within 3 or 4 days. But of course the future is obscure and we do not know what the Hun will do, or if he is where we think he is—if he is, he is having a bad time. I do not mind how bad if it helps to end the war. Goodbye . . .

Ever your loving son | Edwy

*To Helen**

Beaurains | 6 April | 1917

There wasn't a letter . . . but I will add a little more.—the pace is slackening today.

Still not a thrush—but many blackbirds.

My dear, you must not ask me to say much more. I know that you must say much more because you feel much. But I, you see, must not feel anything. I am just as it were tunnelling underground and something sensible in my subconsciousness directs me not to think of the sun. At the end of the tunnel there is the sun. Honestly this is not the result of thinking; it is just an explanation of my state of mind which is really so entirely preoccupied with getting on through the tunnel that you might say I had forgotten there was a sun at either end, before or after this business. This will perhaps induce you to call me inhuman like the newspapers, just because for a time I have had my ears stopped—mind you I have not done it myself—to all but distant echoes of home and friends and England. If I could respond as you would like me to to your feelings I should be unable to go on with this job in ignorance whether it is to last weeks or months or years—I never even think whether it will be weeks or months or years. I don't even wonder if the drawers in the sitting room are kept locked!

Well, I can't get my hair cut this morning, so I shall go over to the battery soon and take a turn for Rubin or Thorburn. Smith is up at the O.P. today.

We have such fine moonlight nights now, pale hazy moonlight. Yesterday too we had a coloured sunset lingering in the sky and after that at intervals a bright brassy glare where they were burning waste cartridges. The sky of course winks with broad flashes almost all round at night and the air sags and flaps all night.

I expect there will be a letter today. Never think I can do without one any more than you can dearest. Kiss the children for me.

All and always yours | Edwy

To Helen

Saturday | Beaurains | April 7 or 8 1917

Dearest,

Here I am in my valise on the floor of my dugout writing before sleeping. The artillery is like a stormy tide breaking on the shores of the full moon that rides high and clear among white cirrus clouds. It has been a day of cold feet in the O.P. I had to go unexpectedly. When I posted my letter and Civil Liabilities paper in the morning I thought it would be a bad day, but we did all the shelling. Hardly anything came near the O.P. or even the village. I simply watched the shells changing the landscape. The pretty village among trees that I first saw two weeks ago is now just ruins among violated stark tree trunks. But the sun shone and larks and partridges and magpies and hedgesparrows made love and the trench was being made passable for the wounded that will be harvested in a day or two. Either the Bosh is beaten or he is going to surprise us. The air was full of aeroplane flights. I saw one enemy fall on fire and one of ours tumble into the enemy's wire. I am tired but resting.

Yesterday afternoon was more exciting. Our billet was shelled. The shell fell all round and you should have seen Horton and me dodging them. It was quite fun for me, though he was genuinely alarmed, being more experienced. None of us was injured and our house escaped. Then we went off in the car in the rain to buy things.

We shall be enormously busy now. Rubin goes off tomorrow on a course of instruction and may be a captain before long, our sergeant major has left with a commission. One officer has to be at the O.P. every day and every other night. So it will be all work now till further notice—days of ten times the ordinary work too. So goodnight and I hope you sleep no worse than I do.

Sunday. I slept jolly well and now it is sunshine and wind and we are in for a long day and I must post this when I can.

All and always yours Edwy

MEMOIRS

In 1914 he was weary, disappointed, saddened, oppressed, but still fighting to keep his spiritual identity. During the eighteen months or so that followed the summer of that year I did not see him. When next I met him he was a changed person, scarcely recognizable for the same man. The war afforded him an opportunity which no lesser event could have given him; he joined up, and went through an intensive course of military training in the Artists' Rifles, and became a Sergeant-Instructor with the duty of teaching map-reading: and in the process laid aside for ever, as it turned out, the anxieties of hack writing and poverty, and domestic irritations. I, too, joined the Artists' Rifles, but, in that large training centre at Gidea Park, it was some time before I learned that he was there. The talks which I had with him there were quite different from our earlier talks. Like most men, I think, I was irked in the extreme by the petty parade-ground severities and the conventionally exacting routine of camp life at Gidea Park; but not so Thomas. He accepted it almost with joy. He threw himself into the mechanical life of this vast military institution with enthusiasm. He identified himself with it in the spirit in which an Etonian is supposed to identify himself with Eton. He grew brown in the open air. His muscles hardened and his limbs strengthened. His eyes cleared and lost their melancholy. He was ready to deliver homilies to anyone on the virtues of the military life. Map-reading, of course, was the ideal subject to have allotted to him as an instructor, but no one could have foreseen that he would have proved so successful in holding the attention of groups of unsophisticated soldier students.

Then, at about the same time, we were both transferred to an artillery cadet school at Trowbridge, from which we were to emerge as officers in the R.G.A. For some weeks we slept in the same barrack-dormitory, he at one extreme end, I at the other. Our life here was not so exacting as it had been at Gidea Park, and there were some opportunities for outside activity. Thomas was insatiable in his desire for more and more physical exertion. No longer were the leisurely walks through the country in which he had once delighted enough to satisfy his mood. He persuaded a few others to join him in long cross-country runs. He seemed bent on acquiring the utmost physical fitness of which the human body is capable. He had escaped from the old literary life, he had apparently weaned himself from the temperament which for him had gone with it.

He had become the perfect soldier of the State, the contented warrior whom the newspapers loved to depict, more completely than any other serviceman I ever met.

R. A. Scott-James

Written about 1945

EDWARD THOMAS claims, and it became generally known, that 'Eastaway' was a disguise deliberately adopted to prevent people from being confined by what they knew or thought of him already. Those who knew him best found it hard to think of him as a soldier at all, since he was a quiet man, a scholar and open-air naturalist. In person he was lean and tall; he had blue eyes and hair of a dull yellow colour; his face was serious and shrewd, but a humorous expression lurked about his mouth. Dressed in what may be described as a 'string' suit, fitting loosely, and hatless, he made a picturesque, though not a self-conscious figure on the roads where he loved to walk. A stick, longer than the ordinary, cut from the hedge, and his dog 'Rags', completes the picture.

Says his friend Frederick Niven:

> You knew the heath-wind flaunts our little ills,
> Of old inn-corners that from sudden gales
> Shelter the traveller.

To one small house he used to arrive on the heels of his post-card, and go with the boys to bathe in he sea. He might be found there listening to a sweet young voice singing 'Land of my fathers' and 'Kelvin Grove', his face intent as he smoked his old clay pipe. And sometimes he himself would sing in the rough style of a countryman taking his turn in the inn-parlour. It might be 'The Raggle-Taggle Gypsies', or some such air.

As a talker, Thomas was excellent. He did not merely utter opinions, or fire off remarks, or deal in small-talk; nor, on the other hand, did he discourse pompously for effect, as some literary men do. He always had interesting thoughts, personal ways of looking at things; and frequently amusing and striking stories to tell. Like all good conversationalists, he knew when to listen also, and how to keep the balance even. It is told how with one silent friend he walked for twelve miles without saying a word—a walk which both men enjoyed hugely.

Easily distracted from his work, he used to go from home when writing a book, and hide himself in some remote place. By that means he could better concentrate upon writing, and then have the pleasure of returning home freshly to his family and garden and the lighter labour of reviewing books. Later he had a study away from the house, where he could be undisturbed. In a letter to W. H. Hudson, he refers to the last time he sat there, idle, where he had never before done anything but work, feeling strangely disconnected. Hard as he had to apply himself to his 'trade' of writing, he disliked 'gas-fire' poets, men who spun out artificial effeminate stuff, poseurs and bores of all kinds. He was in fact, not afflicted with those temperamental vagaries which are so commonly and wrongly attributed to artists.

Twenty years have passed since Edward Thomas died. In the interval his work has received a great deal of attention, and books have been written about him, including two by his widow which were much admired. It is unfortunate that no examples of his poems can be printed with this; but they are, after all, available to anybody who cares to get them. His subject-matter is simply that which would naturally come within the notice of a man who loved nature and was able to express his thoughts and emotions. There is nothing of the sentimental townsman there: he shows people and things as they are, the rain and the wind and the sun also. He used to say, talking of fine writing, that nothing should be written which could not equally be spoken across the table among ordinary people. He admired Swift as perhaps the greatest of prose writers; for he said it was simply fine talk, conversation upon a high level. But as he had great numbers of friends among literary people whose work and character were extremely varied, his sympathies must have been very wide. It might, indeed, be harder to unite his friends than it was for him to bind them to himself with that sincere and deep affection which has already outlasted a good many years and is even now ardent and expressive.

James Guthrie

1937

CAN anything be added to Mr. de la Mare's splendid appreciation of his work, but add my stray memories of what I can recall across the years, of the momentous experience of his friendship.

It was in 1901 that I first met Edward at Duncan Williams's flat in Greys Inn Road. He was just down from Oxford, and joined in the talk of our voluble and amusing circle at intervals, rather remote, kindly, giving the impression of reserves, of knowledge, of perhaps a suppressed anxiety. He was living then at Nightingale Parade, Balham. I went to his rooms there and found the atmosphere of friendliest welcome and sincere pleasure at my visit, to which Helen's hospitality and affectionate character contributed so much. I knew instinctively that by intimacy with him I should find one of the best gifts life has to offer. So subsequently I found, and until I saw him for the last time when he was in camp near Romford and came to see us in our home in Brentwood, I loved and admired him and was ever happy in his company, stimulated to be at my best in sincerity and speech. It was not, I think, chiefly his culture and literary conversation that bound me to him, nor merely his finished and expressive talk, grave humour and beautiful voice, but a strange undaunted honesty in his judgements, an impatience with what was meretricious or superficial in people and things and social arrangements, and a profound love of the simple and the natural that drew me to him.

As our friendship progressed he would at times call for me in the City at the Bank where I was employed, and his unusual appearance, his fine face, light hair, and clothes that evidenced a rural life, made a strange contrast to—all in that restless and commercial environment. I think even then those of us who knew him well might have prophesied his distinction as a poet. His extreme sensitiveness, love of common things and vision of their value and significance, his growing mastery of words and fastidious selection of them, his ear for the music of a phrase as evidenced in his writings, should have indicated the direction his developed powers would take. The early impact of anxiety and the responsibility for others must have deepened and strengthened him, but only on looking back does one feel this to be true. He had much suffering to endure before he found serenity and poise as the happy warrior and the major poet.

We made a number of excursions together, taking bicycles and putting up haphazard at inns,—Avebury, Swindon, Malmesbury, Stroud, Westbury, Bridgwater, Selborne and other places. One of these journeys is recorded in a book he wrote, 'In Pursuit of Spring', though the 'other man', referred to in it as his companion, is 'rather a fraud', as he wrote to me in sending me the volume. As an illustration of his extraordinary gift of creating an intense significance to a single, almost momentary experience, I recall on that occasion lying on the beach at Kilve. We had confirmed the fact that there was no weathercock on the church, and we were resting in peace and almost in silence. Then he turned and bade me listen. A little melodious twitter sounded somewhere, and a tiny bird dipped and swooped between us and the sea. 'A meadow-pippit,' he said, and the moment became unforgettable. But indeed, all things, lightly passed over and unnoticed, he made to possess a value only perceived when he made us see with something of the vision he himself possessed. I hold it to be the spiritual value, and whether he would have acknowledged the word or no, there was something of the mystic in his poet's vision. His poems contain ample illustration of this feeling then awaked in me that I now 'remember in tranquillity'. He would cut walking-sticks from the wood and shape them till they had a character of their own. A knife of mine at least sixty years old, formerly belonging to my father, with a long horn handle so worn with the hand that the white showed through the outer part, had a peculiar fascination for him; somehow I saw it had a soul that his view of it had created. He delighted in sea-songs or chanties I remembered from hearing them sung by the sailors, when as a child I went to Australia in 1880 in a sailing-ship with my father, who commanded her. If a song was new to Edward he would get me to sing it over and over while he learned it, and Helen would sit at the piano and jot down the notes. He loved singing old songs, racy songs, songs that had won the acceptance of a robust democracy as a permanent possession, songs of Tudor fragility and daintiness, but he limited his audience to a family circle. I never heard of him singing or making a speech in public. He would perch a small child on his knee, and clasp his clay pipe with his fine strong hands, and the music that was in him would come forth, wistfully or jauntily. My children delighted in his too rare visits. 'Log-over-leg,' they would demand, and he would comply with the jingle about the fox. I suppose I was just bookish enough to trail some way with him in his literary work and interests, but it was companionship he needed mostly of me, I think. 'Your letter was more to me than praise, and I know you meant it to be, only just now such friendship as yours makes me feel the bitterness of my isolation more.' So he wrote. I suppose I have kept about seventy letters from him, and in the greater part of them there is a suggestion for a meeting or an invitation. 'A three-mile walk tires me just as much as 30 miles with a friend.'

I have referred to him somewhat hesitatingly as a mystic. He would I think have shied at the word and yet one cannot fail to catch the authentic note in some of his poems,—at the close of 'Lights Out', for instance, or in that thrilling lyric 'After You Speak'. In his prose work too, there is so frequently a reminder of this. His own nature reacted to a certain religious chord in the make-up of others, though all who knew him knew how he hated the smug, the pretentious, the self-opinionated, the merely officially religious, and the hardness that sometimes accompanies piety. He was curious about my resolve to take Orders, but I never remember being wounded by anything he said. He was curious too about the mysticism of Richard Jefferies. I have a copy of Behmen Edward gave me, and a Crashaw. He asked me to procure for him St. Teresa's writings, the 'Imitation', the Vulgate, and borrowed Inge's 'Christian Mysticism' several times. He rejected emphatically the easy label of 'anima naturaliter Christiana'. 'Don't label me A.N.C. while I am alive. It seems so particularly a privilege of the unresisting dead to have someone come down upon them and pin that order on their breasts. It can't matter then.' Still, he had written earlier, 'Among my unfertilized plans still lies an "Essay on the Gospel of St. John" by a Devout Agnostic.'

I remember longing greatly that he should experience some awareness of God, especially when I learned he had turned to expressing himself in poetry. He told me of his poems and sent me some in 1915. I may have said something about there being only one cure for his melancholia. He wrote back to say he did not know what I meant. But I still feel that his interest in mysticism was something much more than that of effort towards a literary understanding of Jefferies and Maeterlinck. He had the most exquisite expression of thought of any man I ever knew, but there was something in him ever inexpressible; and the merely romantic side of supernatural experience repelled him particularly, especially when it took literary expression. He once entertained the idea of collaborating with me in a novel, but his honesty, and recognition of the imperatives in his own experience and outlook, would not coalesce with my rather pretentious idealism, and the idea came to nothing.

I have said that as I knew him he was mostly happy, and I can recall many hours of talk, of sitting up at night to go fishing at dawn, hours at Goodwood, at the pantomime even, when life seemed to him something immensely good; but all his intimates have experienced that other side of him, and how sombre it was. I remember calling him 'devious', and how humbly and without irony he accepted the description. It was of course because I found his complexity baffling. He was on one occasion in the depths of depression, and I began to have real fear that his morbidity might affect his reason. He had an idea he had diabetes, and was obsessed with a story he had heard that sufferers from that disease grew so hungry that they ate earth. In imagination he saw himself in that dire condition, and yet the mood passed swiftly as we talked, and he swung quickly to an almost boisterous hilarity over a song we both knew, of dubious decency, with variations and glosses. His sense of the ridiculous often approached hysteria to my sober view, and it was very catching.

I do not know now what more about Edward can be added by me that has not been written elsewhere and better. If I have put in a few touches to the record of the man that may help to give a clearer idea of how his fine and troubled spirit made life a lovelier thing to one friend, and of the capacity for splendid and generous companionship that spirit included, I have not written vainly. Impressions more subtle than those created by ordinary perception remain, when memories of hearing and seeing blur with the years. I repeat that, as I knew him, laughter and joy made up far more of his life than one would ever guess from some of the sombre portraits of him, literary and photographic.

'All is well. All is well between us for ever and ever . . . Remember.' His farewell to Helen sets the significance and truth of his life in the setting of eternity. Poet, soldier, friend, lover, he found and put into final expression the same synthesis of human experience as Julian of Norwich, the mediaeval anchoress, 'a simple unlettered creature', found. 'All shall be well, and all manner of thing shall be well.'

Jesse Berridge

c. *1945*

Of his relations with his contemporaries at Oxford my recollections are misty and confused, for his own accounts of them varied with his various moods. . . . Just because he was so different from the normal, cocksure young men who are prominent in their school and college days, he concluded that he was deficient. He had passed so much of his youth in solitude, observing, and so keenly, all natural objects, but of his fellows he fought shy. He had one or two intimates before I met him, but he had not conquered his fear of intimacy. At Oxford he made a sudden spurt and tried to be social. It seemed to me forced, indeed at times—shall I say?—hysterical . . . It was this diffidence in his attitude towards mankind that possibly accounts for the comparative rarity of portraits in his writing . . . After Oxford, Edwy wrote in quiet intervals and made occasional journeys to town to recommend his work to editors. His success was not striking, for even with letters of introduction, he was not a good go-getter . . . Life in the country certainly seemed to be his best restorative. On the Pilgrims' Way we took the first of a long series of walks together, sometimes for long days, at others for two or three days at a time . . . We just walked in healing silence, Edwy now and then pausing to make brief notes in a pocket book. The open air was his joy and his workshop . . . His habit was, as far as possible, to avoid the highway, and take the most direct route across country . . . His laugh was real, jolly, liberating . . . In social life he was, I imagine, a welcome guest everywhere. Quiet and reserved, his unmistakeable sincerity, his distinguished person, and his responsiveness to light-hearted fun, would add charm to any company. He joined the army and then, to our bewilderment, he became (outwardly) another man. He had no responsibilities, his health and spirits improved with his regular, care-free life, and, in place of a man stoically concealing his burden, we had one who with apparent light-heartedness contributed to the social amenities of any company in which he found himself. But his other (his writing life) went on . . . One day as he left my house he handed me a roll of MS, asking me to read it. It was his first batch of poems . . . Here I recognised was genius; here our confidence in his powers was vindicated. But how crushingly sad! Such complete hopelessness, so simply yet so consummately expressed, may stir the casual admiration of the casual reader; to a friend it cannot be but a legacy of sorrow . . .

H. Hooton

Written about 1945

NOTES

1 *Arthur*. Arthur Hardy.

1 *Mary's*. Helen's younger sister.

2 *old man's company*. E.T. was a frequent visitor to Swindon, home of his paternal grandmother. There he developed his friendship with the old man, David Uzzell.

3 *113 Cowley Road*. At Cowley Road E.T. was an 'unattached' matriculant preparing for an entrance scholarship to the Oxford colleges. He was successful at Lincoln College.

7 *Responsions*. The first of three examinations for the BA (Oxon.)—known as 'smalls'.

7 *ineffectiveness*. 'sterility' was written above.

8 *Goodnight*. A letter card is attached to this letter addressed to Miss Helen Noble, c/o C. Andrews Esq. 33 Bath Road Bedford Park London W: 'Helen, if you can, will you send me, by postal order, 2/6, or even 1/–, posting not later than 5 p.m. on Saturday?' Throughout all their correspondence E.T. kept a rigid control on all their expenses: a marked trait in all his diaries 1902–14.

8 *Pontardulais*. E.T. stayed in Pontardulais at the home of his father's first cousin (Philip Treharne Thomas), a skilled tinplate worker.

9 *a Welsh bard*. Gwili (Revd John Jenkins) was a distant cousin of his first wife.

10 *Pooles*. Helen was a child's governess: first with the Pooles at Ramsgate (where E.T. visited her), then with the Webbs at Margate.

11 *J.C.R.* Undergraduate publication edited by Oldershaw, E.T.'s senior at St Paul's and a friend of G. K. Chesterton.

11 *J.C.R.* For examples of his early verse see *CP*, appendix B; 'Recollections of the Months', *JCR* (25 Apr. 1899) (ETC).

11 *my aunt*. Margaret Townsend.

12 *must my people know*. Helen was pregnant. They were to marry secretly at Fulham Registry Office on 20 June 1899 (*AP* 76–9).

12 *Mrs. Logan*. Beatrice Logan, after her divorce, married John Potbury.

13 *Davies*. A Lincoln friend who later took Holy Orders.

13 *English Literature*. John Morley, *Studies in Literature* (1891), perhaps.

15 *in the streets*. This letter describes the Oxford celebration of the Relief of Mafeking during which E.T. contracted a gonococcal infection (*AP* 87–9).

15 *Maine*. His co-digger. A research student in Anthropology.

15 *Elsey*. A first-year student.

15 *the Davenant*. An undergraduate literary society at Lincoln College.

17 *Haynes and I are collaborating*. The MS of the unfinished novel, *Olivia Patterson*, is in the Berg Collection, New York Public Library (WC 30).

17 *C.O.S.* Unidentified; an Oxford appointments society?

18 *Claudian*. Prolific Latin poet, *c.*395–404.

18 *Mervyn*. E.T. used the English 'v' rather than the Welsh 'f' in most of his letters to English friends and often to his family.

18 *on his paper*. *Manchester Guardian*.

19 *'Tom'*. The great bell of Christchurch, Oxford.

21 *'Chronicle'*. For E.T.'s relations with the *Daily Chronicle* see *GB* and *AP*.

22 *my oldest friend*. Arthur Hardy, E.T.'s friend from school in Battersea.

24 *'Coldstreamer'*. Obscure, possibly *Horae Solitariae*. (RPE 188)

24 *Nightingale Lane S. W.* E.T.'s parents' new home.

24 *nasty letter*. From Bearsted on 28 Aug. 1903 E.T. wrote to Helen, then in London: 'I don't intend to write letters. I couldn't. I suppose my brain is going—it has lasted wonderfully. Anyhow I am not the same person that lived at Rose Acre. So goodbye. The children are well and happy. "Love" to all. Ever and wholly yours Edwy'.

26 *Here are kisses*. Over a hundred crosses simulating two flights of birds. A feature of most of E.T.'s letter to Helen, while the children were small, was his sketches and often elaborate patterns of crosses. ETC has numerous examples of their affectionate replies preserved with Helen's many hundreds of letters to him.

26 *sympathetic London doctor*. Dr Segundo advised E.T. 'for neurasthenia', followed by a Dr T. D. Savitt intermittently in 1907–8 until E.T. met Godwin Baynes (see EF *passim*). E.T. was completely exhausted after writing his *Oxford* (published 15 Dec. 1903) while constantly reviewing for *DC*. On medical advice he spent a month's recuperation away from home, at first with his college friend, J. H. Morgan, and then with his London friends, close to editors and abundant literary journalism. This helped confirm his deep need to live and work in the country.

28 *book*. *Oxford*.

29 *Mr. Bowman*. Possibly the vicar at Bearsted.

29 *Black*. The publisher of *Oxford*.

29 *new literary editor*. 'I am very sorry to say an ignorant Scotchman James Milne.'

29 *handkerchiefs*. A week later E.T. sent Helen 'a short note of business', with instructions: 'Please bank £33 and take out 16/– which ought to enable you to pay Daisy; if not take out another 10/–. Bank it at once.' There follow instructions where to find his 'dress suit—in the little attic; the ties are in the cardboard box in my chest of drawers; the socks are some

where near. You have probably seen the slippers about. Please send them to Irene's, of course . . . Remember I shall be at 13 Rusham Road [his parents' new home] on Friday night and Irene's on Saturday night. I am now busy with accounts and posting cheques. I am ever and wholly yours, Edwy'.

33 *Jesse*. Jesse Berridge, poet and bank clerk preparing for ordination.

33 *Dal and Frank*. Charles Dalmon and Franklin Dyall.

34 *my life in town*. A letter to Bottomley of 7 Mar. 1904 confirms his growing contempt for his London life: 'Work abounded: I could have doubled my income. But I fled and now am beginning to hear music again . . . In health I am no better, though a few pounds heavier, nor am I less depressed, irritable, but I hope I am getting used to it; which is nearly as useful, though not so pleasant, as getting rid of it. I believe I shall never be happy unless I become mad.' Similarly to Hooton, 15 Mar. 1904: 'Well, I got sick of the foolish life; also Helen was in great pain and all alone excepting a nurse. So I returned after a week in town.'

34 *Milne*. James Milne, literary editor of *DC*, and E.T. never saw eye to eye on literary subjects.

35 *soul*. E.T.'s swings of mood are reflected in two letters to Harry Hooton, the most intimate friend of Helen and Edwy, 22 January 1905. 'But now we are both of us being very much surprised by a kind of happiness. At any rate we are out of the wood for the time being.' Followed on 29 May 1905: 'Things—work, health, relation—are at their worst, except work, but temporary improvements in that don't move a scrap.'

37 *Freeman*. A. Martin Freeman.

38 *some more poetry*. Walter de la Mare, *Poems* (1906).

39 *'Keep Innocency' . . . 'Bunches of Grapes' . . . 'The Child in the story awakens'*. Three poems by de la Mare, selected for E.T.'s *The Pocket Book of Poems and Songs for the Open Air* from *Songs of Childhood* (1902).

40 *Davies*. W. H. Davies, *New Poems* (1907).

41 *Dell*. Jesse's son.

41 *Anthology. The Pocket Book of Poems and Songs for the Open Air.*

41 *Ransome*. See *The Autobiography of Arthur Ransome*, ed. Rupert Hart-Davis (1976), 82–217.

41 *Tom . . . Rolf*. Tom and Rolf Clayton—friends of Berridge and E.T.

42 *Dell . . . Denys . . . Incogniti Tertius . . . Quartus*. The Berridge children.

42 *1600 words of reviewing*. E.T.'s diaries record a daily inventory of his method of working and forms of leisure; e.g. this typical entry for 25 Feb. 1904: 'Up 8.30. Writing in morning (700 words-review). Afternoon with Helen to Maidstone and evening reading with Helen. To bed 10.30.' Or, a London entry of 19 Feb. 1903: 'Housework for Mother in the morning. Afternoon 3–7 at the Museum. Then an evening with Dalmon. To bed 12.'

43 *your Gunnar play*. *The Riding to Lithend* (1909), with a dedicatory poem to E.T. and with drawings by James Guthrie, was based on the Old Icelandic *Njálssaga*.

46 *poems*. None of these poems is in *The Complete Poems* of Walter de la Mare.

48 *Isn't Nietzsche magnificent?* Cf. E.T.'s comprehensive review of Nietzsche in the *Bookman* (June 1909), 140.

48 *Trench*. Herbert Trench, *Deirdre Wed and other poems* (1901).

49 *she*. Hope Webb, who was one of Helen's charges at Margate in 1896. See *AP* 144–54 for a discussion of Edward's infatuation with Hope and for quotations from Helen's letters to E.T. who was staying at the Hootons' cottage in Minsmere. On 23 January 1908 E.T. wrote to Hooton: 'I was sorry to lose Hope and have hardly done any work since. It is a good many years since I felt such a strong unreasoning liking for anyone. As for getting to know her, I couldn't even make an effort, and she would naturally not help me. She was Helen's favourite as a child.' (For Hope's subsequent career see The Edward Thomas Fellowship Newsletter No. 26, Feb. 1992.) Later Thomas wrote two thinly disguised accounts of this disturbing episode in *The South Country*, 84–7, and in 'The Fountain', *Rest and Unrest*. Writing to Hooton 7 Mar. 1907, mainly about Jefferies's *Amaryllis* and *The Story of My Heart*, he confessed his inability to understand the experience: 'When we meet you can help me still more. I greatly fear that will never be at Minsmere. For my folly in concealing (or rather in not proclaiming) my letters to and from Hope procured me an awkward interview on my last evening [at which Helen was present] and unhappiness ever since. I was asked not to go on with the correspondence and I am febrile enough to acquiesce and so throw upon myself various burdens of the imagination, of regret, of scheming, of vaguest hope etc. I know I was foolish but the punishment as it always is is excessive. It is small consolation that perhaps Hope is serene enough and even that may not be true. Don't talk about this.' For Helen's much later version see *Under Storm's Wing*, 119–21. (I now believe that in writing her two books Helen drew on the preserved complete two-way correspondence between herself and Edward.)

49 *my Pocket Book*. *The Pocket Book of Poems and Songs for the Open Air*, compiled by E.T. in 1907.

51 *Goodwood races*. See *The Icknield Way*, ch. 4: 'There were dusty tracks for exercising horses on both sides of the road. I like to see fine horses running at full speed. To see this sight, or hounds running on a good scent, or children dancing, is to me the same as music, and therefore, I suppose, as full of morality and beauty. I sat down for some time watching the horses.'

52 *tales and sketches*. The basis of his *Rest and Unrest* and *Light and Twilight*.

52 *your Icelandic play*. *The Feud*, which first played in matinée at the Haymarket in 1907.

52 *the book. Richard Jefferies*, published 26 Jan. 1909. See David Garnett, *The Golden Echo* (1953).

54 *thrust upon editors*. Tales and sketches later included in *Rest and Unrest* and *Light and Twilight*.

54 *if it lives*. The *English Review* accepted E.T.'s work until 1915–16.

55 *Symons*. Arthur Symons.

55 *the later poems*. *The Fool of the World, and other Poems* (1906).

55 *London Nights*. Published 1895, rev. 1897.

55 *near here*. In Froxfield. Ivy Ransome and Helen became firm friends.

55 *spirited and clever*. There follow two quite indecipherable lines heavily scored out by E.T.

56 *diaries*. Now in NLW Aberystwyth.

56 *the Book*. Bottomley's *Riding to Lithend*, with drawings by James Guthrie.

56 *Our other neighbours*. Arthur and Ivy Ransome.

56 *Arthur Wor*. Waugh, literary editor of the *Daily Chronicle*.

56 *Garnett's play acted*. *The Feud*.

56 *The Playboy*. Synge's *Playboy of the Western World*.

57 *some day*. Mostly in *Light and Twilight* (1911); a few in the posthumous *Cloud Castle and Other Papers* (1922).

58 *much material by the way*. It seems E.T. abandoned this guide.

58 *little book of sketches*. *Rest and Unrest*.

58 *Ezra Pound's second book*. *Exaltations*, reviewed by E.T. in *DC* (23 Nov. 1909).

59 *'Home'*. 'Home' and 'The Castle of Lostormellyn' were eventually published in *Light and Twilight* (1911). The foreword notes that all but one of these tales had appeared in magazines.

60 *strange piece of work*. This became *Feminine Influence on the Poets*. As usual E.T. failed to carry out the original conception submitted to his agent.

60 *I come that way*. In preparation for *The Icknield Way*.

61 *Bill . . . Charley*. Dad's sons.

61 *the wind and rain*. The memoir of Winifred Roberts, a neighbour, recorded in 1949: 'The house stood on a high ridge, it was never out of the sound and feel of wind. Whatever the compass point, the wind sighed or whined or shrieked round the house until Thomas became almost obsessed by it. After a while, he took to doing much of his work in a summer house, at the end of the garden, out of the reach of the tormenting winds' (ETC).

61 *change of diet*. In January he began to follow a strict vegetarian diet.

61 *the Arabs and the Celts*. *Feminine Influence on the Poets*, published Oct. 1910,

Maurice Maeterlinck, completed in Jan. 1911, and *Celtic Stories*, written during the autumn of 1911, are relevant here.

63 *Mary and the Bramble*. By Lascelles Abercrombie, reviewed by E.T. in *DC* (9 Aug. 1911).

64 *your friend*. Arundel del Re, later sub-editor of *Poetry Review*.

64 *an editor*. H. W. Nevinson at the *Daily Chronicle*.

66 *your poems*. H. Monro, *Before Dawn: Poems and Impressions* (1911).

67 *proofs of two others*. *Celtic Tales*, *Isle of Wight*, *Lafcadio Hearn*, *Maurice Maeterlinck*.

68 *don't think I shall go away now*. This refers to a letter to Garnett of 20 Sept. 1911: 'Gibbon's plan is just what I wanted, and I will write to him. I am staying a night in Sevenoaks next week and will go on to see him probably. The route will be decided for me when I hear of a ship. I think things look very well now. The *English Review* also might take something. Of course I dare not be away more than a month, or not much more, especially at the busiest part of the year.' Eventually he dithered more and more and insulted many of his closest friends until E. S. P. Haynes paid for E.T. to spend two or three months at Laugharne to write his delayed book on Borrow.

68 *big batch of proofs*. Of *The Icknield Way*, which was dedicated to Hooton.

69 *Llaugharne*. The text follows E.T.'s varied spelling of Llaugharne and Laugharne.

69 *young brother*. Ernest, an artist-designer.

69 *G.B.* Gordon Bottomley.

69 *Gerald*. Giraldus Cambrensis.

70 *Muirhead Bone*. An artist friend of E.T.

70 *nobody wants it*. See 'Swansea Village' in *The Last Sheaf*.

70 *Dewar*. An editor and naturalist.

70 *Milne*. Literary editor of the *DC*.

71 *Davies*. W. H. Davies, *Song of Joy and Others* (1911).

71 *Miss T.* In *Peacock Pie: A Book of Rhymes* (1913).

73 *your book*. *The Listeners and Other Poems* (1912).

74 *The Cherry Trees*. Walter de la Mare, *Collected Poems*, 387.

74 *Ellis*. E.T. later spent two periods with Ellis as a paying guest (*AP* 213–14 and 223–4). On this cycling trip he and Merfyn also stayed with de la Mare at Cowden and Hooton at Coulsdon.

75 *Slinfold*. Near Horsham.

76 *Cowden*. De la Mare's home.

76 *proofs*. Proofs of E.T.'s *Swinburne: A Critical Study*.

77 *Welsh walk*. See W. H. Davies, *A Poet's Pilgrimage* (1918).

77 *ridiculously thin-spired church*. This letter includes a sketch of Farthing Down church on the side.

78 *Jones*. A former colleague and friend of Hooton, then in a Paris bank.

78 *Julian*. E.T.'s younger brother.

78 *for the whole of the time*. For E.T.'s friendship with Bax, Farjeon, and Baynes see *AP* 193–5, 199–200, and EF.

79 *Dermot O'Byrne*. A literary pseudonym of Sir Arnold Bax.

79 *a fiction*. *The Happy-Go-Lucky Morgans*.

79 *Holmbury*. Leith Hill, the home of R. C. Trevelyan. There is a note by Bottomley among the ETC papers: 'I seemed to be laid up all winter . . . Our friends Mr and Mrs Robert C Trevelyan suggested we should use their empty house on Leith Hill in Surrey . . . from the end of October 1912 until April 1913. While there ET visited us at intervals and my wife went to the Petersfield house, while I was never able to undertake the journey.'

82 *D.C. Daily Chronicle*.

84 *typewriting*. Mostly done for E.T., first by John Freeman and then by Eleanor Farjeon. E.T. later learned to type himself.

84 *my MS*. *The Happy-Go-Lucky Morgans*.

84 *Davies's last book*. W. H. Davies, *Foliage: Various Poems* (1913).

85 *Hodgson's poem*. This was submitted for a *Poetry Review* prize. E.T. was one of the judges. He wrote to Monro in Jan. 1913: 'I have found it very hard to choose among your poets. I should like to give four names instead of one, but as I mustn't I have come to the conclusion I ought to name "The Stone" by W. W. Gibson. Perhaps I shall want to correct this decision.' He did not. The other judges chose Brooke's *Grantchester*.

85 *Irene*. Helen's elder sister.

86 *Ecstasy*. This was intended for Batsford's Fellowship Books series. It was abandoned and the unfinished typescript is in the Berg Collection.

86 *my fiction*. *The Happy-Go-Lucky Morgans*.

86 *cheaper here*. E.T. found Yew Tree Cottage, the small cheaper house in Steep village, too cramped for working. He sought Hooton's advice, as usual, on 12 Oct. 1913: 'I must get the cheapest possible place since the expenses here will be practically the same and I have already broken into my nest-egg to make up for the steady descent in my earnings. What I want is a place to work till about the end of the year.'

87 *Proverbs*. Later published as *Four-and-Twenty Blackbirds* (1915).

88 *'Times'*. E.T. was not accepted as a reviewer for *The Times*.

88 *Frost*. Cf. *Selected Letters of Robert Frost*, ed. L. Thompson (London, 1964), 50–220.

89 *the States*. Gwili had spent 3 months in the summer of 1913 lecturing and preaching (in English and Welsh) at expatriate USA churches.

89 *Celtic Stories*. The second edition of *Celtic Stories* was slightly emended by Gwili.

89 *George*. Watcyn Wyn's son.

90 *hurried flustered fashion*. See *AP* 199–200 for the background to this letter.

91 *Frost*. With the prospect of a Royal Literary Fund grant and offers of more congenial work from many editors, E.T. returned to live at Yew Tree Cottage and to work in his hilltop study. I believe Frost was urging him to write a fictitious biography. Half of it, entitled 'Fiction', is in ETC (*AP*).

92 *Meredith's Homes and Haunts*. *A Literary Pilgrim in England* (1917).

92 *We*. E.T. was on a cycling tour with Merfyn and Bronwen, which ended with the Frosts in Herefordshire. Frost had moved to Ledington from Beaconsfield on 26 Mar. as a neighbour of Lascelles Abercrombie and W. W. Gibson.

93 *T.P. article*. 'How I Began', *Last Sheaf*, 15–25. Frost's poems referred to are in *A Boy's Will* (1913).

94 *your poems*. *North of Boston* (1914). For E. T.'s reviews see *GB* 233.

95 *sketches*. *Cloud Castle and Other Papers* (1922).

95 *Homes and Haunts*. *A Literary Pilgrim in England* (1917).

96 *Peter*. Mrosowsky.

96 *unvarnished reports*. See *Last Sheaf*.

97 *Ryton*. Where E.T. was staying with the Frosts.

97 *War Poetry article*. *Poetry and Drama*, 2/8 (Dec. 1914), 341–5.

98 *Lesley*. Frost's daughter.

100 *Collected Poems*. *Poetical Works of Wilfred Scawen Blount* (1914), i and ii.

101 *what he went for*. Eventually Garnett served as a civilian ambulance orderly.

102 *unprofitable writing*. E.T. began the prose versions of his first poems on 16 Nov. 1914.

102 *Hardy's new poems*. *Satires of Circumstance*; no published review.

102 *'wings' light word'*. Cf. final version of 'November Sky', *CP* 10–13.

104 *for saying it*. Monro rejected E.T.'s poems. E.T. had sent his first ten poems to Monro on 15 Dec. 1914: 'I enclose some poems which I should like you to look at. . . . I deliver myself into your hands. Only one other person [E. Farjeon] except my wife has seen them. This is my only complete copy.'

104 *Kenneth Morris's book*. Kenneth Morris, translator and commentator on the *Mabinogion*, helped R. P. Eckert with his book on E.T.

106 *Anthology*. *This England*.

106 *New Numbers*. Poems by W. W. Gibson, Rupert Brooke, Lascelles Aber-

crombie, and John Drinkwater. E.T. reviewed Part I in *New Weekly* (21 Mar. 1914), but I have not traced any review by him of Part II.

107 *Frost. North of Boston*, reviewed by E.T. in *Daily News* (22 July 1914) and *English Review* (Aug. 1914).

107 *his first book. A Boy's Will* (1913).

108 *'May 20'*. Originally the last 2 lines of the poem, later entitled *May 23*, read:

> A fine day was May the twentieth,
> The day of old Jack Norman's death.

See alterations in *CP* 112.

109 *Mt. Blanc.* A restaurant.

109 *3 Henrietta St.* Duckworth's office.

110 *Rupert Brooke.* E.T.'s article appeared in *English Review*, 20 (8 June 1915), 325–8.

111 *Harry Hooton.* The following typescript poems accompany this letter in the Colbeck Collection, UBC, Vancouver: 'Tears', 'The Huxter', 'A Cat', 'Adlestrop', 'Two Pewits', 'Digging', 'The Path', 'After Rain', 'The Mountain Chapel', 'November', 'The Chalk Pit', 'Beauty', 'The Sign-post', 'An Old Song', 'March the Third', 'Interval', 'The Lofty Sky', 'Over the Hills', 'Ambition', 'April', 'Fifty Faggots', 'Song', 'Health', 'But these things also', 'A Gentleman', 'The Penny Whistle', 'The Barn', 'Good-Night', 'The Bridge'. This is the present order of the typescripts. 'The Huxter' is signed 'Edward Eastaway' in Helen's hand.

112 *'The Road not Taken'*. 'The Road not Taken' in Frost's *Mountain Interval* makes oblique reference to E.T.'s halting between prose and verse. 'Two Roads' is the same poem. Later Frost altered the printed text to 'the passing there | Had worn them really about the same.'

115 *Civil List.* E.T. was awarded a Civil List grant (£300) on 10 June 1916.

115 *David.* Garnett's son. Garnett served abroad as a civilian nursing orderly from July to Dec. 1915.

117 *real work again.* E.T.'s initial response to military service given in a letter to W. H. Hudson, 24 Oct. 1915: 'Camp life is very uncomfortable, especially indoors at night, cold, badly-lighted, noisy, the food ill-cooked, and ill-served. But it does not disagree with me. In fact, I never grumbled less, I believe. And I got to like the men much better as soon as we had to depend on one another.'

119 *verses. CP*, Nos. 99 and 101. These particular poems, I believe, sparked off the series of 'Household Poems', E.T.'s name for them, Nos. 98–118.

120 *things.* 'Eastaway' poems in *This England*.

120 *Anthology. This England.*

120 *Annual. An Anthology of New Poetry.*

120 *Lawrence.* Frost's parents' home where he was in High School.

121 *my birthday*. 3 Mar.

121 *I rhymed some*. 'Celandine', *CP*, No. 103.

123 *N.C.O.'s.* See Biographical Register, Army colleagues, for these NCOs with E.T. in Artists' Rifles.

123 *trying to draw me*. John Wheatley's unfinished sketch of E.T. is reproduced in *GB* facing p. 138.

125 *Bottomley's 'Lear'*. For Bottomley's *King Lear's Wife* see *GB* 255–7, 267.

129 *50 faggots*. Poem 73 in *CP*.

129 *'The Old Cloak'*. E.T. had planned an anthology of narrative verse with Frost.

130 *small new publisher*. Selwyn and Blount with whom E.T.'s friend Roger Ingpen was connected. They published E. S. P. Haynes, *Personalia* (1918), with a memoir of E.T.

132 *the 2nd thing*. 'The Trumpet', *CP*, No. 137.

133 *Miss . . . aski*. Kzementarski.

133 *Ingpen*. Roger Ingpen wrote to Frost on 17 Apr. 1917: 'My name may probably be unknown to you, but I am arranging the publication of his poems under the name of "Edward Eastaway" and he gave me your address and told me that you had a duplicate M.S. of the poems which you were trying to get published on your side. I gave Walter de la Mare particulars of the book and while he was on his visit to the States he spoke of it to Mr Christopher Morley of Doubleday, Page and Co. and I have since had a letter from Mr Morley asking me to send proofs of this book to him. The book is now in proof and I shall send him a copy at once . . . Doubleday also asked for some of the poems of John Freeman whom I think you have met. Both of these books are in the hands of Selwyn and Blount of 27 Chancery Lane, London with which firm I am connected. If you can help me in regard to "Eastaway's" Poems I shall be very glad. The reviews of his contributions to Constable's Annual of New Poetry have been most laudatory and deservedly so, I think. His book is dedicated to yourself.' Two postscripts follow: 'I shall suggest to Mr Morley that we supply him with an edition in sheets'; 'In his last letter to me Thomas wrote "I beg you not to make use of my situation, as a publisher might be tempted to, now or in the event of any kind of accident to me, to advertise the book."' In the event E.T.'s father disclosed the identity of 'Eastaway' in a letter to *The Times*.

134 *Gordon's list*. Poems by 'Edward Eastaway' published in *An Anthology of New Poetry*.

134 *Baba is very well*. Myfanwy (Baba) was staying with her aunt Mary at Chiswick.

134 *your letter and your poem 'France, France'*. Frost's letter and his poem are not included in his published works:

Franconia N.H. | December 7 1916

Dear Edward:

I have been down sick in bed for a week and a half: thats where I have been and thats why you haven't heard from me. Port wine is what I need now if I am going to shine. But I'm not. I find that the chief thing on my mind is not a personal one, what's going to become of you and me—nothing like that—but a political one—the change in the government in England and the possibilities of great changes in France. What becomes of my hopes of three months ago when the drive on the Somme began? Something has gone wrong. How can we be happy any more—for a while? Lloyd George is the great man and he belongs where he now takes his place. But would he ever have arrived there with Bonar Law and Carson on his right and left, but for some desperate need. Silly fools are full of peace talk over here. It is out of friendliness of a kind to the Allies: they act as if they thought you were waiting for them to say the word to quit. It's none of my business what you do: but neither is it any of theirs. I wrote some lines I've copied on the other side of this about the way I am struck. When I get to writing in this vein you may know I am sick or sad or something.

Robert

Suggested by Talk of Peace at This Time

France, France, I know not what is in my heart.
But God forbid that I should be more brave
As watcher from a quiet place apart
Than you are fighting in an open grave.

I will not ask more of you than you ask,
O Bravest, of yourself. But shall I less?
You know the extent of your appointed task,
Whether you still can face its bloodiness.

Not mine to say you shall not think of peace.
Not mine, not mine. I almost know your pain.
But I will not believe that you will cease,
I will not bid you cease, from being slain

And slaying till what might have been distorted
Is saved to be the Truth and Hell is thwarted. R.F.

135 *your book*. *Mountain Interval*.

137 *Scotch philosopher*. J. M. Thorburn.

140 *to my diary*. See *CP*, appendix.

141 *T—*. Thorburn.

144 *ghostly village'*. Beaurains.

146 *my book*. 'Edward Eastaway', *Poems* (1917).

147 *Frost*. De la Mare visited Frost during his USA lecture tour.

148 *13 March 1917*. This letter, not in EF, was found among Helen's letters in 1967.

150 *Hooper*. See EF 255.

151 *Beach Thomas*. Sir William Beach Thomas (1868–1957) was a constant writer on the countryside and the open air for the *Daily Mail*. His successful *The English Year* (1913–14) was a book E.T. was once expected to write. He was a war correspondent in France for the *Mail*; his *With the British in the Somme* (1917) was highly acclaimed.

152 *Jesse*. Jesse Berridge was now rector of Little Baddow.

152 *that chimney*. An exposed, often targeted observation post which E.T. (and some other officers) failed to climb.

153 *old chalk pit*. This would carry many memories for Helen and Edward of their open-air courtship days. Cf. 'The Chalk Pit', *CP*, No. 72 and the notes to it in *CP* 396–7. Also 'Chalk Pits' (1911) in *The Last Sheaf*, 27–37.

154 *village*. Beaurains.

156 *rotten time*. As a Civil Servant, Julian's call-up was being delayed.

156 *Salisbury*. Julian toured with E.T. when he was preparing *In Pursuit of Spring*.

156 *the Annual*. *An Anthology of New Poetry*.

157 *the old man*. Dad Uzzell.

158 *B*. Beaurains.

161 *gamekeeper*. See EF 603–4.

161 *small city*. Arras.

163 *respectable review*. In *The Times Literary Supplement* (23 Mar. 1917), 151: 'He is a real poet, with the truth in him. At present, like most of his contemporaries, he has too little control over his eyes . . . Or is the new method an unconscious survival of a materialism and naturalism which the tremendous life of the last 3 years has made an absurdity.'

163 *To Helen*. A continuation of a letter of 5 Apr., which begins 'This is the second day' and ends 'The Somme pictures are absurd, compared with what I could tell you in five or six minutes and shall do someday I hope. Goodbye. I am all and always yours Edwy. | If there is a letter today I shall write more.'

INDEX

Note: In the Index E.T. refers to Edward Thomas